Adobe
Illustrator™

CLASSROOM IN A BOOK

Library of Congress Catalog No.: 93-73010

ISBN: 1-56830-056-5

10 9 8 7 6 5 4 3 2   First Printing: February 1994

The information in this book is furnished for informational use only, is subject to change without notice, and should not be construed as a commitment by Adobe Systems Incorporated. Adobe Systems Incorporated assumes no responsibility for any errors or inaccuracies that may appear in this book. The software and typefaces mentioned in this book are furnished under license and may only be used or copied in accordance with the terms of such license.

PANTONE®* Computer Video simulations used in this product may not match PANTONE-identified solid color standards. Use current PANTONE Color Reference Manuals for accurate color. *Pantone, Inc.'s check-standard trademark for color. PANTONE Color Computer Graphics" © Pantone, Inc. 1986, 1993.

Pantone, Inc. is the copyright owner of PANTONE Color Computer Graphics and Software which are licenced to Adobe to distribute for use only in combination with Adobe Illustrator. PANTONE Color Computer Graphics and Software shall not be copied onto another diskette or into memory unless as part of the execution of Adobe Illustrator.

PostScript™ is a trademark of Adobe Systems Incorporated ("Adobe"), registered in the United States and elsewhere. PostScript can refer both to the PostScript language as specified by Adobe and to Adobe's implementation of its PostScript language interpreter.

Any references to "PostScript printers," "PostScript files," or "PostScript drivers" refer, respectively, to printers, files, and driver programs written in or supporting the PostScript language. References in this book to the "PostScript language" are intended to emphasize Adobe's standard definition of that language.

Adobe, the Adobe logo, the Adobe Press logo, Acrobat, Adobe Dimensions, Adobe Garamond, Adobe Illustrator, Adobe Photoshop, Adobe Premiere, Adobe Type Manager, Adobe Separator, Adobe Streamline, Adobe Teach, ATM, Classroom in a Book, Classroom in a Box, Distiller, Madrone, Minion, and PostScript are trademarks of Adobe Systems Incorporated which may be registered in certain jurisdictions. Barmeno, Bellvue is a trademark and Berthold City is a registered trademark of H. Berthold AG. Fruitiger, Helvetica, and Times are trademarks of Linotype-Hell AG and/or its subsidiaries. Gill Sans is a trademark of The Monotype Corporation registered in the US Patent and Trademark Office and elsewhere. Agfa is a registered trademark of Agfa division, Miles, Inc. Apple, Macintosh, and LaserWriter are registered trademarks, and Quadra, QuickDraw, QuickTime, System 6, System 7, and TrueType are trademarks of Apple Computer, Inc. MacroMind Director is a trademark of Macromedia, Inc. CameraMan and Movie Play are registered tradmarks of Vision Software. All other brand and product names are trademarks or registered trademarks of their respective holders. Photograph liscensed from THE BETTMAN ARCHIVE.

Printed in the United States of America by Shepard Poorman Communications, Indianapolis, Indiana.

Published simultaneously in Canada.

Adobe Press books are published and distributed by Hayden Books, a division of Prentice Hall Computer Publishing. For individual orders, or for educational, corporate, or retail sales accounts, call 1-800-428-5331. For information, address Hayden Books, 201 W. 103rd Street, Indianapolis IN 46290.

CONTENTS

INTRODUCTION

The Adobe Illustrator™ program is one of the most popular illustration software programs sold today. The Adobe Illustrator *Classroom in a Book*™ is a set of lessons designed to teach you how to use Adobe Illustrator.

Created by the Educational Services group at Adobe Systems, Inc., *Classroom in a Book* is a project-based series of lessons that you can complete at your own pace. You can expect to spend between 30 and 40 hours with this product.

HOW DOES IT WORK?

Classroom in a Book consists of a series of design projects with complete information for creating them. Once you've learned some pen-tool basics, you'll spend time creating projects for a fictitious travel agency named *Navigations*. Within this context, you'll work on a corporate logo, posters, postcards, advertisements, letterhead—all of the kinds of tasks you might do when working for a typical upscale company.

Working in the context of actual projects, you'll learn different techniques for putting together your knowledge of many different Adobe Illustrator techniques.

Each lesson contains step-by-step instructions for creating the projects, along with lots of explanation and tips and techniques. Every third lesson is a review project that will reinforce what you've learned in prior lessons.

Lesson 1 gives you an overview of the Adobe Illustrator program's latest features and gets you started using the pen tool to draw simple shapes. In Lesson 2 you'll draw and paint a corporate logo. By the time you finish Lesson 2, you'll be ready to review everything you've learned up to that point by drawing a postcard in Lesson 3.

Lesson 4 teaches you how to use the transformation tools to scale, rotate, reflect, and shear the company logo for letterhead, envelopes and stationery. You'll also learn to use gradient fills and create type on a path. In Lesson 5, you'll take a trip to the beach and spend some time learning about importing and masking. By the end of Lesson 6 (halfway through the book), you'll be able to create this three-fold brochure that includes gradients, type on a path, type outlines, imported text and, graphics.

In Lesson 7 you'll create an 18 by 24 inch poster of the French wine country. You'll learn about blending and use some of the new plug-in filters that come with Adobe Illustrator 5.0. You'll also see how to use layers to work with complex artwork. Lesson 8 teaches you how to create and use custom graph designs. In Lesson 9, you'll review all of these techniques while you create a complex chart for an annual report.

Lesson 10 gives you information about using custom colors. You'll also spend some time learning about color separations. In Lesson 11 you'll create a corporate newsletter. In Lesson 12 you'll get some tips on multimedia presentations that use Adobe Photoshop™ and Adobe Dimensions™.

WHO SHOULD USE IT?

Classroom in a Book is designed for users at many levels. If you're new to Adobe Illustrator, you'll get a good grounding in all the basic features. If you have been using Adobe Illustrator for a while, you'll find *Classroom in a Book* teaches many advanced features that are included with the latest version of Adobe Illustrator.

This book is meant to be used in conjunction with the documentation provided with Adobe Illustrator. You'll still need to refer to the *Adobe Illustrator User Guide*, *Tutorial*, and *Beyond the Basics*.

SELF-PACED LEARNING

Using *Classroom in a Book* is similar to taking a 30-hour training course. In this case, you get to choose when and where you do the work. Final exam scheduling is also up to you.

When you have completed the projects in this book, you'll know all the basic features and most of the advanced features of the Adobe Illustrator program.

GETTING STARTED

Before you begin using Adobe Illustrator Classroom in a Book, you need to make sure that your system is set up correctly and that you have installed all the necessary software.

Although we can't include an Adobe Illustrator *Instructor* in a Book, we will provide all the help we can to get your system set up and ready to go.

WHAT YOU NEED TO DO

To get ready to use *Classroom in a Book*, you need to do the following things. (We'll give you more details later.)

• Check the system requirements.

• Install Adobe Illustrator and Adobe Type Manager, as described in the *Getting Started* booklet that came with Adobe Illustrator.

• Install the fonts that we have included with the *Classroom in a Book* software. (If you have already installed the fonts that came with Adobe Illustrator 5.0, you can skip this part. Note that the fonts that came with Adobe Illustrator are not automatically installed when you run the installer; they are only copied to your hard disk.)

• Copy the *Classroom in a Book* files that come with this package to your hard drive.

CHECKING THE SYSTEM REQUIREMENTS

The system requirements are the same as those for the Adobe Illustrator 5.0 program, except that you need a CD-ROM drive. If you are already running Adobe Illustrator 5.0, skip down to the section named "Special considerations."

System requirements

More specifically, the Adobe Illustrator 5.0 system requirements are

• A Macintosh® computer with a hard disk drive with a minimum of 3.1 megabytes of free application random-access memory (RAM). At least 5 megabytes is recommended.

• Apple® System software 6.0.7 or higher; System 7™ is recommended. If you are running System 6™, 32-bit QuickDraw™ is required.

• Any PostScript™ printer or other Macintosh-compatible graphic output device.

Special considerations

In addition to the general requirements, there are several more that apply only to *Classroom in a Book.*

• To use the *Classroom in a Book* files, you need a CD-ROM drive

• To take advantage of the lessons in this book, you need a color monitor.

• To watch the Adobe Teach™ movies included with this package, you need to have QuickTime™ installed in your system. (QuickTime is not a part of Adobe Illustrator and must be obtained separately.)

• To use the Pathfinder filters included with the Adobe Illustrator software and used in some of the *Classroom in a Book* lessons, you'll need to have a math coprocessor in your computer. (In most cases, we have provided a work around for those of you who do not have a math coprocessor.)

INSTALLING THE SOFTWARE

You need to install the Adobe Illustrator program with Adobe Type Manager™, the special *Classroom in a Book* student fonts, and the *Classroom in a Book* files.

Installing Adobe Illustrator and the Adobe Type Manager program

Install the Adobe Illustrator and Adobe Type Manager programs. *Adobe Illustrator Classroom in a Book* does not include the Adobe Illustrator program software. You must purchase the software separately. The *Getting Started* guide that comes with Adobe Illustrator 5.0 includes complete instructions for installing both Adobe Illustrator and the Adobe Type Manager (ATM™) program.

Installing the fonts

The *Classroom in a Book* electronic files use several special Adobe™ Type 1 fonts. These fonts (both outline and bitmapped) are included in a folder named *Student Fonts*. You must install these fonts in your system before you can use the electronic files. The Student Fonts folder includes

Adobe Garamond™
Bellevue™
Berthold City®
Gill Sans®
Madrone™
Times

If you have previously installed the fonts that came with Adobe Illustrator 5.0, you do not need to install the *Classroom in a Book* Student Fonts.

Installation instructions vary depending on whether you are using System 6, System 7 or System 7.1.

Reminder: You need to remove from your system any TrueType™ and existing bitmapped versions of the Student Fonts you may already have. These would include Helvetica and Times. If you do not remove them, you may experience font conflicts when you open the Classroom in a Book *files.*

Complete instructions for installing Adobe Type 1 fonts are included in the *Getting Started* guide that comes with Adobe Illustrator 5.0. See the section named "Using the ATM Program," and the subsection named "Using Adobe Type 1 fonts."

Copying the *Classroom in a Book* files

The *Classroom in a Book* CD-ROM disc includes folders containing all the electronic files for the *Classroom in a Book* lessons. These folders are included:

*Project	Lesson06
Adobe Teach	Lesson07
Extras	Lesson08
Lesson01	Lesson09
Lesson02	Lesson10
Lesson03	Lesson11
Lesson04	Lesson12
Lesson05	Student Fonts

To copy all of these files, drag the Adobe Illustrator CIB folder icon onto your hard disk drive.

If you have limited hard disk space, you may want to copy only the files for one or two lessons at a time.

Creating a Project folder

While you're working through *Classroom in a Book*, you will create and save many Adobe Illustrator files.

We recommend that you make a Project folder and put your work files there. In fact we've included one in the Adobe Illustrator CIB folder. The asterisk (*) at the beginning of the name keeps the folder at the top of the list for easy access. (If you ever want to keep a file or folder at the end of a list, you can put a ~ in front of the name.)

You can also make a new folder from within the Adobe Illustrator program by choosing the Save As command from the File menu. You can click the New Folder button in the dialog box and name the new folder.

Throwing away your Preferences file

We recommend that you throw away your Preferences file before you begin the lessons. Complete instructions for doing this are included in Lesson 1.

GETTING READY TO ROLL

Now that you've got everything installed, there are a few more things you need to know before you begin.

You should know Macintosh basics before you use *Classroom in a Book*. If you can use a menu, resize a window, and open and save files, you know enough to use this book.

Watching the movies

Adobe Teach movies are QuickTime movies included with *Classroom in a Book*. You can watch a movie to see a preview of what's to come in a lesson, or you can go back and review the movie after you've tried a new technique. You can even watch a movie right now if you want. You'll see the Adobe Teach movie icon whenever it's time to watch a movie.

Depending on the amount of memory you have, you may have to close the Adobe Illustrator program while you watch the movie.

To watch an Adobe Teach movie:

1 Make sure that QuickTime is installed in your system.

2 In the Finder (not in Adobe Illustrator), locate the folder named Adobe Teach.

The movies are named Adobe Teach followed by a number. You watch the movies with an application called Movie Player, which is also included in the folder.

3 Double-click an Adobe Teach file icon to open a movie.

4 When the application opens, choose Start from the Movie menu.

5 To play the movie again, choose Rewind from the Movie menu. Then choose Start from the Movie menu.

6 To close the application, choose Quit from the File menu.

You can control the movie by using the control bar at the bottom of the movie window.

Use the Volume Control button (speaker) on the left to change the volume. Position the pointer on the button, and hold down the mouse button to drag and change the volume.

The triangle just to the right of the Volume Control button is the Play button. You can click this button instead of choosing Start from the Movie menu. When you click the Play button during play, the triangle changes to a Pause button (double bar), and the movie pauses. Click again to continue.

Using the final files

A completed file for each project in this book is included in each lesson folder. You will take a look at the final file before you begin the project. We recommend that you resize the final file and leave it open in case you want to refer to it while you are working on a project.

The final files for the lessons are locked. You will not be able to save any changes to the final files.

6

Using the interim files

An interim file is a file that contains portions of the final artwork file. We have included interim files for several reasons.

Perhaps you don't want to do everything in a long lesson. Or maybe you did part of a lesson and lost your working file.

To use the interim files, first find their location noted in a specific lesson. If you open the interim file at the specified point, all the steps in the lesson up until that point will have been completed. You can then continue the lesson from that point. Interim files are included in the Extras folder.

Moving on

Now that your system is set up and ready to go, it's time to begin learning Adobe Illustrator. Lesson 1 begins with a quick overview of the Adobe Illustrator program's features. If you're new to Adobe Illustrator, you'll see a little bit about how it works. If you've used Adobe Illustrator before, you'll get to see many of the latest features.

The Art of Travel

THREE 3 REASONS TO TRAVEL

Painting
One great reason to travel to Europe is the inspired painting in the Louvre.

Crafts
Another great reason to travel to Europe is the vibrant textiles you may find .

Another reason to travel is to explore the classic architecture in the city of Athens.
Architecture

Lesson

1

LESSON 1: EXPLORATIONS

Part of learning any software program is getting an eye for the kinds of things that the program can do. In the first part of this lesson, you'll examine some artwork from Navigations—The Ultimate Travel Service. Navigations is a fictitious travel agency we've created to provide a context for the lessons in this book. You'll work in the world of travel and create the kinds of projects a high-quality travel service might pay you to do.

Navigations began in the early fifties as a small service agency with a single site. Today the company has an ultra-chic worldwide clientele.

Of course, Navigations is continuously exploring new ways to capture business. One of those ways is visually to grab the attention of armchair travelers and turn them into customers.

Extensive market research has led the ad execs to focus on print media. They've chosen print for two reasons: because you can't fast-forward through it, and if the art is high quality, clients may keep it around the house.

Navigations wants to achieve a completely new look and feel for the corporate image. Projects will include a new company logo, new letterhead, a postcard, a poster—even an international newsletter. You'll work on the kinds of design projects an upscale worldwide travel corporation might need.

But first, you need to refine your skill at using the Adobe Illustrator program. So let's get started. You'll begin by taking a quick look at the program. Then you'll move on to learning how to draw lines and curves with the pen tool.

Completing this lesson may take anywhere from 2½ to 3½ hours, depending on your current pen tool expertise, the kind of computer you have, and any previous experience with the Adobe Illustrator program.

THROWING AWAY THE PREFERENCES FILE

But first, some nuts and bolts.

The Adobe Illustrator Prefs file determines certain settings when you open the program. If you have already used the program, it's a good idea to throw away your Preferences file so that the defaults will be restored. Adobe Illustrator will create a new Preferences file when you start the program.

To throw away the Prefs file:

1 Quit the Adobe Illustrator program if it is running.

2 Open the System folder, and open the Preferences folder.

3 Locate the Adobe Illustrator Prefs file, and drag it to the Trash.

4 Choose Empty Trash from the Special menu.

5 Close all the folders.

6 Double-click the Adobe Illustrator icon to start the program.

EXPLORING ADOBE ILLUSTRATOR

In the first part of this lesson, you'll explore some fairly complex artwork and look at some of the Adobe Illustrator program's latest features. For now, you won't do any drawing; you'll just check things out.

After this quick tour, you'll get down to the basics of creating line art. Once you learn how to use the pen tool, you will be able to draw exquisitely smooth curves with a few clicks of the mouse. At the end of the lesson, you'll draw some shapes that will help you get started with Navigations projects.

To open the file:

1 If the program is not open, double-click the Adobe Illustrator icon in the Adobe Illustrator folder.

2 Choose Open from the File menu. A dialog box appears.

3 Locate the Adobe Illustrator CIB folder, and open it.

The *Classroom in a Book* files are stored in individual lesson folders. The files you'll use in this lesson are in the Lesson 1 folder.

4 Open the Lesson 1 folder.

5 Open the folder named *01Demo*.

6 Open the file named *01Sample*.

You will learn how to create this three-fold travel brochure later in these lessons.

The document opens in Preview view. In this view you see the drawing as it will be printed, with all the colors displayed.

We'll take a look at the entire window area to see the different features.

Drawing Area

The default Artboard is letter size (8.5 by 11 inches), but you can specify dimensions up to a maximum size of 120 by 120 inches.

The two rectangles that surround the brochure define the page boundary and the *imageable* area. The outer rectangle represents the paper size, and the inner (dotted) rectangle represents the *imageable* area of the currently selected printer. The size of the imageable area can vary from printer to printer.

You can use the area outside the imageable area for practice sketching. All objects drawn in the file will be saved with the file, but only those inside the inner (dotted) rectangle will be printed.

Toolbox

The first time you open a document, the toolbox appears on the left side of the screen. In addition to the tools you see, the toolbox contains several other tools. You can see the other tools by positioning the pointer on a tool in the toolbox and holding down the mouse button on those tools that have a small black triangle.

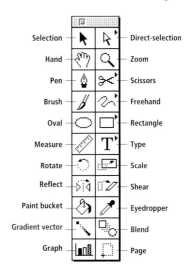

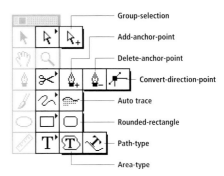

To select a tool in the toolbox, you click it. To select one of the additional tools, you position the pointer on the current tool in the toolbox and drag to the right to highlight the tool of your choice. When you release the mouse button, the selected tool replaces the tool currently in the toolbox.

Note: *You can restore all the default tools to the toolbox by holding down the Command and Shift keys and double-clicking any tool in the toolbox.*

Zooming

 You can use the zoom tool to zoom in on a specific area of the art.

1 Move the mouse pointer to the toolbox, and click the zoom tool. The status line at the bottom of the window tells you you've got the zoom tool.

2 Move the pointer into the drawing area.

3 Hold down the mouse button and drag a marquee around the airplane in the lower-left corner of the brochure.

The area you selected is enlarged. You can see the zoom factor in the title bar of the window.

Note: You can also zoom by selecting the zoom tool in the toolbox and then clicking in the drawing area.

4 Choose Actual Size from the View menu. The document is displayed at its actual size.

5 Choose Fit In Window from the View menu. The view is zoomed out so that the complete document is displayed inside the window.

Status line

The status line is displayed at the bottom of the window. You can set the status line to display the current tool or several other options.

1 Locate the status line at the bottom of the window. It probably says *Zoom*, because the currently selected tool is the zoom tool.

2 Move the pointer to the status line, and hold down the mouse button.

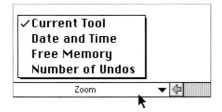

You see different options for what you can display in the status line.

3 Use the mouse and drag to check out the different options.

4 When you have finished, choose Current Tool as the status line option.

Paint Style palette

The Paint Style palette is where you set the paint attributes for the objects you draw. You can fill objects with colors, patterns, or gradient fills. When you fill an object, everything inside the object is filled. You can also stroke an object. When you stroke an object, only the outline is painted.

1 Choose Show Paint Style from the Window menu. The Paint Style palette appears.

2 Move the pointer to the small downward-pointing triangle near the top right corner of the palette, and hold down the mouse button.

This opens the Panel Display pop-up menu. The icons indicate different ways you can display the Paint Style palette. Try them out.

You can also change the size of this palette by clicking the panel icon just to the left of the pop-up menu arrow. Click different panels to display them.

3 Choose the second option in the pop-up menu, so that the two side-by-side panels are displayed in the Paint Style palette.

4 Drag the Paint Style palette by its title bar to the right side of your screen.

You'll use the selection tool to select an object in the drawing so that you can take a look at the paint attributes.

5 Click the selection tool (solid arrow) in the toolbox.

6 Move the pointer inside the large *A* in *Art* on the first panel of the brochure, and click the mouse button.

7 Look at the Paint Style palette to see how the object is filled and stroked.

The Fill box shows you the object is filled with a green gradient. The Stroke box shows the object is stroked with black. Directly below the paint swatches, you see the current Fill and Stroke attributes in words—F: art gradient, S: 100% Black. In the right panel, near the bottom, you can see that the Stroke Weight is .8 points.

8 Click the blue circle near the bottom of the left panel of the brochure, and look at its paint attributes.

9 Choose Hide Paint Style from the Window menu to close the palette. The palette is closed.

Character palette

The Character palette is where you can set type attributes.

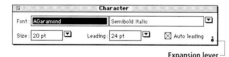 You'll use the type tool to select some type in the drawing so that you can take at look at the type attributes in the Character palette.

1 Click the type tool in the toolbox.

2 Drag the I-beam pointer across the word *Painting* in the center panel to highlight the text.

3 Click the zoom tool in the toolbox.

4 Drag a marquee around the selected word *Painting* to zoom in on it.

5 Choose Show Character from the Window menu.

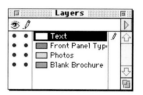

You can see that the font is AGaramond Semibold Italic, the size is 20 and the leading is 24.

6 Click the lever in the bottom right corner of the Character palette to expand the palette.

The Character palette expands to show additional type options. If you want to move the Character palette to a different location on your screen, you can drag it by its title bar.

7 Click the selection tool in the toolbox.

8 Now you see the baseline below the type, indicating the entire text object is selected.

9 Choose Select None from the Edit menu so that nothing is selected in the drawing.

10 Choose Hide Character from the Window menu. The palette is closed.

11 Choose Fit In Window from the View menu so that you can see the entire drawing.

Layers palette

This document was created on four different layers. The different layers provide an easy way to group and arrange objects in the document. For example, a given layer can be locked or hidden.

1 Choose Show Layers from the Window menu.

Notice the four different layers.

2 Drag the palette by its title bar so it is near the edge of the window and so you can see most of the drawing as well as the palette.

3 Take a look at the dots in the left column.

A dot beneath the eye icon indicates you can view that layer. A dot beneath the pencil icon indicates you can write to that layer.

Next, you'll turn off all of the layers. Then you'll turn them back on, one by one, so you can see which objects are on each layer.

4 Click the dot below the eye icon for each of the layers, until none of the drawing is displayed.

5 Click below the eye icon, to the left of the Blank Brochure layer, to turn the view of that layer back on.

6 Click below the eye icon to the left of the Photos layer to view that layer.

7 Click below the eye icon to turn on the other two layers.

8 Make sure that all the layers have been turned on.

9 Choose Hide Layers from the Window to close the palette.

Artwork

So far, you've looked at what is called Preview view, where all the colors of the objects are shown. When you work in Artwork view, you see only the *paths* for the objects. The path is the basic element of the Adobe Illustrator program. A path can be a single straight line or a curve, a combination of lines and curves, a square or a circle, or an irregular shape.

Working in Artwork can sometimes be faster, because it doesn't take as much time to redisplay the screen as you work. Sometimes you want to see only the paths, especially when objects are drawn on top of other objects.

1 Choose Artwork from the View menu, and take a look at the artwork.

You see that the objects in the drawing are a series of paths.

2 Click on different lines to select them.

Notice that the lines you click are selected with different colors. The colors indicate the layer of the selected object. If you click the large A on the front panel, the selection is red, the same color as the Front Panel Type layer in the layers palette.

3 Choose Show Paint Style from the Window menu. You can see what the paint attributes are, even though they are not shown in the artwork.

Don't be intimidated by the paths in the artwork of the drawing. By the end of Lesson 6, you'll be able to create all of them.

Custom views

You can create custom views and save them with your documents. A custom view can include the current zoom level, whether you are working in Artwork or Preview, different layer options, and of course, different portions of the artwork.

1 Hold down the mouse button on the View menu. The custom views created for this document are listed at the bottom of the menu.

2 Choose Painting Closeup from the View menu, and take a look. This custom view is a Preview view and has been zoomed to 300%.

3 Look at the other views at the bottom of the View menu.

Get ready to go to work

Next you'll put everything away so you can begin learning how to draw.

1 Choose Close from the File menu to close the file. When the program asks if you want to save the changes, click Don't Save.

2 Close any open palettes. Make sure the toolbox is displayed. (If you closed the toolbox, you can open it by choosing Show Toolbox from the Window menu.)

Before you begin drawing, you'll open a new file and save it.

1 Choose New from the File menu.

2 Choose Save As from the File menu.

3 Name the file *01Work1*, and save it in the Project folder. (See the "Getting Started" section of this book for information about the Project folder.)

Now that you've had a quick look at the program, it's time to get started learning how to use it. The rest of this lesson will focus on drawing paths.

TIP: IF YOU DON'T SEE THE TOOLBOX, CHOOSE SHOW TOOLBOX FROM THE WINDOW MENU.

DRAWING STRAIGHT LINES

The pen tool is used for drawing both straight lines and smooth flowing curves. You begin with lines. Later on, you'll learn about curves.

Drawing a line

You draw a line by clicking at the points where you want to begin and end the line. For this part of the lesson, you'll work in Artwork view.

1 Choose Artwork from the View menu (Command-E). For now, you'll be working in Artwork view, since you won't be painting any paths.

2 Click the pen tool in the toolbox.

Note: If you don't see the toolbox, choose Show Toolbox from the Window menu.

3 Move the pointer to the drawing area. Since you won't be printing these practice lines, you can use parts of the drawing area outside the dotted rectangles.

The pen tool pointer has a small *x* next to it. This indicates that you can begin a new path.

4 Click the mouse button once. Do not drag, just click.

When you clicked the mouse button, you created an anchor point, a small solid square. This first click indicates where to begin the line.

Notice the *x* has disappeared, indicating that you are now continuing a path rather than beginning a new one.

5 Move the pointer an inch or two diagonally up and, right and click the mouse button.

The second click creates a second anchor point, and a line is drawn between the beginning anchor point and the second anchor point.

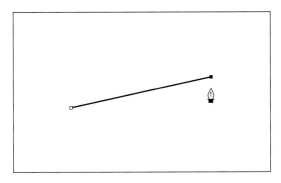

6 Click the pen tool in the toolbox to end the path.

Whenever you draw an open path, you need to indicate when you have finished a particular path. You do this by clicking the pen tool in the toolbox. An *open path* is one that has a distinct beginning and end. *Closed paths* are loops and have no endpoints. You'll learn more about closed paths later in this book.

You can draw a line that has as many connected points as you want.

To draw several connected lines:

1 With the pen tool selected, move the pointer to the drawing area, and click the mouse button.

2 Move the pointer, and click again.

3 Move the pointer, and click again. The program will draw a line to every place that you click.

4 Continue moving the pen tool and clicking until you have a dozen or so anchor points. *Do not click the pen tool to end the path.* (Your path may look quite different from the one below.)

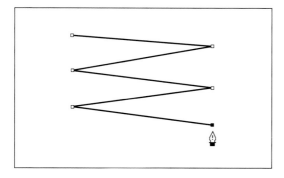

Undoing, selecting, and erasing

As you learn the basic drawing techniques, you'll want to erase paths you've drawn.

Undoing the last operation

1 Choose Undo pen from the Edit menu (Command-Z).

Note: The keyboard command for the Undo command (Command-Z) is probably one of the first shortcuts you'll want to memorize.

The last segment of the path is erased.

2 Press Command-Z to undo another segment. The next-to-last segment of the path is erased.

3 Move the pointer to the status line at the bottom of the window.

4 Hold down the mouse button and choose Number of Undos from the pop-up menu.

This shows you how many undos and redos you have left. Each time you use the Undo command, another segment is undone. The number of Undos you can perform is a preference you can set in the General Preferences dialog box. The default is 10. This means you can undo 10 operations. See the *Adobe Illustrator User Guide* for more information about setting preferences.

Although you won't change it now, you can specify the number of undos to be as many as 200.

5 Press Command-Z two or three more times.

6 Choose Redo Pen from the Edit menu (Command-Shift-Z). The last line you erased is restored.

7 Choose Redo Pen from the Edit menu again. The next segment is restored.

8 Continue to choose Redo or press Command-Shift-Z until the entire path is restored. At this point, the Redo command is dimmed in the Edit menu.

9 Move the pointer to the status line at the bottom of the window.

10 Hold down the mouse button and choose Current tool from the pop-up menu so you can see what tools you select.

Erasing an entire path

Of course, you'll sometimes want to erase an entire path, not just the last segment. Before you can erase the path, you must select it.

1 Click the pen tool in the toolbox to end the current path.

2 Click the selection tool in the toolbox.

3 Position the pointer on the zigzag path, and click the mouse button. The entire path is selected. You can tell the entire path is selected because all the anchor points are selected; that is, they are solid.

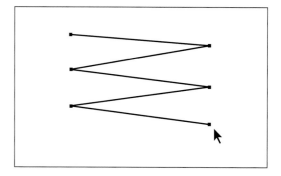

TIP: USE THE SELECTION
TOOL TO SELECT AN
ENTIRE PATH. USE
THE DIRECT SELECTION
TOOL TO SELECT ONLY
A PART OF A PATH.

4 Choose Cut from the Edit menu (Command-X).

The path is deleted.

If you want to restore the path, you can choose Undo from the Edit menu to undo the cut operation.

5 Press Command-Z to undo the cut and restore the path.

Erasing part of a path

The selection tool selected the entire path. Suppose you want to remove only a part of the path. You can use the direct selection tool to select path segments. A *segment* is the line between two anchor points.

1 Click the direct selection tool (hollow arrow) in the toolbox. Check the status line at the bottom of the toolbox to make sure that you have the direct selection tool.

2 Click away from the path to deselect everything. When nothing is selected, you don't see any of the anchor points on the path.

3 Click one of the segments in the path.

Although you don't see any difference on your screen, the segment that you clicked is selected. (The anchor points on the path are not selected; they are hollow.)

4 Choose Cut from the Edit menu (Command-X). The segment is deleted. Now, the rest of the path is selected.

As you can see, you can use the direct selection tool to select just a segment of a path rather than the entire path.

5 Click away from the path to deselect everything.

6 Click another path segment; then press Command-X to delete the segment.

7 Choose Undo Cut from the Edit menu (Command-Shift-Z) to restore the deleted segments.

8 Use the direct selection tool to drag a marquee around the entire path.

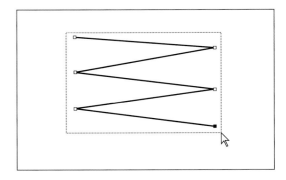

When you release the mouse button, all of the anchor points inside the marquee are solid, indicating that they are selected.

9 Choose Cut from the Edit menu (Command-X) to delete everything you selected.

Keeping lines vertical, horizontal, or diagonal

You can draw lines that are vertical, horizontal, or diagonal by holding down the Shift key. This is referred to as *constraining* the line. When you hold down the Shift key, you can draw directly to the right or left (horizontal), directly up or down (vertical), or at a 45-degree angle.

To draw constrained lines:

1 Click the pen tool in the toolbox.

2 Move the pointer to the drawing area, and click the mouse button.

3 Hold down the Shift key.

4 Move the mouse to the right about an inch, and click the mouse button. Keep the Shift key down.

5 Move the pointer down about an inch. Keep the Shift key down.

6 Click the mouse button.

7 Keep the Shift key down and click the mouse button to see how lines are constrained.

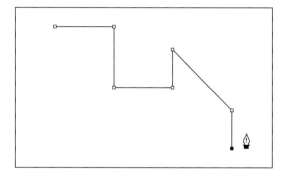

8 Click the selection tool in the toolbox.

9 Click the path to select it.

10 Choose Cut from the Edit menu (or press the Delete key) to delete the path.

11 Choose Close from the File to close this file.

DRAWING CURVES

In this part of the lesson, you'll learn how to draw smooth curved lines with the pen tool. Just as drawing a curve on paper is a bit more difficult than drawing a straight line, drawing a curve with the program is a bit more difficult.

You'll begin by drawing a single curve and continue by learning how to draw a series of curves together. You'll also learn how to draw a path that has both lines and curves.

First you'll open a file that contains some guidelines to help you learn.

To open the file:

1 Choose Open from the File menu.

2 Open the Lesson 1 folder and the file named *01Paths*. You see some gray curves and shapes. (We've created this file with the gray lines on a separate, locked layer. You'll do your practice drawing on the top layer.)

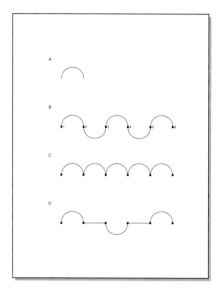

3 Choose Save As from the File menu.

4 Name the file *01Work2*, and save it in the Project folder.

Drawing a single curve

For starters, you'll draw a single curve that has two anchor points. We've provided some custom views with the file to make it easier to zoom in on the curve you want to work on.

To draw a single curve:

1 Choose Curve A from the View menu.

2 Click the pen tool in the toolbox. The pen should have the small *x* beside it.

3 Move the pointer to the bottom left end of curve A.

4 Hold down the mouse button and drag straight up to the dot.

5 Release the mouse button.

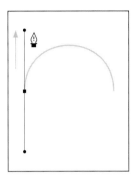 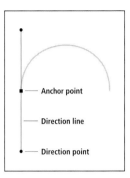

No, it's not a curve yet. What you've done is create the first anchor point, where the curve will begin. Attached to the anchor point are *direction lines*. The circles at the ends of the direction lines are *direction points*.

The anchor points, direction points, and direction lines are aids that will help you draw. These aids are always displayed in the current selection color, in this case, light blue. Anchor points, direction points, and direction lines are never printed.

Much of the editing you will do involves moving anchor points and direction lines. Try to remember that anchor points are square and direction points are round.

Next, you indicate where you want the curve to end.

6 Move the pointer to the end of the curve.

7 Hold down the mouse button and drag downward to the dot.

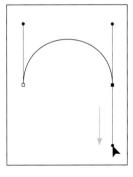

Now you see the curved line (black). You also see the direction lines and points (blue) associated with the second anchor point.

When you release the mouse button, the pointer turns back to the pen.

8 Click the pen tool in the toolbox to end the current path.

You always need to indicate when you have finished drawing a path. You do this by clicking the pen tool in the toolbox. Alternatively, you can choose Select None from the Edit menu.

Editing curves

It's possible you didn't draw the curve you wanted the first time you tried. That's what the anchor points and direction lines are all about. You can use them to edit the curves.

First, you'll learn a quick way to make copies of the curve, so you'll have some spares around.

To move and copy the curve:

1 Click the selection tool in the toolbox.

2 Click the curve to select it.

Notice that the two anchor points are selected and that the direction lines and points are not displayed.

3 Position the pointer on the curve, and drag to the right until there is about a quarter-inch between the two curves. Release the mouse button. You have moved the curve. Now you'll put it back and try a different technique.

4 Choose Undo Move from the Edit menu.

5 Position the pointer on the curve, and drag to the right until there is about a quarter-inch between the two curves. Do *not* release the mouse button.

6 Hold down the Option key. Notice the change in pointer shape. A hollow pointer is adjacent to the solid pointer. This indicates that you are making a copy.

7 Release the mouse button.

8 Release the Option key. The original curve remains in place, and a copy is displayed at the point where you moved it.

9 Choose Repeat Transform from the Arrange menu (Command-D).

Your screen should look like this:

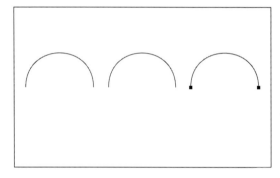

The Repeat Transform command lets you repeat many operations. In this case you repeated the move and copy operations that you just performed.

Changing curves by moving anchor points

You can change the shape of a curve by moving the anchor points of the curve.

1 Click the direct selection tool in the toolbox. You use the direct selection tool because you want to work only with segments of the path rather than with the entire path.

2 Click the curved line of the leftmost curve. The anchor points and some of the direction lines are shown. The anchor points are hollow, indicating they are not selected.

3 Click the anchor point on the right side of the curve. The anchor point is solid, indicating that it is selected. You also see both blue direction lines.

4 Hold down the mouse button and drag to move the selected anchor point up and down, then back and forth, to see the changes made to the curve.

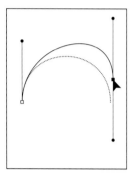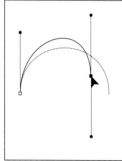

5 Release the mouse button.

Changing curves by moving segments

You can change the shape of a curve by moving the line itself.

1 Click away from the artwork to deselect everything.

2 Choose a curve you have not edited, and click the curved line.

In this case, the anchor points are hollow (de-selected), and the upper direction lines appear. You have selected the line segment and not the anchor points.

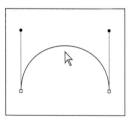

3 Move the pointer to the curved line, and hold down the mouse button.

4 Drag the segment up and down to see the effects. The anchor points remain stationary, and the segment changes shape.

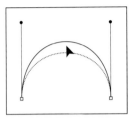 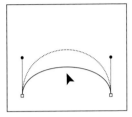

Changing curves by moving direction points

You can change the shape of a curve by moving the direction points.

1 Click away from the artwork to deselect everything.

2 Choose a curve you have not edited, and click an anchor point.

3 Move the pointer to the upper direction point on the right, hold down the mouse button and drag upward. Notice how the curve changes.

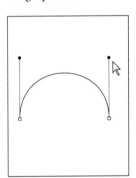 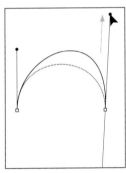

4 Drag a direction point to the right or the left and notice how the slope of the curve changes.

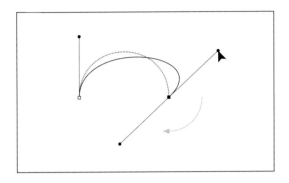

To clean up your screen:

1 Choose Select All from the Edit menu (Command-A) to select all the artwork.

2 Choose Cut from the Edit menu (Command-X) to delete all the artwork.

Tips for drawing curves

When you first begin drawing curves with the pen tool, you may wonder where to put an anchor point and how far or which direction to drag a direction point. Here are some answers to common questions about drawing curves.

In what direction do I drag?

Drag in the direction of the bump on the curve you are about to create. For an upward curve, drag up. For a downward curve, drag down.

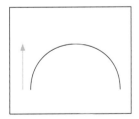 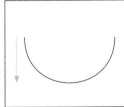

How far should I drag?

Use the One-Third rule. Imagine that the line forming a final curve is stretched out flat into a straight line. Drag your direction point about one-third of the straight-line length of the curve.

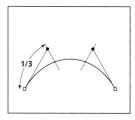

Where do I put anchor points?

Put anchor points at the sides of the curve rather than on the top of the bump. When you put them on the sides, it is easier to edit the smooth part of the curve.

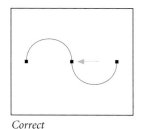

Correct   Incorrect

Place anchor points as far apart as possible while still fitting the curve. Take big steps when you draw curves.

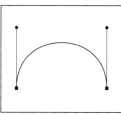 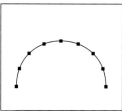

Correct   Incorrect

Drawing multiple curves

Now that you've learned how to draw a single curve, you're ready for several curves on the same path.

To draw a path with multiple curves:

1 Choose Curve B from the View menu. The view is changed to Curve B.

2 Click the pen tool in the toolbox.

3 Move the pointer to the left end of the curved line near Point 1.

4 Hold down the mouse button and drag upward about an inch.

Dragging the direction line indicates the direction of the curve you are about to create. Since you are dragging upward, the bump of the curve will be on the top.

5 Release the mouse button.

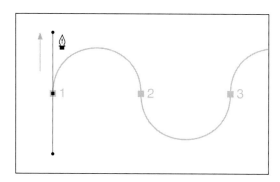

6 Position the pointer at Point 2.

7 Hold down the mouse button and drag downward. Don't worry if your curve doesn't match the drawing exactly. This is just for practice.

8 Release the mouse button.

9 Move the pointer to Point 3. Hold down the mouse button and drag upward to create the second curve. Release the mouse button.

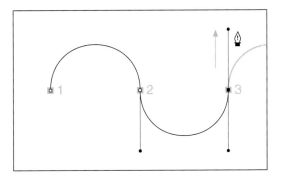

10 Finish tracing the outline by positioning the pointer on each numbered point and dragging to create the curves.

11 Click the pen tool in the toolbox to indicate that you have completed the path.

Drawing curves with corner points

All curves are not alike to the Adobe Illustrator program. The curves you have just drawn—paths along a continuous wave shape—are connected by anchor points called *smooth points*. Noncontinuous curves are joined by *corner points*. Corner points are more easily seen than described.

1 Choose Curve C from the View menu.

Take a look at the curves in Curve C of the drawing. These curves are all joined by corner points. A corner point is created differently from a smooth point.

2 Click the pen tool in the toolbox.

3 Position the pointer on the left end of the path.

4 Hold down the mouse button and drag upward to create the first anchor point.

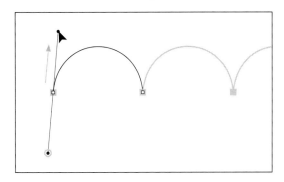

5 Move the pointer to the end of the first curve and drag downward to set the second anchor point and create the first curve.

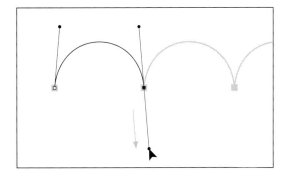

Next, you make the second anchor point a corner point.

6 Move the pointer over the second anchor point, the one you just drew. The caret next to the pen tool pointer indicates that you can make this anchor point a corner point.

7 Hold down the Option key. Notice that the status line reads "Pen: Make Corner."

8 Hold down the mouse button and drag upward to establish the direction of the outgoing curve.

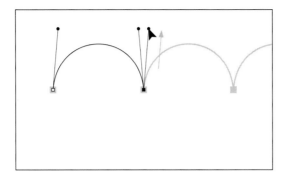

9 Release the mouse button, and then release the Option key.

10 Move the pointer to the third anchor point, and drag downward to establish the second curve.

11 Reposition the pointer over the third anchor point, hold down the Option key, and drag upward to establish the corner point.

12 Continue until you have drawn the entire path.

13 Click the pen tool in the toolbox to end the path.

Drawing curves and lines together

When you draw lines and curves together in the same path, you need to create corner points where the path changes from a line to a curve and vice versa. These corner points are created by moving the pointer back over the existing anchor point and clicking or dragging. You'll practice this next.

Time-out for an Adobe Teach movie

If your system is capable of running Adobe Teach movies, you can see a preview of the techniques taught in this section.

Depending on the amount of memory you have, you may have to close the Adobe Illustrator program while you watch the movie.

To play the movie:

1 From the Finder, locate the Adobe Teach folder in the Adobe Illustrator CIB folder and open it.

2 Double-click the file named *Adobe Teach 1.*

3 When you see the splash screen, choose Start from the Movie menu.

4 You can use the Rewind command in the Movie menu to rewind the move and start it again.

For more information on playing the Adobe Teach movies, see the "Getting Started" section of this book.

5 Choose Close from the File menu.

6 Return to the Adobe Illustrator program.

And now, back to the lesson

1 Choose Curve D from the View menu.

2 Click the pen tool in the toolbox.

3 Draw the first curve in the usual way—by dragging up, then moving the pointer to the second anchor point and dragging down.

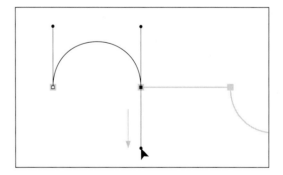

Next, you make the second anchor point a corner point.

4 Move the pointer back over the second anchor point, and click the mouse button. You click, rather than drag, because you want to create a line next.

5 Move the pointer to the right, where the end of the line will be, and click the mouse button.

Now you must create a corner point because you are switching from a line to a curve.

6 Position the pointer on the last point you drew, and drag the direction point down to set the direction of the next curve.

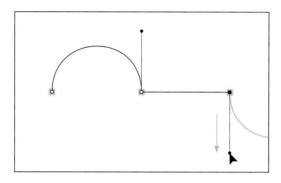

7 Finish drawing the curve by moving the pointer to the other side of the bump and dragging upward.

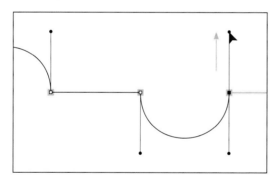

8 Make the last anchor point you drew into a corner point by clicking that anchor point.

9 Draw the end of the straight segment by clicking the mouse button.

10 Make a corner point for the last curve. Then draw the curve.

11 Click the pen tool in the toolbox to end the path.

EDITING PATH SEGMENTS

There may be a time or two when you want to remove part of a path and replace it. You'll learn how in this part of the lesson.

1 If necessary, scroll to see all of the last set of lines and curves that you drew.

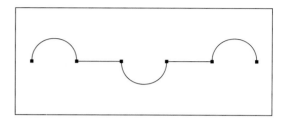

Suppose you want to delete the curve in the center and change it to a straight line.

2 Choose Select None from the Edit menu (Command-Shift-A) to deselect everything.

3 Click the direct selection tool in the toolbox.

4 Click the bump of the center curve to select it.

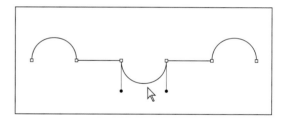

5 Choose Cut from the Edit menu (Command-X), or press the Delete key.

6 Click the pen tool in the toolbox.

7 Position the pointer over the left anchor point (where the curve you deleted used to begin). Notice that the *x* next to the pointer changes to a slash when you are over the point. The slash indicates that you are continuing an existing path.

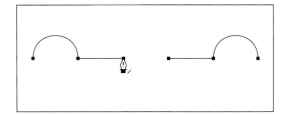

8 Click the mouse button.

9 Move the pointer across the gap to the anchor point where the curve used to end. Notice that the pen pointer now has a small box with a line, indicating a merge from one path to another.

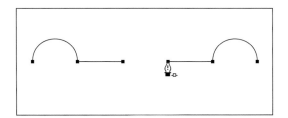

10 Click the mouse button. The new line is part of the existing path.

GIVE ME A BREAK

Using the pen tool to draw curves takes practice. It's a little bit like riding a bicycle; once you get it, you've got it forever. The more you draw, the easier it gets. We've provided some drawings to help you practice using the pen tool.

But first, take a look at something you can do right now, without any practice at all.

Seven ways to draw a rectangle

Drawing curves might seem tough. It may seem like *you* do more work than the computer does. But take a look at a different feature—the rectangle tool. Here are not one, not two, but seven ways to draw a rectangle.

You can find the rectangle tool in the toolbox, right next to the oval tool.

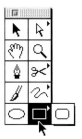

To draw a rectangle by dragging edge to edge:

1 Click the rectangle tool in the toolbox.

2 Scroll to find some empty space on the screen. Any white space will do, since this is just practice.

3 Move the pointer to the drawing area, hold down the mouse button, and drag diagonally down and right an inch or two. Then release the mouse button.

To draw a rectangle by dragging from the center:

1 Make sure the rectangle tool is selected.

2 Hold down the Option key and drag.

Note: *Another way to draw a rectangle from the center is to double-click the rectangle tool in the toolbox. A plus sign appears in the toolbox. All the rectangles you draw will be from the center.*

To draw a rectangle that is a square:

1 Make sure the rectangle tool is selected.

2 Hold down the Shift key and drag. The rectangle is constrained to a square.

Keep in mind that all squares are rectangles, but not all rectangles are squares.

To draw a rectangle by the numbers:

1 Make sure the rectangle tool is selected.

2 Click the mouse button in the drawing area. The Rectangle dialog box appears.

3 Enter 200 for the Width.

4 Enter 100 for the Height.

Note: You can move from one field to another in any dialog box by pressing the Tab key.

5 Leave the Corner Radius at zero.

6 Click OK.

To draw a rectangle with round corners:

1 Choose the rounded rectangle tool from the toolbox. This tool is next to the rectangle tool. Position the pointer on the rectangle tool; hold down the mouse button and drag right.

2 Drag a rectangle, or click and enter a height and width. Leave the Corner Radius value at the default of 12, and click OK.

To copy an existing rectangle:

1 Click the selection tool in the toolbox.

2 Click a rectangle to select it.

3 Position the pointer on the edge of the rectangle, and begin dragging.

4 While the mouse button is down, hold down the Option key.

5 Release the mouse button and then the Option key.

To repeat the copy of the last rectangle:

1 Choose Repeat Transform from the Arrange menu (Command-D).

2 Do it again.

Actually, these are not the only ways to create rectangles. You can also create scaled, rotated, reflected, and sheared copies of the original. We'll save that for a later lesson.

To delete all of your rectangles:

1 Use the selection tool and drag a marquee to select all the rectangles. (You can also choose Select All from the Edit menu to select everything on the screen.)

2 Choose Cut from the Edit menu (Command-X), or press the Delete key.

Drawing ovals

Everything you just learned about rectangles applies to ovals as well, with one exception. *There is no rounded oval tool.* Try creating ovals by dragging, by the numbers, and from the center. Use the Shift key when you want a circle.

EDITING ANCHOR POINTS

Next you'll practice splitting paths and adding, deleting, and converting anchor points.

Splitting paths

You can use the scissors tool to produce a break in a path. Cuts made with the scissors tool must be on a line or a curve rather than on an endpoint.

1 Select the rectangle tool in the toolbox. (Because the rounded rectangle tool was used last, you'll have to position the pointer on the rounded rectangle tool, hold down the mouse button, and drag right. Check the status line to make sure that you have the rectangle tool.)

2 Move the pointer to the drawing area, and drag to draw a small square.

3 Click the scissors tool in the toolbox.

4 Click the top edge of the rectangle.

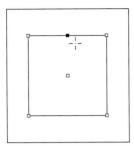

You see a new selected anchor point where you clicked. Actually, the scissors tool has created *two* anchor points. Because they are one on top of the other, you can see only one. Both are selected.

5 Click the direct selection tool in the toolbox.

6 Click away from the artwork to deselect everything.

7 Click the right edge of the rectangle so you can see the anchor points.

8 Move the pointer over the anchor point you just created. Hold down the mouse button and drag upward.

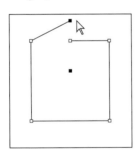

You can see that the path has been split.

Adding anchor points

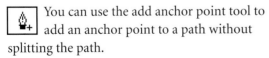 You can use the add anchor point tool to add an anchor point to a path without splitting the path.

1 Click the rectangle tool in the toolbox.

2 Click in the drawing area.

3 Enter 120 for Width, 120 for Height, and click OK.

4 Select the add anchor point tool in the toolbox. (You'll have to drag out from the scissors tool.)

5 Position the pointer at the center of the top edge of the square, and click the mouse button. A new anchor point appears.

6 Click the center of each side of the square to add an anchor point on each of the other three sides.

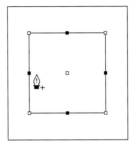

7 Click the direct selection tool in the toolbox.

8 Drag the anchor point at the center of the top segment down about halfway toward the center point.

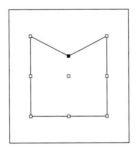

9 Drag the other new anchor points toward the center to make a star shape.

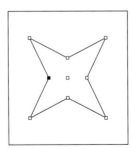

Converting direction points

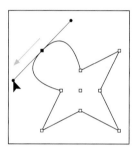 You can use the convert direction point tool to convert corner points to smooth points and vice versa.

1 Select the convert direction point tool in the toolbox. You'll have to drag from the add anchor point tool.

2 Position the pointer on the top left anchor point of the star.

3 Hold down the mouse button and drag left and down. The anchor point is converted to a smooth point.

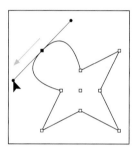

4 Position the pointer on the bottom left anchor point, and drag down and right.

5 Work your way around the star, and drag the remaining points of the star into smooth points until you have a four-leaf clover shape.

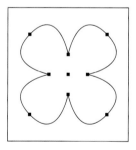

You can also use the convert direction point tool to convert smooth points to corner points.

6 Position the pointer on the top left anchor point of the four-leaf clover.

7 Click the mouse button. (Do not drag.) The anchor point is converted to a corner point.

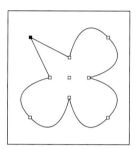

8 Click the remaining sides of the four-leaf clover shape to convert all the points back to corner points.

Deleting anchor points

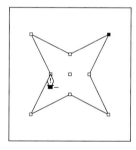 You can use the delete anchor point tool to delete an anchor point in a path.

1 Select the delete anchor point tool in the toolbox. (You'll have to drag.)

2 Position the pointer on one of the inner anchor points of the shape, and click the mouse button. The anchor point is deleted.

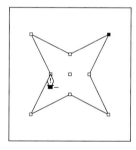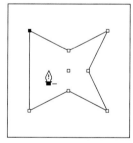

3 Click the remaining anchor points near the center of the star. The anchor points are deleted, and the shape returns to a square.

4 Click the top right corner of the square. The anchor point is deleted, and the shape becomes a triangle.

SUMMARY OF PEN TOOL POINTERS

Now that you've spent some time with the pen tool, you've noticed that there are several symbols that appear next to the pointer while you are drawing.

Here's a quick review of these pen tool pointers.

PEN TOOL POINTERS	
✎ₓ	Begin drawing a path
✎ₒ	Close a path
✎⁄	Continue on an existing path
✎ᵤ	Merge from one path to another
✎₊	Add an anchor point
✎₋	Delete an anchor point

Resetting the toolbox and closing the file

You'll reset the toolbox back to the default tools.

1 Hold down the Command key and the Shift key and double-click any tool in the toolbox. The default tools are restored.

2 Check to see that the rectangle and oval tools do not have plus signs, If they do, double-click them to remove the plus signs so that the regular tools are restored.

3 Choose Close from the File menu. Save your changes if you want.

PUTTING IT ALL TOGETHER

The best way to learn to use the pen tool is to practice. Once you get a feel for it, it will be easy. To help you practice, we've provided some different shapes for you to trace.

Drawing closed paths

The paths you have drawn so far with the pen tool have all been open paths. In a *closed* path, the final anchor point is drawn on the first anchor point of the path. Ovals and rectangles, for example, are closed paths.

1 Open the Lesson 1 folder and the file named *01Shapes*.

2 Choose Save As from the File menu, name the file *01Work3*, and save the file in the Project folder.

Each shape has been saved as an enlarged custom view. You can choose the different views from the bottom of the View menu. Remember that you can choose Fit In Window to see the entire file.

Here are some tips for drawing the shapes.

Cloud

You might want to start with the cloud because it doesn't have any corner points. Begin with the large bump at the top of the cloud. Drag up to begin the first curve. Move the pointer to the other side of the bump, and drag down. Then move the pointer more or less around in a clockwise direction, and continue to drag and create curves.

End the path by dragging on the first anchor point you created. You will see a small circle next to the pen tool when the pointer is over that anchor point.

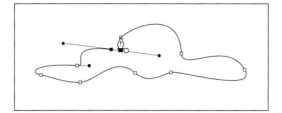

Don't worry if your curves don't exactly match the underlying shapes. It's the practice that counts. Remember that you can use the direct-selection tool if you want to edit your paths by moving segments, anchor points, and direction points.

Seashell

Choose Seashell from the View menu to see the zoomed version.

The seashell is mostly curves, but it does contain two straight lines. Make corner points when you switch from lines to curves, and vice versa. You can make these corner points by moving the pointer back over an anchor point and either clicking or dragging, depending on whether you want to draw a curve next or a line next. If you have trouble, see "Drawing Curves and Lines Together," earlier in this lesson.

You'll also need to create corner points when you draw the scallops at the top. If you have trouble, see "Drawing Curves with Corner Points," earlier in this lesson.

Be sure to close the path at the end.

Note: If you're trying to close path where the first anchor point is a curve, you can hold down the Option key while you create the final anchor point. The first curve's direction points and lines will remain unchanged.

Truck

Choose Truck from the View menu to see the zoomed version.

Remember that you can constrain straight lines to be vertical or horizontal by holding down the Shift key when you click the second point of the line. Use the oval and rectangle tools for the window and the wheels.

Umbrella

Begin by drawing the smooth curve at the top as one large curve with an anchor point at each end. Then make corner points to draw the three scallops at the bottom. Hold down the Option key when you close the path so that you won't change the original curve. If you have trouble, see "Drawing Curves with Corner Points," earlier in this lesson.

Palm tree

Most of the palm tree leaves can be created by clicking the pen tool. We have thrown you a couple of curves. Be sure to make a corner point when you need to.

Sailboat

By now you should be a pro.

Waves

Are they waves or is it a school of sharks? In any case, you're right; this is an *open* path and yet another opportunity to draw corner points. If you can draw this path without any help, you're definitely out of the jaws of the pen tool.

Practice makes perfect

When you have drawn all the shapes in this file, choose Select All, press the Delete key, and draw them one more time. If you can draw all of the shapes in this file, you're definitely a pen tool expert, and you'll be capable of drawing every object in the rest of this book.

Close your files, and save the work if you want to.

And now, off to work

Imagine you're in a place where there are waves and beach umbrellas and seashells. Maybe you'll get an image of something you'd like to draw. If you do, take a crack at it. If not, move on to Lesson 2 where you'll design a new logo for them.

Lesson

2

LESSON 2: DESIGNING A LOGO

Your task in this lesson is to create a design for a new corporate logo for Navigations. While designing and drawing the logo, you'll

• use the pen tool techniques you learned in Lesson 1 to draw the basic shapes

• learn how to use a template for tracing

• learn to paint paths with various levels of gray

• use the auto trace tool to trace part of a drawing automatically

• learn to paint paths with different colors

• get acquainted with the stacking order and learn how to move different levels of the drawing in front of one another

• add some type to the logo

• learn how to mix and save a color

Completing this lesson may take anywhere from 2 to 3 hours.

BEGINNING THIS LESSON

In this lesson, you'll open a file and a template. A template is a PICT file that you open when you open the Adobe Illustrator file. The template images are shown on the screen but do not print. Templates are most commonly used for tracing paths. You can create your own templates by scanning images with a scanner and saving them in the PICT format. (PICT is a bitmapped Macintosh format.)

1 Open the Lesson 2 folder and the file named *02Begin*.

Although this looks like an empty file, it has a template for you to trace, as well as some special paint settings in the Paint Style palette.

2 Use the scroll bars to scroll down below the page rectangle to see the airplane template. You'll use the template later in the lesson. (If you don't see the airplane, choose Show Template from the View menu.)

3 Choose Save As from the File menu, and name the file *02Work*. Save the file in the Project folder. Notice that the file name in the title bar is 02Work:02Templ, indicating that both the working Illustrator file and the template are open.

Note: The template is actually a separate file named 02Templ. *Whenever you open the Adobe Illustrator file, the template is also opened as long as the PICT file remains in its original location. If you move the PICT file, the program will ask for the location of a template when you open the Adobe Illustrator file.*

PLANNING THE PROJECT

Before you begin drawing, you'll take a look at the finished artwork and examine its components. Later, you can use this file as a reference as you draw in your work file.

1 Open the Lesson 2 folder and the file named *02Final*. This file contains the completed artwork.

TIP: IF DIALOG BOX UNITS ARE IN INCHES AND YOU WANT TO ENTER POINTS, TYPE THE VALUE AND ADD "PT." IF DIALOG BOX UNITS ARE IN POINTS AND YOU WANT TO ENTER INCHES, TYPE THE VALUE AND ADD "IN."

There is a rectangle in the background. Different paths are drawn for the clouds, the mountain, and the lake at the bottom of the drawing. The airplane is in front of the clouds and obscures part of them.

2 Choose Artwork from the View menu.

In Artwork view, you get a better sense of how the different shapes are placed in relation to one another.

3 Choose Preview from the View menu.

4 To resize the window, move the pointer to the size box in the bottom right corner of the window. Hold down the mouse button and drag upward and to the left until the window is about one-fourth the size of your screen.

5 Choose Fit In Window from the View Menu (Command-M).

6 Drag the window by its title bar to the upper right corner of your screen so that it is out of the way but available for you to see as you use the working file.

Note: Any time you want to view the final file, you can choose 02Final from the Window menu.

7 Choose 02Work:02Templ from the Window menu to make that file the active window.

CREATING THE ARTWORK

You'll create the artwork in several stages. First, you'll draw the background, lake, and mountains. After that, you'll create the clouds and the airplane.

Drawing the background rectangle

You begin by drawing the rectangle in the background.

To draw the rectangle:

1 Choose Artwork from the View menu (Command-E) to switch to Artwork view.

2 Scroll so that you can see the entire page

3 Click the rectangle tool in the toolbox.

4 Hold down the Option key, and click inside the window, at roughly the center of the page. The Rectangle dialog box appears.

5 Enter 246 for Width.

6 Click the word Height to select the height field, and enter 406 for Height.

7 Click OK to close the dialog box.

If you want to reposition the rectangle in the drawing area, click the selection tool (solid arrow), and drag the rectangle by its edge to the center of the page.

Depending on the size of your monitor, you may want to use the zoom tool to enlarge the drawing. Make sure that you can see the bottom half of the rectangle.

Moving and zooming while drawing

In addition to using the scroll bars to move the drawing, you can use the hand tool to drag sections of the drawing into view.

Sometimes you want to zoom in and out or move the image while you are in the middle of drawing a path. Here are some shortcuts for zooming and moving while you are using another tool.

To try out the zoom shortcuts:

1 Click the pen tool in the toolbox, and move the pointer into the drawing area.

2 Hold down the spacebar on the keyboard with your index finger. The hand tool appears. Holding down the spacebar has the same effect as clicking the hand tool.

3 Hold down the mouse button and use the hand tool to drag inside the drawing.

The hand tool is selected as long as you hold down the spacebar. When you release the spacebar, the tool changes back to the currently selected tool, in this case, the pen tool.

4 Hold down the spacebar with your index finger and hold down the Command key with your middle finger. The zoom-in tool appears.

5 Click the mouse button to zoom in a level. Releasing the keys returns the pen tool.

6 Hold down the spacebar with your index finger, the Command key with your middle finger, and the Option key with your ring finger. The zoom-out tool appears. Click the mouse button to zoom out a level.

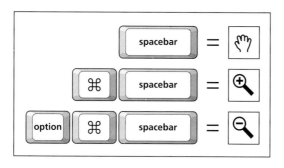

Important: When using these keyboard shortcuts, it's a good idea to press the Command key first, and then press the other keys. The reason for this has to do with editing text. When you are entering text, if you press the spacebar, you won't get the hand tool; instead, you will get a space in your text.

7 Try out the different combinations to get a feel for them. With all three fingers down, you see the zoom-out tool. Lift your ring finger and you see the zoom-in tool. When only the spacebar is pressed, you see the hand tool. When no keys are pressed, the currently selected tool is shown.

A note about precision

The lake, mountain, and cloud shapes in this lesson are free-form shapes that allow for your own style. You don't need to match the suggested shapes perfectly. Practice making shapes that you like while using the provided shapes as a reference.

After you draw rough versions of the lake and the mountain, you will practice editing these shapes.

Drawing the lake

The lake is the shape at the bottom left of the rectangle. The top of the shape is the curved lake shore; the left and bottom edges are straight lines. You can see the complete path for the lake in this figure.

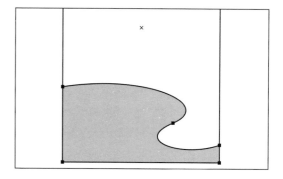

To draw the lake:

1 Choose Actual Size from the View menu to change the zoom factor to 100%.

2 Click the pen tool in the toolbox.

3 Position the pointer on the left edge of the rectangle, about one-third of the way up from the bottom.

4 Hold down the mouse button and drag slightly upward and to the right, a little past halfway across the rectangle. Then release the mouse button. Use the figure below as a reference.

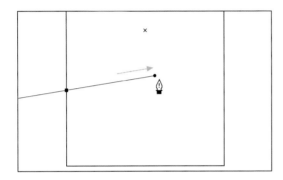

5 Position the pointer about halfway between the direction line and the bottom of the rectangle. Hold down the mouse button and drag downward and left, as shown. Release the mouse button.

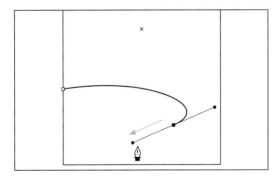

You have created the first part of the S-curve.

6 Position the pointer on the right edge of the rectangle about a quarter of an inch from the bottom, and drag right and slightly upward. This creates the second curve of the lake.

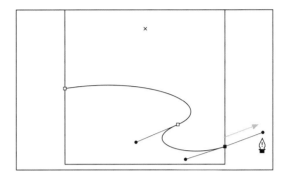

Next you will add a straight line to the existing curve.

7 Position the pointer on the last anchor point you drew, the one that is on the rectangle's edge. A small carat appears next to the pointer.

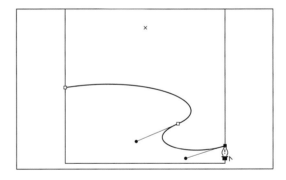

8 Click the mouse button. The direction line disappears.

9 Move the pen tool pointer to the bottom right corner of the rectangle, and click the mouse button.

10 Move the pointer to the bottom left corner of the rectangle, and click the mouse button.

11 Move the pointer to the first point in the lake path. A small circle appears next to the pointer when you are over the original anchor point. Click the mouse button to close the path. The circle changes to an *x*.

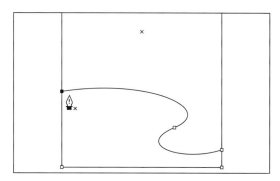

12 Choose Save from the File menu (Command-S) to save your work.

If you'd like to edit the path, you can do that after you draw the mountain.

Drawing the mountain

The mountain shape is similar to the lake in that it consists of some curves and some straight lines.

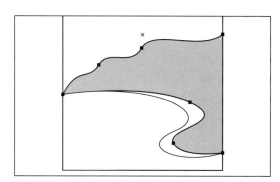

To draw the mountain:

1 Click the pen tool in the toolbox.

2 Position the pointer on the left edge of the rectangle, just above the first anchor point of the lake path. Drag right and slightly upward; then release the mouse button.

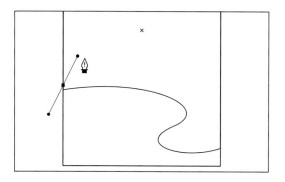

3 Move the pointer, and drag to create the first curve; then release the mouse button.

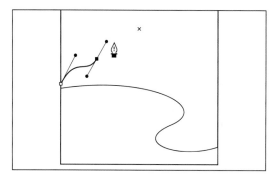

4 Continue to drag curves. When you are at the right side of the rectangle, drag to create an anchor point that is exactly on the edge of the rectangle.

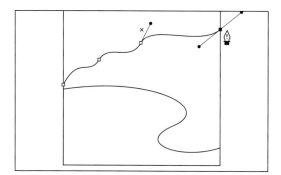

5 Move the pointer back over the anchor point you just created, and click the mouse button. You do this because you are switching from curves to lines.

6 Move the pointer down to near the top edge of the lake and, click again.

7 Move the pointer to the left, and drag left to create the curve of the shoreline. Continue using the pen tool to follow loosely the lake shore line.

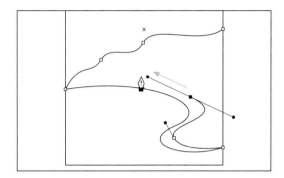

8 When you have drawn all the way to the left side, click the last anchor point you drew; then click the first anchor point of the path to close the mountain path. Make sure that you see the circle next to the pen tool when you close the path.

9 The figure below shows a complete path for a mountain.

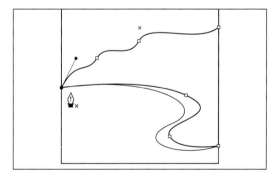

10 Choose Save from the File menu (Command-S) to save your work.

Editing paths

You can use the direct selection tool to edit the path you have just drawn.

You can edit paths by moving the anchor points, by moving the path segment itself, or by moving the direction lines.

Use the techniques below to practice editing your paths.

Before you can move an anchor point, direction line, or path segment, you must select it. You use the direct selection tool to select these different parts of a path.

Moving anchor points

1 Click the direct selection tool (hollow arrow) in the toolbox. You see Direct Selection in the status line, indicating that is the selected tool.

2 Click away from the artwork to deselect everything.

3 Click a path you want to edit to select it. You see the anchor points.

You can drag a selected anchor point to a new location. The rest of the path is still connected to the anchor point.

Changing curve shapes by moving direction points

You can change the shape of a curve by moving the direction points associated with that curve. First, select the curve. When a curve is selected, you see the direction lines and direction points. The anchor points are hollow.

1 Click the direct selection tool (hollow arrow) in the toolbox.

2 Click away from the artwork to deselect everything.

3 Click the path so that you can see the anchor points.

4 Click an anchor point that is part of a curve. You see the direction lines associated with the anchor point.

You can drag a direction point to change the shape of a curve. You can also drag to shorten the length of the direction line, reducing the size of the curve.

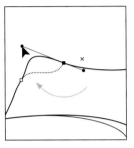 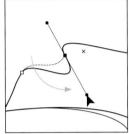

Moving path segments

A path segment is the part of the path between two anchor points. You can select and move a path segment.

1 Click the direct selection tool (hollow arrow) in the toolbox.

2 Click away from the artwork to deselect everything.

3 Click a path to select it. You see the hollow anchor points and the direction lines.

You can drag the segment to a different position. The anchor points remain in their original location.

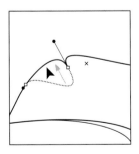 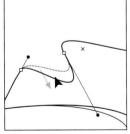

4 Practice editing by changing the shapes of the mountain and lake.

5 When you have finished editing, choose Save from the File menu (Command-S).

Painting paths

Next you will add shades of gray to the three shapes you have created. First, you'll take a closer look at the Paint Style palette.

To open the Paint Style palette:

1 Choose Select None from the Edit menu so that nothing is selected.

2 Choose Paint Style from the Object menu (Command-I). (You can also open this palette from the Window menu.) The Paint Style palette opens.

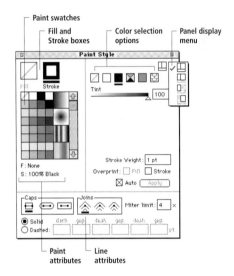

The colors currently selected for filling and stroking will be those of the last object that you selected.

This palette is a floating palette and will remain in front of the window until you close it.

You can change how much of the palette is displayed. To change the palette size, hold down the mouse button on the small triangle in the top right corner of the palette and drag to choose an option.

3 Try out different panel display options; then set the palette so that you can see both of the top panels.

The Color Selection options are shown near the top of the right panel.

4 To examine the Color Selection options, click the Fill box in the left panel. A solid line appears below the box.

5 Click the first Color Selection box (the one on the left, with a slash through it).

Notice the line below the box and the word *None* above the boxes.

6 Click the other Color Selection options to see what they are (White, Black, Process, Custom, Pattern, and Gradient).

You can move the Paint Style palette to a different location by dragging its title bar.

7 Drag the palette to a place where it is not obstructing the artwork.

To fill the paths:

1 Click the selection tool (solid arrow) in the toolbox.

2 Click the edge of the background rectangle to select it.

So far in this lesson you have been working in Artwork view. Now you will switch to Preview view to see what the printed artwork would look like.

3 Choose Preview from the View menu (Command-Y).

The fill and stroke of the objects you have drawn will depend on what you have filled or stroked previously. They may be difficult to distinguish from each other if they are all the same color.

The rectangle should still be selected.

4 In the Paint Style palette, check to see that the Fill box at the top of the window has a solid line under it. This indicates this option is selected. If it is not selected, click to select it.

5 Position the pointer over the light gray color swatch, the first swatch in the second row. The pointer changes to an eyedropper. Click the mouse button to fill the rectangle with a light gray.

The paint swatches contain colors that you can use to fill or stroke objects. The four swatches at the top of the palette (the None, White, Black, and Process White) color swatches cannot be modified. Other colors can be created and added to the swatches.

You'll change back to Artwork view so you can easily see the paths.

6 Choose Artwork from the View menu (Command-E).

7 Click the edge of the mountain shape to select it.

8 Click the medium gray color swatch (the second swatch in the second row) to fill the mountain with a medium gray.

9 Click the edge of the lake shape to select it.

10 Click the dark gray color swatch (the third swatch in the second row) to fill the lake with a dark gray.

11 Choose Preview from the View menu (Command-Y) to see how the painting looks.

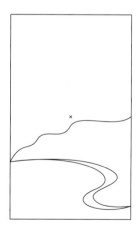

You can draw and edit in Preview view as well as in Artwork view. For now, you'll switch back to Artwork view.

12 Choose Artwork from the View menu (Command-E).

13 Choose Save from the File menu (Command-S) to save your work.

To draw the clouds:

1 Choose Select None from the Edit menu (Command-Shift-A) to deselect everything.

2 Click the pen tool in the toolbox.

3 Use the pen tool to draw a cloud shape. Be sure to close the path when you have finished. Refer to the finished art file as a reference for drawing the cloud shapes.

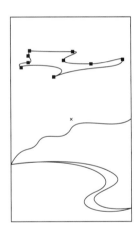

Although you can't see it in Artwork view, the cloud you drew is filled with whatever color you used to paint your last filled object, in this case, the gray you used for the lake.

4 In the Paint Style palette, click the white paint swatch (the second swatch in the first row). This fills the cloud with white.

5 Use the pen tool to draw a second cloud.

The second cloud will be filled with white.

6 Choose Preview from the View menu (Command-Y) to see how the painted clouds look.

7 If you want to select the clouds to move them, click the selection tool, click inside a cloud shape, and drag the cloud to a new location.

8 Choose Save from the File menu (Command-S).

Drawing the airplane

Next you draw the airplane by tracing the shape from a template.

1 Choose Artwork from the View menu (Command-E) to return to artwork mode.

2 Scroll down until you see the airplane shape in the center of your screen.

As mentioned earlier, the airplane is in a separate file called a template. You can see the airplane, but you cannot change it. You'll use the airplane template as a guide to help you draw the airplane.

3 If necessary, use the zoom tool to enlarge the plane so that you can comfortably trace it.

When you are drawing the plane, try to go all the way around the plane and make a closed path before you start editing. It's easier to go back and edit once you have completed the path.

4 Click the pen tool in the toolbox.

5 Begin tracing by placing an anchor point about three-quarters of the way up the top wing and then dragging up and right.

6 Move the pointer to the other side of the wing at about the same distance from the tip, and drag down and left, as shown below.

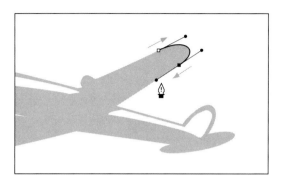

7 Position the pointer on the second anchor point you created, and click the mouse button to create a corner point. (Remember to click the *anchor point*, not the direction point at the end of the direction line.)

8 Move the pointer to the intersection where the wing meets the body of the plane and click. This creates a straight line between the two anchor points.

9 Move the pointer to where the tail meets the body and, click the mouse button.

To switch from the straight line along the body to the curve of the tail, you must change the last anchor point.

10 Position the pointer on the last anchor point you drew, and drag a direction point up and right along the length of the tail.

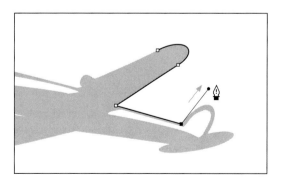

11 Move the pointer to the other side of the tail, and drag down and left to make the curve for the tail.

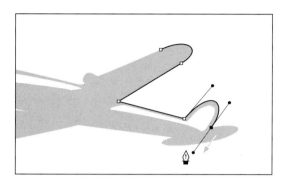

12 Move the pointer to the anchor point at the bottom of the tail; hold down the Option key and drag right along the bottom tail piece.

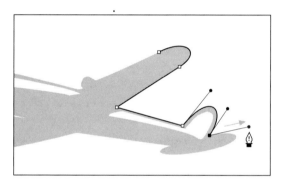

13 Move the pointer around the curve, and drag to create the curve for the bottom tail piece

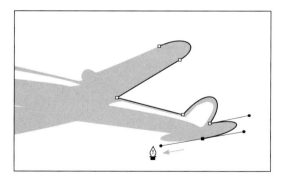

14 Move the pointer around the curve; then drag up and right to create the last curve on the bottom tail piece.

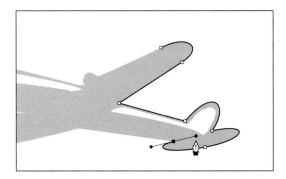

15 Click the last anchor point.

16 Continue tracing the plane until you are back at the beginning.

17 Make sure you create a closed path by ending the path on the original anchor point of the path.

If you want to edit the airplane path, you can use the direct selection tool to move anchor points, direction points, or segments of the path.

Painting the airplane

1 If the Paint Style palette is not open, choose Paint Style from the Object menu.

2 With the airplane path selected, click the Fill box in the Paint Style palette.

3 Click the Black swatch to paint the plane black.

4 Choose Preview from the View menu (Command-Y) to see the results.

5 Choose Artwork from the View menu (Command-E).

Autotracing and painting the plane highlights

Instead of drawing the white plane highlights with the pen tool you can trace them automatically with the auto trace tool.

1 Select the auto trace tool in the toolbox.

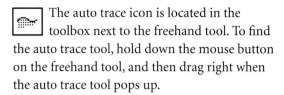 The auto trace icon is located in the toolbox next to the freehand tool. To find the auto trace tool, hold down the mouse button on the freehand tool, and then drag right when the auto trace tool pops up.

2 Move the pointer to one of the airplane highlights, the white shapes inside the body. Click inside the white area, close to the gray edge.

The program automatically traces the shape.

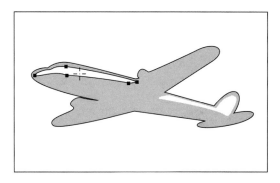

3 Move the pointer to the other inside shape just inside the white edge, and auto trace it.

4 Click the selection tool in the toolbox.

5 Click the edge of one of the autotraced paths.

6 Hold down the Shift key, and click the edge of the other autotraced path. Both shapes are now selected.

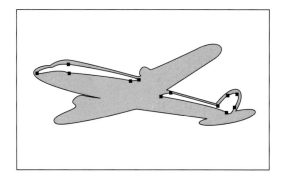

When you make a selection and then hold down the Shift key, you can add additional objects to what is selected. If you add something you don't want selected, you can deselect that object by clicking it again with the Shift key held down.

1 Click the Fill box in the Paint Style palette.

2 Click the White swatch (the second swatch in the first row) to paint the airplane highlights.

Grouping and moving the airplane

Now that the airplane is drawn and painted, you want to move it into the drawing. Before you move it, you will group the different pieces to make it easy to move the airplane around.

1 With the selection tool (solid arrow), click the edge of the airplane.

2 Hold down the Shift key and click one of the highlight paths; then click the other highlight path.

3 Choose Group from the Arrange menu (Command-G). The airplane parts are grouped, so you can drag the entire airplane to a new location.

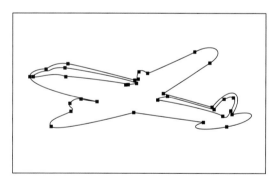

4 Drag the airplane by an edge up to its location above the mountain and lake artwork. The window will scroll automatically as you drag.

5 Choose Preview from the View menu (Command-Y) to see the results.

6 Choose Save from the File menu (Command-S).

Adding the speed lines to the airplane

1 Click the pen tool in the toolbox.

2 Using the original artwork as a reference, click where you want the line to begin. Then click where you want the line to end in order to draw the straight line at the top right of the drawing.

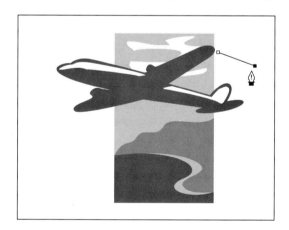

3 Click the Fill box in the Paint Style palette, and click the None swatch.

4 Click the Stroke box in the Paint Style palette.

5 Click the Black swatch (the third swatch in the first row) in the Paint Style palette.

6 Click *Stroke Weight* to select the Stroke Weight field. Set the stroke weight to 4 points, and press Return to apply the new stroke weight.

7 Click the selection tool in the toolbox.

8 Position the pointer on the line. Hold down the mouse button and begin dragging. With the mouse button held down, hold down the Option key. The pointer changes to a solid arrow with a hollow arrow.

9 Continue dragging the line to a new location. Release the mouse button before you release the Option key.

You have created a copy of the line in a new location.

10 Use the Option+drag procedure to create the two speed lines on the other side of the airplane.

Grouping other parts of the artwork

In a complex drawing, you sometimes want to group parts of the drawing to make them easier to work with.

To group the speed lines with the airplane:

To complete the airplane part of the drawing, you group the speed lines with the airplane. Remember that the airplane and its highlights are already grouped.

1 With the selection tool (solid arrow), click the airplane. Notice that in Preview view, you can simply click anywhere inside the shape rather than having to click the edge of the path.

2 Hold down the Shift key and click each of the speed lines. Then release the Shift key.

3 Choose Group from the Arrange menu (Command-G).

To group the two clouds together:

1 With the selection tool click one of the clouds to select it.

2 Hold down the Shift key and click the other cloud to add it to the selected items.

3 Press Command-G to group the clouds.

4 Choose Save from the File menu (Command-S) to save your work.

Understanding the painting order

The Adobe Illustrator program paints objects in the order that you create them. This is referred to as the *stacking* or the *painting order*. In the artwork you just drew, the background rectangle was created first and is the "bottom" or "back" level. The other objects were painted in succession in front of one another. If you had drawn the rectangle last, it would be displayed on top of all the other objects in the drawing.

Because you won't always draw artwork in the exact order it is displayed, the program provides commands to let you change the stacking order. In a simple case, you can move an object to the front or back of the stack. In a more complex case, you cut an object and paste it in front or in back of another object.

The stacking order pertains to the order in which objects are painted on a single *layer*. Each document contains at least one layer, and you can add additional layers. You will learn more about layers in a future lesson. For now, you'll learn how to change the stacking order on a single layer.

Changing the painting order

This drawing has five different objects. The rectangle is at the back of the stack, and the airplane (grouped with the highlights and speed lines) is at the front of the stack.

Suppose, just for practice, that you want to move the rectangle in front of the other objects.

To move an object in front or back of all the other objects in a layer:

1 With the selection tool, click the rectangle. You can click inside the edge of the rectangle in Preview view, as long as you don't click inside any other shape.

2 Choose Bring To Front from the Arrange menu (Command-Equal sign).

The rectangle is moved to the front and obscures the other artwork.

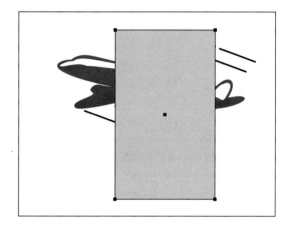

3 Choose Send To Back from the Arrange menu (Command-hyphen).

The rectangle is moved to the back layer.

Sometimes you will want to move an object to a level that is not the front or the back. In this case, you first cut the object so that it is copied to the clipboard. Then you select another object and paste the original object back into the drawing, using the second object as a reference point.

Suppose, for example, you want to place the airplane behind the clouds. The plane is currently on the topmost level.

To move an object between two other objects:

1 Use the selection tool, and click to select the airplane.

2 Choose Cut from the Edit menu. This removes the airplane from the drawing and copies it to the clipboard.

3 Use the selection tool to select the clouds.

4 Choose Paste In Back from the Edit menu.

The plane is pasted onto the level behind the clouds, and you see the clouds in front of the airplane.

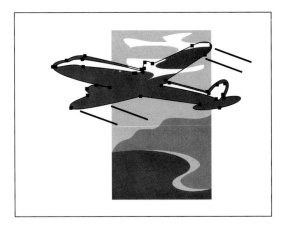

You could move the clouds back to their original position by choosing Undo from the Edit menu, by selecting the airplane and using the Bring to Front command, or by cutting the clouds and pasting them in front of the mountain.

5 Use the selection tool, and click the clouds to select them.

6 Choose Cut from the Edit menu.

7 Use the selection tool, and select the mountain.

8 Choose Paste In Front from the Edit menu.

The clouds are pasted in front of the mountains and behind the airplane.

9 Try moving the different levels of this drawing.

10 When you have finished, restore the levels to their original status.

11 Choose Save from the File menu (Command-S).

ADDING THE TYPE AND LINE

To complete the logo, you'll add the name of the company to the drawing. In this lesson, you'll simply add a word and change the font and size. In a later lesson, you'll learn more about using type.

To add type:

1 Click the type tool in the toolbox.

2 Scroll down so you can add the type below the artwork. You can drag it into position later.

3 Click below the artwork.

You see the blinking insertion point.

The size of the insertion point reflects the size of the last type you created, or if you have not used type, the default of 12-point Helvetica.

4 Type in all capital letters **NAVIGATIONS**.

If you see gray shading rather than typed letters, zoom in a level or two.

5 Click the selection tool in the toolbox. Clicking any tool in the toolbox, after you create type, selects the type object. You see the text *baseline* and *alignment point* (the anchor point on the left end of the line), indicating that the text is selected.

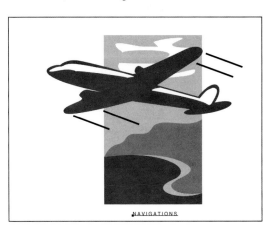

To modify the type:

1 With the type selected, choose Character from the Type menu (Command-T). The Character palette appears. This palette lets you change a variety of type attributes.

Font pop-up menu

Lever

2 Drag the palette to reposition it so you can see both the palette and the type you just created.

3 Use the pop-up font menu in the Character palette to choose a font. You can access this pop-up menu by placing the pointer on the triangle to the right of the current font and holding down the mouse button. Drag to choose City in the menu and Bold in the submenu. (If you don't see City in the menu, you will have to install it. See the "Getting Started" section of this book for more information about installing fonts.)

4 Double-click the size field in the Character palette. Enter 60, and press Return. The type size is changed.

5 Click the lever at the bottom right of the Character palette. Clicking the lever expands the palette.

Font pop-up menu

Lever

6 In the Tracking field, enter 240 and press Return. Changing the *tracking* inserts uniform spacing between the characters you selected.

7 Click the close box to close the Character palette.

8 If necessary, use the selection tool to drag the type by the baseline to its position in the drawing, using the final art as a reference.

9 Choose Save from the File menu (Command-S).

Adding the line

Next you will add the line that is under the word *Navigations.*

To add the line:

1 Click the pen tool in the toolbox.

2 Click under the N. (Do not drag, just click.)

3 Hold down the Shift key and click under the S.

Holding down the Shift key constrains the line to a straight line.

To paint the line:

1 With the line selected, click the Fill box and the None swatch in the Paint Style palette.

2 Click the Stroke box in the Paint Style palette. The line under the Stroke box indicates that it is selected.

3 Click the Black swatch (the fourth swatch in the first row) to stroke the line with black.

4 Enter a value of 8 in the Stroke Weight field.

5 Press Return to apply the new stroke weight.

6 If you want to reposition the line, use the selection tool to drag it to a new location.

7 Choose Save from the File menu (Command-S).

ADDING COLOR

Finally, you will select the objects in the drawing and paint them with process colors.

1 Click the zoom tool in the toolbox, hold down the Option key, and zoom out so that you can see the entire drawing.

2 Click the selection tool in the toolbox.

3 Click the edge of the background rectangle to select it.

4 In the Paint Style palette, scroll all the way down to the bottom row of swatches to see the special row of colored swatches created for this file. This row contains colors that were specifically created for this drawing and were saved with the file.

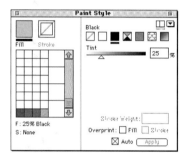

5 Click the Fill box.

6 Click the light blue color swatch.

7 Click to select the lake. Then click the medium blue color swatch to paint the lake.

8 Click to select the mountain. Then click the tan color swatch to paint the mountain.

9 Click the direct selection tool in the toolbox. Because the airplane, airplane highlights, and speed lines are all grouped, you use the direct selection tool to select only parts of the group.

10 Click the airplane to select it.

11 In the Paint Style palette, click the green swatch.

About color

The paint swatches provided with this file are process colors. *Process color* is made up of four colors: cyan (C), magenta (M), yellow (Y), and black (K, to avoid confusion with blue). The Adobe Separator program is used to print these four colors on separate pieces of paper or film; they are then ready for printing on a four-color printing press. An object that has been painted red in the Adobe Illustrator program will appear on both the magenta page and the yellow page. At printing time, the magenta ink is printed on top of the yellow ink, creating red.

Custom color may be a process color mix you've named and saved as a custom color. Custom color may also be a predefined color from a color matching system, such as those in the PANTONE® MATCHING SYSTEM, FOCOLTONE COLOUR SYSTEM, TRUMATCH color swatching system, and TOYO Color Finder 1050. Every ink color is printed as an individual separation. To use custom colors, you must first open the special files that are provided with the Adobe Illustrator program. See the *Adobe Illustrator User Guide* for further information.

Mix a process color

You can assign colors that will be printed with process inks by indicating percentages for cyan, magenta, yellow, and black. Next you will create a process color and stroke the line under the type with it.

To mix a process color:

1 Click the line under Navigations.

Remember that the line has an 8-point stroke. You can see the attributes listed in the Paint Style palette. You should see the line under *Stroke*.

2 Click the Process color option at the top of the palette. The Process box is the fourth from the left, the one with the four triangles. You see the word *Process* above the boxes.

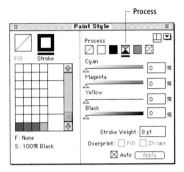

Four sliders and text boxes appear, one for each of the four process colors.

You can change color values by dragging the sliders, or by entering values in the text boxes.

3 Hold down the mouse button, and drag the triangle slider below Cyan back and forth. Notice that as you drag, the color is shown in the Stroke box at the top of the palette.

4 Leave the Cyan slider about in the middle.

5 Drag the triangle below the Yellow slider back and forth. The Stroke box displays the composite process color.

6 Play with the sliders until you have a color you like.

If you want to adjust the color saturation, you can hold down the Shift key and drag any slider to adjust all triangles simultaneously. This procedure lets you adjust overall color tint without affecting the CMYK proportions.

You can add the color you created to the swatches. The color will be saved with the file.

To define a paint swatch:

1 Use the sliders to create a color you like.

2 Drag the new color from the Stroke box to any unfilled paint swatch. You can now use this color to paint objects in the drawing.

You can also add the current color to the swatches by holding down the Option key and clicking a swatch. If the swatch has an existing color, that color will be replaced with the new color.

If you like, you can experiment with different colors. Select different shapes and paint them. Try creating colors that you like and saving them.

To clear a paint swatch, you hold down the Command key and click the swatch. To clear a group of swatches, hold down the Command key and drag over the swatches. Note that you cannot use the Undo command to restore deleted swatches.

3 Choose Save from the File menu (Command-S) to save your work.

4 Close the working file and the final file.

Lessons 1 and 2 have shown you the Adobe Illustrator procedures you need to complete a corporate logo for Navigations. You've used the pen tool to draw paths, and the Paint Style palette to add color, and you've practiced changing the stacking order in the drawing. You've used the type tool and the auto trace tool. In the next lesson, you'll review these techniques while drawing a postcard.

The Art of TRAVEL

NAVIGATIONS

THREE
3
REASONS
TO TRAVEL

① Painting
One great reason to travel to Europe is the inspired painting in the Louvre.

② Crafts
Another great reason to travel to Europe is the vibrant textiles you may find .

Another reason to travel is to explore the classic architecture in the city of Athens. ③
Architecture

Lesson

3

LESSON 3: PROMOTIONAL POSTCARD

This lesson provides a project that you can use to practice the techniques you learned in Lessons 1 and 2. You'll draw a postcard for Navigations.

THE TASK

Navigations wants to send their summer travelers a postcard enticing them to take a vacation. Your job is to create some designs for them to review. To help you get started, we've drawn a complete postcard that you can use as practice.

This lesson provides step-by-step instructions for creating the postcard. If you find you need more explanation than a step provides, refer back to the more detailed information in Lessons 1 and 2.

Completing this lesson may take anywhere from 1½ to 2½ hours.

PLANNING THE PROJECT

You'll have two documents open on the screen. One is the finished artwork that you can use as a reference. The other is the file you will be working with.

To open the reference file:

1 Open the Lesson 3 folder and the file named *03Final*. The document opens in Preview view.

Take a look at the postcard file to see what the components of the drawing are.

Notice how the objects are stacked on top of one another. The background rectangle behind all the other objects creates a border. A second rectangle is inside the first. The mountains, city skyline, and the water all have highlights. Any highlights will be drawn after the underlying object has been created.

2 Choose Artwork from the View menu, and take a look at the paths in the drawing.

3 Use the selection tool to click the edge of the path for the tan central mountain to select the path.

4 Choose Preview Selection from the View menu. (Command-Option-Y). The mountain is previewed, while the other objects are displayed as paths.

You can use the Preview Selection command to see a preview of whatever is selected in the artwork. This can save time and memory, because the program does not have to display the entire drawing in Preview.

5 Choose Preview to return the entire drawing to its painted Preview.

The tan mountain remains selected. Notice the bottom path of the tan mountain. In Preview view, you see that this path overlaps the green mountain to the left as well as the city skyline. You don't see the overlapping parts because they are behind the other objects.

This means you don't have to be as precise with the bottom of the tan mountain, since you won't see it in the final drawing.

Take a look at the type. There is a painted version of the type that is on top of, and slightly offset from, a black version of the type. This effect creates a drop shadow. The type is stacked on the top level of the drawing.

6 To resize the window, move the pointer to the size box in the bottom right corner of the window. Hold down the mouse button and drag upward and to the left until the window is about one-fourth the size of your screen.

7 Click the zoom tool in the toolbox; hold down the Option key and click to zoom out until the postcard fits inside the window

8 Use the scroll bars to center the postcard inside the window.

9 Drag the window by its title bar to the upper right corner of your screen so that it is out of the way but available for you to see as you use the working file.

Note: Any time you want to view the final file, you can choose 03Final from the Window menu.

10 Choose Select None from the Edit menu (Command-Shift-A) to deselect everything in the reference file.

To open the working file:

1 Open the Lesson 3 folder and the file named *03Begin*.

This file contains an airplane shape outside the page boundary. You will use this shape for tracing. The file also contains some special paint swatches you will use when painting.

2 Choose Save As from the File menu, locate the Project folder, and name the file *03Work*.

DRAWING AND PAINTING RECTANGLES

You'll begin by drawing three rectangles, one for the border, one for the sky, and one for the water.

To create the border rectangle:

1 Click the rectangle tool in the toolbox.

2 Click inside the drawing area near the top left corner of the page rectangle.

3 Enter 430 for Width.

4 Enter 250 for Height, and click OK.

5 Use the selection tool to center the rectangle in the top part of the drawing area.

6 Use the scroll bars to center the window on your screen. You don't need to see the airplane right now.

Notice that you are working in Preview view, and the rectangle is painted.

To paint the rectangle:

1 Choose Paint Style from the Object menu (Command-I).

2 Drag the Paint Style palette to a convenient location so that you can see both the palette and the rectangle.

3 Use the scroll bar to scroll down all the way to the bottom of the paint swatches. You should scroll past the empty swatches until you see the three rows of colored swatches at the very bottom.

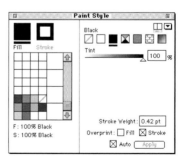

4 With the rectangle selected, click the Fill box in the Paint Style palette. Then click the burgundy paint swatch in the next-to-last row of swatches.

5 With the rectangle selected, click the Stroke box in the Paint Style palette, and click the None swatch (the swatch with the diagonal line through it).

You'll draw the rectangle for the sky from the center outward.

To create the sky rectangle:

1 With the rectangle tool selected, position the pointer on the center point of the original rectangle.

2 Hold down the Option key. Notice that the current tool shown in the status line at the lower left of the window changes from *Rectangle* to *Centered Rectangle*. The pointer also changes shape.

3 Hold down the mouse button and drag outward until you have created a second rectangle that is about a half inch smaller than the first rectangle.

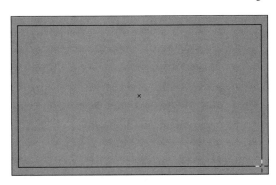

4 Release the mouse button and then the Option key.

5 With the rectangle selected, click the Fill box in the Paint Style palette. Then click the light blue paint swatch in the bottom row of swatches.

Next you create a third rectangle for the water.

To create the water rectangle:

1 With the rectangle tool selected, move the pointer to the bottom left corner of the inner rectangle. Drag diagonally up and right until the new rectangle is about one-fourth the height of the drawing.

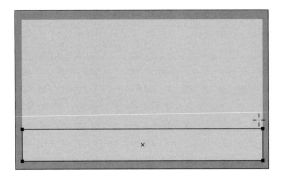

2 With the rectangle selected, click the Fill box in the Paint Style palette. Then click the medium blue paint swatch in the next-to-last row of swatches.

3 Choose Save from the File menu to save your work (Command-S).

DRAWING AND PAINTING THE MOUNTAINS

The green and the tan mountains in the drawing are drawn as separate filled paths.

First, you draw the tan mountain near the center.

To create the tan central mountain:

1 Choose Select None from the Edit menu (Command-Shift-A) to deselect everything.

2 Click the pen tool in the toolbox.

3 In the Paint Style palette, click the Fill box; then click the None swatch (the swatch with the diagonal line through it) so the path won't be filled as you draw.

When you work in Preview, it is sometimes difficult to draw irregularly shaped objects that are filled. Turning off the fill while you draw solves this problem.

4 In the Paint Style palette, click the Stroke box; then click the Black swatch. Set the Stroke Weight to 1. Although the final mountain does not have a stroke, it is easier to draw the mountain with a stroke weight assigned.

You will draw the mountain as a closed path, with the final anchor point created on top of the first anchor point.

5 Begin drawing on the left side of the mountain. Hold down the mouse button and drag right and upward. Move the pointer up and to the right, and drag again.

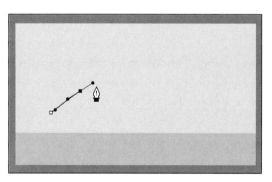

6 Continue to add curves to draw the mountain.

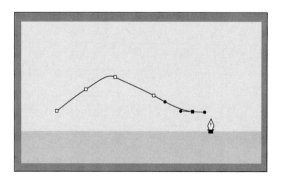

If you don't like a particular curve, you can choose Undo from the Edit menu (Command-Z) to remove the last curve drawn. The next curve you draw will still be connected to the original path.

If you want to erase the entire path and start over, you can use the selection tool to select the path, and then choose Cut from the Edit menu or press the Delete key.

7 Continue to draw the mountain until you have an anchor point that is exactly on the right edge of the inside of the border. Move the pointer back over that point, and click to make that point a corner point so you can switch to a straight line.

8 Move the pointer down below the water line, hold down the Shift key to make a straight line, and click the mouse button.

9 Move the pointer to the left, below the water line, and click the mouse button.

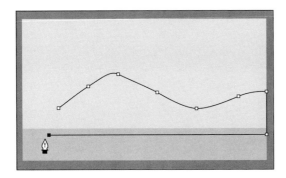

10 Move the pointer to the first anchor point you created. A small *o* is added to the pointer when you are over that point. Click the mouse button to close the path. The *o* changes to an *x.*

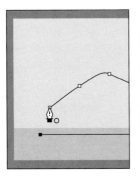

11 Click the Fill box in the Paint Style palette. Then click the tan swatch.

12 Click the Stroke box, and click the None swatch.

To move the mountain behind the water:

1 Click the selection tool in the toolbox.

2 Click the mountain path to select it.

3 Choose Cut from the Edit menu (Command-X).

4 Click the water rectangle to select it.

5 Choose Paste In Back from the Edit menu (Command-B). The mountain is moved behind the water and remains in front of the background rectangles.

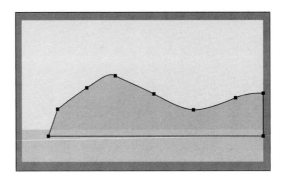

To create the green mountain:

1 Choose Select None from the Edit menu (Command-Shift-A) to deselect everything.

2 Click the pen tool in the toolbox.

3 In the Paint Style palette, click the Fill box; then click the None swatch.

4 Click the Stroke box, and set the stroke to black with a 1-point stroke weight.

5 Begin drawing the second mountain on the left edge of the inside rectangle, about halfway up the drawing. Hold down the mouse button and drag. Continue creating anchor points and dragging to draw the mountain until you are down below the water line near the right side of the drawing.

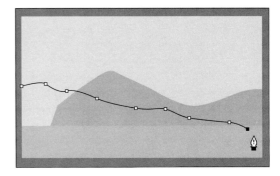

6 Move the pointer to the left edge of the inner border below the water line, and click the mouse button. Then, move the pointer up to the original anchor point, and click to close the path.

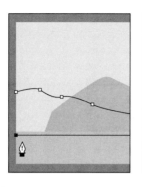 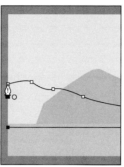

7 Click the Fill box in the Paint Style palette. Then click the light green color swatch in the bottom row of swatches.

8 Click the Stroke box, and click the None swatch.

To move the mountain between the water and the first mountain:

1 Click the selection tool in the toolbox.

2 Click the path of the mountain you just drew to select it.

3 Choose Cut from the Edit menu (Command-X).

4 Click the tan central mountain to select it.

5 Choose Paste In Front from the Edit menu (Command-F). The mountain is moved in front of the first mountain and behind the water.

6 Choose Save from the File menu (Command-S).

DRAWING AND PAINTING THE SKYLINE

Next you draw the city skyline.

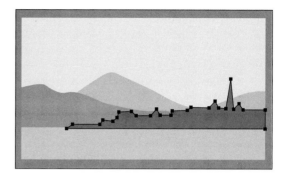

1 Choose Select None from the Edit menu (Command-Shift-A) to deselect everything.

2 Click the pen tool in the toolbox.

3 In the Paint Style palette, click the Fill box, then click the None swatch.

4 Click the Stroke box, and set the stroke to black with a 1-point stroke weight.

The city skyline is another filled shape. The skyline consists of a series of lines and curves drawn with the pen tool. The bottom part of the shape, which is hidden below the water, can be any irregular shape, as long as the path is closed at the end.

5 Begin by positioning the pointer just below the water line, about one-fourth of the way from the left edge of the inner rectangle.

6 Click the mouse button.

7 Move the pointer up and right, and click again.

8 Move the pointer about an inch to the right, and click again. Then move up and right, and click.

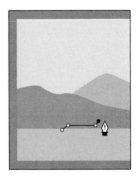

9 Continue to move the pointer and click or drag to draw the skyline shape. Use the Option key when you want to change a corner point to a smooth point. Use the Shift key when you want straight lines. Don't worry about matching the reference shape exactly; just draw what you like.

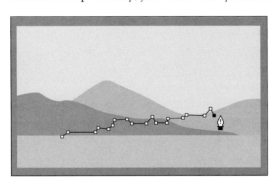

10 Continue drawing until you are at the right side of the drawing. Make the anchor on the edge a corner point. Then move the pointer downward to create the path that will be below the water line.

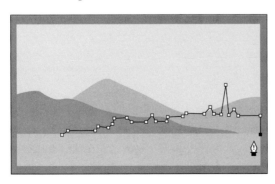

11 Be sure to close the path at the end of the drawing by clicking the original anchor point.

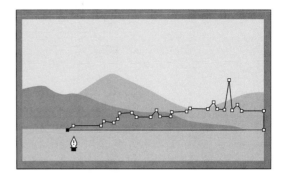

12 In the Paint Style palette, click the Fill box, and click the dark gray swatch to paint the skyline black with a 75% tint.

13 In the Paint Style palette, click the Stroke box, and click the None swatch.

To move the skyline behind the water:

1 Click the selection tool in the toolbox.

2 Click the path of the skyline to select it.

3 Choose Cut from the Edit menu (Command-X).

4 Click the water to select it.

5 Choose Paste In Back from the Edit menu (Command-B). The skyline is moved behind the water.

6 Choose Save from the File menu (Command-S) to save your work.

ADDING HIGHLIGHTS TO THE SKYLINE

The highlights in the city skyline are a series of irregular shapes you can draw with the pen tool.

To draw the skyline highlights:

1 Click away from the artwork to deselect everything (or press Command-Shift-A).

2 Choose Artwork from the View menu (Command-E.)

3 Use the zoom tool to zoom in for a better view.

4 Click the pen tool in the toolbox.

5 Use the pen tool to draw one of the skyline shapes.

You can draw a rectangular shape by clicking the four corners. To draw a triangle shape, click the mouse button at each point on the triangle, making sure to click the original anchor point at the end to close the path.

When you move the pointer over the original anchor point, the small circle appears next to the pen tool pointer, indicating you can close the path. After the path is closed, the circle turns into an *x*, indicating you can begin a new path.

6 Use the pen tool to draw the other skyline shapes. Remember to close the paths.

You can use the selection tool to drag shapes to different locations.

You can use the direct selection tool to select points or line segments on a shape and edit them.

When you have finished drawing the different city highlight shapes, you can paint them all at the same time.

To paint the skyline highlights:

1 Click the selection tool in the toolbox.

2 Click the edge of one highlight shape.

3 Hold down the Shift key and click the edge to select a second highlight shape.

4 Keep the Shift key down and click other highlight shapes until all are selected. Then release the Shift key.

5 In the Paint Style palette, click the Fill box and click the light gray swatch.

6 In the Paint Style palette, click the Stroke box and click the None swatch.

7 Choose Preview from the View menu (Command-Y) to see your work.

8 Choose Artwork from the View menu (Command-E).

ADDING SHADOWS AND HIGHLIGHTS

Take a look at the shadow and highlights in the reference file. These shapes are free-form paths drawn with the pen tool. The green mountain has a darker green shadow. The tan mountain has two white snow highlights.

To create the mountain shadow:

1 Click away from the artwork to deselect everything (or press Command-Shift-A).

2 Click the pen tool in the toolbox.

Next you'll draw the shadow for the green mountain on the left.

3 Begin dragging on the inside edge of the border rectangle. Then move the pointer, and continue to draw curved shapes. Remember to draw a straight line when you are next to the border. Also, be sure to close the path.

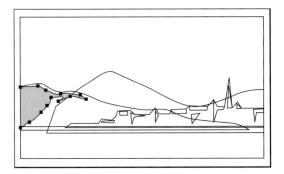

4 Click the Fill box in the Paint Style palette. Then click the dark green color swatch.

To create the snow highlights:

1 Draw the snow highlights on the other mountain tops.

2 Use the selection tool to select both snow highlights by using the Shift key while you click.

3 Paint the snow highlights white by clicking the White swatch in the Paint Style palette.

4 Choose Preview from the View menu (Command-Y) to see the results.

5 Choose Save from the File menu (Command-S) to save your work.

To create the water highlight:

1 Click away from the artwork to deselect everything (or press Command-Shift-A).

The water highlight is a combination of broad curves and straight lines. You will leave the fill turned on while you create the water highlight so you can get a feel for filling while working in Preview view.

2 Click the pen tool in the toolbox.

3 Take a look at the reference file to see where the water highlight begins, in relation to the skyline.

4 Click the bottom edge of the city skyline near the left side of the skyline.

5 Move the pointer to the right; hold down the Shift key, and click to draw the straight line for the top of the highlight. Release the Shift key.

6 Position the pointer on the last anchor point you drew; hold down the mouse button, and drag down and left (about half an inch) to make the last anchor point a corner point.

7 Move the pointer below the water line. Hold down the mouse button and drag to the right.

8 Notice the path is being filled with white, the last color you used.

Important*: When you paint a filled shape in Preview, the fill does not directly follow your path. When a path is not closed, the path is painted as if a straight line were drawn between the first and last points of the path. Every time you add a new anchor point, the shape of the fill changes. When you close the path, the shape is filled as you want it to be.*

9 Continue drawing the curves.

When you get to the bottom of the highlight on the right side, you want to switch from curves to straight lines.

10 Click the anchor point on the border.

11 Move the pointer to the left; hold down the Shift key and click to create the straight line at the bottom of the highlight.

12 Convert to curves by dragging on the last anchor point you created.

13 Continue to draw the large sweeping curves of the water highlight.

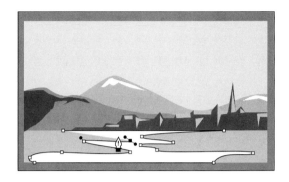

14 Be sure to close the path.

15 Choose Save from the file menu (Command-S) to save your work.

DRAWING AND PAINTING THE AIRPLANE

Included in the working file is an airplane shape that you can trace. The airplane is just to the left of the page rectangle.

The airplane has been saved as a separate view named Plane to Trace. Instead of zooming and scrolling, you can choose the view from a menu.

To draw the plane:

1 Choose Plane to Trace from the View menu. This is the last item in the menu.

2 Choose Select None from the Edit menu (Command-Shift-A) to deselect any artwork.

3 In the Paint Style palette, click the Fill box, and then click the None swatch.

4 Click the Stroke box and set the stroke to black with a 1 point stroke weight.

5 Click the pen tool in the toolbox.

6 Use the hints in the figures below to help you draw the airplane shape.

Start here

Clicks

Drags

Click again to convert point

More clicks

Finish

Keep in mind that you can use the direct selection tool (hollow arrow) to move any anchor points or segments you want to edit.

To position the plane in the drawing:

1 Click the selection tool in the toolbox.

2 Click the path of the airplane to select it.

3 Click the zoom tool in the toolbox.

4 Hold down the Option key and click to the left of the tail of the airplane to zoom out. Click until the zoom factor is 100%.

5 If necessary, scroll so that you can see the airplane and the postcard.

6 Click the selection tool in the toolbox.

7 Drag the airplane to its location in the postcard. Use the final artwork as a reference.

8 With the plane selected, click the Fill box in the Paint Style palette, and click the medium gray swatch. Set the Stroke to None.

9 Add the speed lines by selecting the pen tool and clicking at the beginning and end of the lines. Remember to click the pen tool in the toolbox after you create the first line.

10 Paint the speed lines by first selecting them and then clicking the Stroke box in the Paint Style palette. Click the white paint swatch and set the Stroke Weight to 1 point.

11 Choose Save from the File menu (Command-S) to save your work.

CREATING TYPE WITH A DROP SHADOW

The final task in creating the postcard is adding the type. First you create and paint the type; then you make a copy and move it; and finally you paint the copy.

To create the type:

1 Click the Type tool in the toolbox.

2 Click in the drawing near where you want the type to begin. You can drag the type to its final position later.

The blinking insertion point represents the size of the last type you created.

3 Type **NAVIGATIONS** in all capital letters.

4 Click the selection tool in the toolbox. The type you just created is selected.

TIP: TO SELECT A TEXT OBJECT, IMAGINE THE INVISIBLE BASELINE ON WHICH THE TEXT RESTS. USE THE SELECTION TOOL TO CLICK THAT BASELINE.

5 Choose Character from the Type menu (Command-T).

6 Choose City from the Font pop-up menu and Bold from the submenu.

7 Click the word *Size* to select the Size field, enter 42, and press Return.

8 Click the lever at the bottom right of the Character palette if you don't see the Tracking field.

9 Click the word *Tracking* to select the Tracking field, enter 240, and press Return. The type spacing is expanded. (If the Tracking was already at 240 from the previous lesson, you won't see a change.)

10 Drag the type by the baseline to its proper position. Use the final file as a reference in positioning the type.

Note: If the text object is not selected, click the position of the baseline so that you can see the alignment point and the baseline.

11 Click the Fill box in the Paint Style palette, and then click the dark gray swatch.

12 Choose Save from the File menu (Command-S) to save your work.

To copy and move the type:

1 With the type selected, position the pointer on the baseline, and begin dragging *just slightly* up and right. Then hold down the Option key to make a copy.

2 Move the copy of the type so that it is three or four points up and three or four points to the right of the original type. Release the mouse button and the Option key.

3 Fill the copy of the type by clicking the Fill box in the Paint Style palette and then clicking the yellow swatch.

Note: You can make fine adjustments to the position of the selected type (or any selected object) by using the arrow keys. Pressing the up arrow key once moves the selected object one point upward. Pressing the down arrow key once moves the selected object one point downward. The right and left arrow keys move the selected object one point to the left or right.

4 Choose Save from the File menu (Command-S) to save your work.

This completes the postcard. If you would like additional practice, try drawing different kinds of city skylines. You can make an industrial skyline or one with a foreign flair. You can also experiment by painting different objects with different colors.

5 Close the file named *03Final*.

6 If you want to print your working file, make sure that your printer is turned on and that it is selected in the Chooser. The choose Print from the File menu and click Print.

7 Close any open files.

LESSON 4: CREATING A CORPORATE LOOK WITH STATIONERY AND BUSINESS CARDS

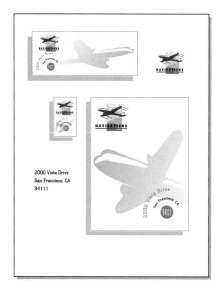

avigations has selected your logo as the best of all the preliminary designs. Unfortunately, they're not sending you to the South Seas to look for visually interesting scenery. Instead, they want you to work on establishing the corporate identity. It's time for letterhead, envelopes, and business cards.

This will be a great opportunity for you to learn about the Adobe Illustrator transformation tools. Without having to do any redrawing, you can use these tools to modify the logo for the different elements involved.

While adapting the logo, you'll

• resize the logo to fit on letterhead, envelopes, and business cards

• learn to rotate, reflect, and shear the airplane to create a different look and feel

• create a gradient fill and apply it to the airplane

• get acquainted with the different ways to create and spec type

Completing this lesson may take anywhere from 2 to 3 hours.

PLANNING THE PROJECT

First we'll take a look at the finished product.

1 Open the Lesson 4 folder and the file named *04Final*.

This file contains the finished artwork. The drop shadows have been added to the different pieces of stationery to enhance the presentation to the customer.

Notice the Navigations logo in the upper right corner. Every other logo and modified airplane is taken from this original. The logo has been resized for the stationery and the business card.

Take a look at the airplane in the background of all three elements. The airplane is filled with a gradient and has been resized, reshaped, and rotated for each item.

Finally, notice the type on the curved path with the company address.

2 Choose Artwork from the View menu (Command-E). Take a look at the artwork.

3 Choose Preview from the View menu (Command-Y).

Next you'll resize the window and reposition it so you can access it while you are working on the artwork in the working file.

4 Use the size box in the lower right corner of the window to resize the window so that it's about one-fourth the size of your screen.

5 Choose Fit In Window from the View menu (Command-M).

6 Drag the window to a convenient location on your screen.

7 Open the file named *04Begin*.

8 Choose Save As from the File menu, and name the file *04Work*. Save the file in the Project folder.

COPYING AND TRANSFORMING THE LOGO

You'll begin by copying the original logo and scaling it for the letterhead.

To copy the logo:

1 Click the selection tool in the toolbox.

2 Click the logo to select it. All of the parts of the logo have been grouped, so the entire logo is selected.

3 Begin dragging the logo; then hold down the Option key to make a copy as you drag.

4 Drag the logo downward to the upper left corner of the letterhead. Release the mouse button, and then release the Option key.

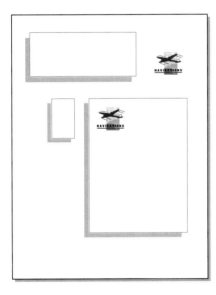

To scale the logo:

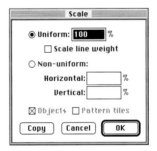 You'll use the scale tool to resize the logo. You can scale by choosing percentages or by dragging so that you can see the results and choose the size you want.

When you scale an object, you enlarge or reduce it horizontally (along the x axis) and vertically (along the y axis) relative to a fixed point of origin that you designate. If you do not designate an origin, the object is scaled from its center.

1 Click the scale tool in the toolbox.

2 Move the pointer to the center of the selected logo in the letterhead.

3 Hold down the Option key and click the mouse button.

Clicking in the center of the selected logo sets the point of origin in the center. Holding down the Option key displays the Scale dialog box.

4 In the Scale dialog box, make sure that Uniform is selected.

5 Enter 120 for the percentage.

6 Make sure that the Scale Line Weight option is selected. When you choose this option, all of the line weights of stroked paths are scaled along with the objects.

7 Click OK.

The logo is resized according to the specifications.

8 Choose Save from the File menu (Command-S) to save your work.

Next you'll use the same procedure to place the logo onto the envelope and the business card.

To make additional copies:

1 Click the selection tool in the toolbox.

2 Select the original logo.

3 Begin dragging; then hold down the Option key and drag a copy to the upper left corner of the envelope.

4 Select the original logo, and drag a copy to the top half of the business card. Remember to hold down the Option key.

5 With the logo on the business card selected, double-click the scale tool in the toolbox.

Shortcut: *When an object is selected and you double-click the scale tool in the toolbox, the object will be scaled exactly from its center.*

6 In the Scale dialog box, select Uniform scale and enter 65%. Make sure that the Scale Line Weight option is checked. Click OK.

7 Click the selection tool in the toolbox.

8 Select the logo on the envelope, and use the scale tool to scale to a 70% Uniform scale with scaled line weights.

9 Choose Save from the File menu (Command-S) to save your work.

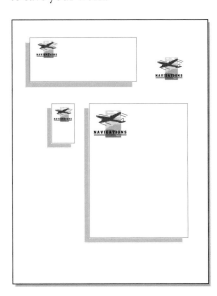

Next you'll scale the airplane for the lighter background versions. You'll begin with the business card. In this case, you'll scale by dragging, rather than by using the dialog box.

1 Click the zoom tool in the toolbox.

2 Hold down the mouse button and drag a marquee around the business card to zoom in on it.

3 Use the selection tool to select the logo on the business card.

4 Center the logo in the upper half of the business card.

5 Choose Ungroup from the Arrange menu (Command-U).

You ungroup the logo because you want to use only a part of it.

6 Click away from the artwork to deselect everything.

7 Click the plane to select it.

8 Hold down the Shift key, and click the two inner highlights of the plane to add them to the selection.

9 Begin dragging; then hold down the Option key to make a copy. Drag the copy to the bottom part of the business card. Leave the airplane selected.

10 Click the scale tool *once*, in the toolbox.

11 Click the nose of the airplane *once*. This sets the scale origin at the nose instead of at the center.

12 Move the pointer to the tail of the plane. Hold down the Shift key to constrain the scale so that the vertical and horizontal scaling is proportionate. With the Shift key down, hold down the mouse button and drag down and right to scale the plane until it's about twice as big as the original.

13 Release the mouse button; then release the Shift key.

Next you'll use the rotate tool to rotate the airplane. As does the scale tool, the rotate tool rotates around a point of origin.

To rotate the airplane:

1 Click the rotate tool in the toolbox.

2 Click the nose of the airplane to set the origin around which you will rotate.

3 Move the pointer to the tail of the airplane.

4 Hold down the mouse button and drag downward so that the nose of the plane is pointing toward the upper left corner of the window. Release the mouse button.

5 Choose Save from the File menu (Command-S) to save your work.

Time out for a movie

 If you are able to run Adobe Teach movies on your system, you can see a preview of the shearing technique taught in this section. Play the movie named *Adobe Teach 2*. For information on how to play Adobe Teach movies, see the "Getting Started" chapter at the beginning of this book.

And now, back to the lesson

The shear tool slants or skews an object along an axis you specify. You'll use the shear tool to reshape the airplane.

To shear the airplane:

1 Make sure the airplane and highlights are still selected.

2 Click the shear tool in the toolbox.

3 Position the pointer just above the nose.

4 Hold down the mouse button and drag *slowly*. Drag diagonally down and right about a quarter of an inch. Release the mouse button.

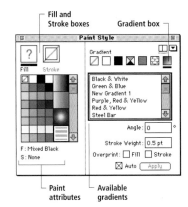

It's easy to shear too much. Be sure to drag slowly. Remember that you can use the Undo command and try the shear again.

Later in the lesson, you'll use the transformation tools on the background airplane for the envelope and the stationery. Right now, you'll create a gradient fill for the business card.

USING A GRADIENT FILL

You can fill a closed path with a *gradient fill*, a graduated blend between colors. In this part of the lesson, you'll paint the background airplane with an existing gradient fill. Then you'll create and name a new gradient fill and apply it to the background airplane.

To paint with a gradient fill:

1 Click the selection tool in the toolbox.

2 Use the selection tool to select the airplane you just sheared in the business card. *Do not select* the airplane highlights.

Note: *If the airplane and the highlights are all selected, you can hold down the Shift key and click the highlights to deselect them. Alternatively, you can deselect everything and then click the plane outline to select it.*

3 Choose Paint Style (Command-I) from the Object menu to display the Paint Style palette.

4 Click the Fill box.

5 Click to select the Gradient box at the top of the palette. The Gradient box is on the far right side of the color selection options.

The list of available gradients appears.

6 Click Black & White in the list.

The selected airplane is filled with the gradient.

Using the gradient vector tool

The gradient vector tool lets you modify the direction of gradient fills in your artwork. You can use the gradient vector tool to "repaint" the gradient along an imaginary line you create. You can change the direction of the gradient or change the starting and ending point of the gradient fill.

To use the gradient vector tool:

1 Make sure that the airplane is selected.

2 Click the gradient vector tool in the toolbox.

3 Hold down the mouse button and drag from the tip of the top wing to the tip of the bottom wing.

4 Experiment with the gradient vector tool by dragging to and from different points on the airplane. Try dragging just a little way, instead of across the entire plane.

Creating a gradient fill

1 Choose Select None from the Edit menu (Command-Shift-A) to deselect everything.

2 Choose Gradient from the Object menu. The Gradient palette is displayed.

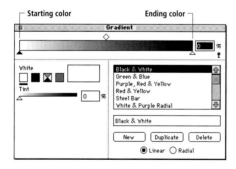

3 Click New. The name, *New Gradient*, followed by a number, appears in the list.

4 Type *Plane Gradient*, and press Return.

When you create a gradient, you define the starting color and the ending color. These colors are represented by the small triangles below the gradient bar in the Gradient palette. A solid triangle is the selected triangle. By default, the starting triangle is selected when you open the palette.

5 With the starting triangle selected, click the Process box to indicate you'll create a process color. The Process box is the third from the left. You see the word *Process* above the boxes when you click the Process box.

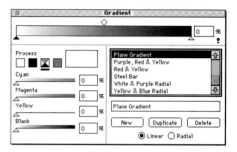

6 Define the starting color as follows. (Be sure to press Return when you have finished.)

Note: You can use the Tab key to move between the fields.

    Cyan ....0 %
    Magenta ......4 %
    Yellow ....17 %
    Black............0 %

7 Click the triangle at the right end of the gradient bar to select it for defining the ending color of the gradient.

8 Click the Process box in the Gradient palette. All color values should default to zero, indicating Process White. Leave the values at the defaults.

9 Press the Return key.

10 Choose Hide Gradient from the Window menu to close the Gradient palette.

Now you'll apply the Plane Gradient to the airplane.

To apply the gradient fill:

1 Use the selection tool to select the airplane you just sheared on the business card. *Do not select* the airplane highlights.

2 Click the Fill box in the Paint Style palette.

3 Click to select the Gradient box in the Paint Style palette.

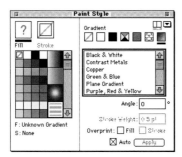

4 Click *Plane Gradient* in the list.

The selected airplane is filled with the gradient.

5 Click the gradient vector tool in the toolbox.

6 Drag from the nose of the airplane to the tail to make the gradient match the final artwork.

To group and position the airplane:

1 Click the selection tool in the toolbox.

2 Select the airplane and both highlights by holding the Shift key down and clicking.

3 Choose Group from the Arrange menu (Command-G).

4 Use the selection tool to position the airplane on the business card. The tail of the airplane can overlap the edge of the card.

5 Choose Save from the File menu (Command-S) to save your work.

MAKING ADDITIONAL TRANSFORMATIONS

To complete the airplane transformations, you'll make copies of the background airplane for the envelope and letterhead and use the transformation tools to distort the copies.

First, you'll copy the background airplane from the business card to the letterhead.

1 Make sure that the background airplane is selected.

2 Choose Copy from the Edit menu (Command-C).

3 Choose Fit In Window from the View menu (Command-M).

The Fit In Window command is useful if you have done a lot of zooming and need to reorient the drawing.

4 Choose Paste from the Edit menu (Command-V).

5 Drag the selected airplane to the center of the bottom half of the letterhead.

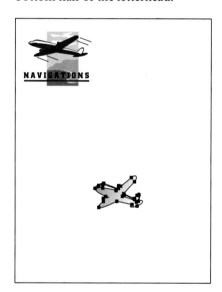

6 Double-click the scale tool and scale the airplane to 500%.

7 Click the selection tool in the toolbox.

8 Center the larger airplane in the lower half of the stationery. It's all right if part of the tail is outside the rectangle.

9 Click the shear tool in the toolbox.

10 Position the pointer on the right wing; hold down the mouse button, and drag about a quarter inch to the left to distort the plane.

Next you'll copy the background airplane from the letterhead to the envelope. Then you'll scale, reflect, shear, and rotate the background airplane.

11 Click the selection tool in the toolbox.

12 Select the airplane if it is not selected.

13 Begin dragging the airplane upward, and hold down the Option key to make a copy. Put the copy over the center of the envelope.

To scale the airplane:

1 Double-click the scale tool to set the scale origin in the center of the selected airplane.

2 Scale the airplane to a 50% uniform scale.

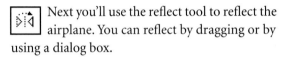 Next you'll use the reflect tool to reflect the airplane. You can reflect by dragging or by using a dialog box.

To reflect the airplane:

1 Double-click the reflect tool in the toolbox.

2 In the Reflect dialog box, click Vertical; then click OK.

The reflect tool creates a mirror image of the airplane.

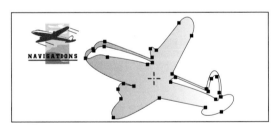

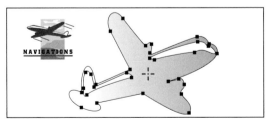

3 Zoom in on the envelope if you want.

To shear the airplane:

1 Click the shear tool in the toolbox.

2 Click the tail of the airplane.

3 Position the pointer on the left wing; hold down the mouse button, and drag a little bit down and to the right to distort the plane.

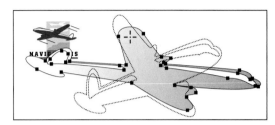

If you don't like the look of the sheared airplane, use the Undo command, and repeat the shearing process.

To rotate the airplane:

1 Click the rotate tool in the toolbox.

2 Position the pointer on the nose of the airplane, hold down the mouse button, and drag up or down to rotate the airplane properly.

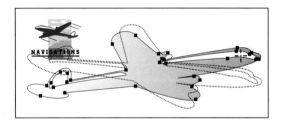

3 If necessary, use the selection tool to position the airplane in the envelope so that the tail of the plane is under the logo.

Note: You can use the arrow keys to move the selected airplane in small increments.

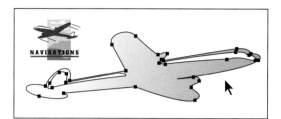

4 If you have been working steadily on this lesson and haven't saved your work, now would be a good time to do that.

WORKING WITH TYPE

The final part of creating the stationery is to design the address. You'll practice using different fonts, leading, and alignment. You'll color the type and learn to create type on a path.

There are several different ways to create type with the Adobe Illustrator program. You can create *point* type just by clicking the type tool and clicking in the window. You can create *rectangle* type by dragging a rectangle with the type tool. Type can also be contained in any area, and type can be placed on a path.

There are three type tools in the toolbox: the type tool, the area type tool, and the path type tool.

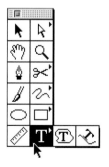

Creating rectangle type

You'll do your preliminary work in the open area just below the business card. First, you'll zoom in for a better view. Then you'll create a text rectangle to work in.

To create rectangle type:

1 Click the zoom tool in the toolbox.

2 Click a couple inches below the business card. Click again, until you have zoomed to 150%. You can see the zoom factor in the title bar of the window.

3 Click the type tool in the toolbox.

4 Move the I-beam pointer below the business card; then drag to create a rectangle that is about half as tall as the business card, and about twice as wide as the business card.

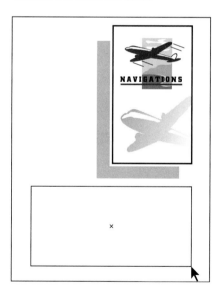

Notice that (in Preview view) you don't see the rectangle once you release the mouse button. The blinking insertion point is at the top left of the rectangle area. This is where the type you enter will begin.

You have created a text rectangle. This rectangle is neither filled nor stroked. It simply defines an area in which you can type, and you don't see it when you print. Text rectangles are particularly useful in creating columns of text.

The type you create will be the same size and font as the last type you created. If you recently used a particularly large font size, the type may not fit in the rectangle. You'll change the size before you begin typing.

5 Choose Size from the Type menu and 8 from the submenu.

6 Enter the following text. Put a Return at the end of each line.

> **2000 Vista Drive**
> **San Francisco, CA**
> **94111**

Don't worry if all of the type doesn't fit inside the box.

7 Click the type tool in the toolbox.

When you click the type tool after typing, the rectangle and the type are selected. You know type is selected when you see the alignment point and the baseline under the type.

Setting type attributes

You can set the font, size, leading, and other type attributes in the Character palette or by choosing commands from the Type menu.

In this part of the lesson, you'll experiment with different type attributes just to see how they affect the type. After that, you'll set the type to the right specs for this job.

1 Choose Character from the Type menu (Command-T).

The Character palette appears.

2 If the entire palette is not displayed, click the lever to expand the palette. Drag the palette so you can see both the palette and the type.

Note: If the Tracking value is still at 240 from the previous lesson, click the word Tracking to restore the default value of 0.

3 Experiment with different fonts. Use the pop-up font menu in the Character palette to choose a font. You can access this pop-up menu by placing the pointer on the triangle to the right of the current font and holding down the mouse button. Try different fonts to see how they look.

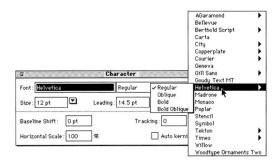

4 Try changing the type size. You can select the Size field, type a value, and press Return or Tab. You can also use the size pop-up menu from the pop-up menu next to the Size field.

5 Change the leading by typing values or by using the pop-up menu. Try out leading of 36 and 10.

Leading specifies the amount of vertical space between type baselines and is measured in points.

6 Experiment with the tracking by entering values of 50 and -50 (minus 50). Press Return to see the results.

Tracking inserts uniform spacing between the selected characters when more than two characters are selected. You can use tracking when you want to adjust the spacing of a word or of an entire text object. Positive values move type apart; negative values move characters closer together.

7 Use the I-beam pointer and drag to select a single letter. Enter different values for Baseline Shift. Try 10 and -10. Press Return after you change values.

Baseline Shift controls the distance that type appears from its baseline. You can use this feature to create subscripts or superscripts, or to move type on a path above or below a path.

8 Click the type tool in the toolbox to select all the type.

9 Try values of 50 and 200 for Horizontal Scale. This feature specifies the proportion between the height and width of the type. Adjustments have no effect on the character height.

10 When you have finished experimenting, set the following values for all the type:

> Font: City-Medium
> Size: 16 points
> Leading: 24 points

11 Set the Baseline Shift, Horizontal Scale, and Tracking back to their defaults. You can return these fields to the defaults by clicking the word before the field. For example, to return Baseline Shift to its default of 0 points, click the word Baseline. Use the same procedure for Horizontal Scale (default is 100%) and Tracking (default is 0).

12 Close the Character palette.

Changing the size of a text rectangle

You can adjust the size of any rectangle you have created to hold type. Because the rectangle and the type are grouped together, you use the direct selection tool to select only parts of the rectangle.

1 Choose Artwork from the View menu (Command-E).

2 Click the direct selection tool in the toolbox.

3 Click away from the artwork to deselect everything.

4 Click the right edge of the text rectangle.

5 Position the pointer on the right edge of the selected rectangle.

6 Begin dragging to the left, then hold down the Shift key to constrain the rectangle. Drag until you can see only the *2000* in the top line. Then release the mouse button and Shift key.

7 Notice the box with the + sign on the lower right side of the text rectangle.

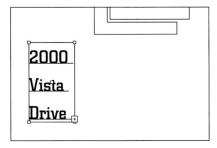

8 The plus sign indicates an overflow of type. You can see the plus sign only in Artwork view.

9 Use the direct selection tool and hold down the Shift key to drag the right side of the box back to the rectangle's original size so that the entire address is seen inside the box.

Changing alignment

You can change the type alignment with the Type menu. (You can also change alignment with the Paragraph palette, which we haven't explored yet.)

1 Click the type tool in the toolbox.

2 Drag the I-beam pointer across the type to select it.

3 Choose Alignment from the Type menu and Center from the submenu.

4 Try different alignment options to see how they look.

5 When you have finished, return the alignment to Left.

6 Choose Preview from the View menu (Command-Y).

Painting type

You can paint type with different colors.

1 Click the type tool in the toolbox. The text rectangle is selected.

Note: Although the text rectangle is also selected, it will not be painted.

2 Choose Show Paint Style from the Window menu. (This is an alternative to using the Object menu to open the Palette.)

3 By default, type is filled with black and not stroked. Change the color of the selected type by clicking different swatches in the Paint Style palette to fill the selected type with a color.

You can also change the color of a single letter or word.

4 Click the type tool in the toolbox.

5 Double-click a word to select it. (Double-clicking selects a word, triple-clicking selects a paragraph.)

6 Click a paint swatch in the Paint Style palette to change the color of the word. Then click the I-beam pointer somewhere else in the text to deselect the painted word and see the color. (You don't see the actual fill color until you deselect the word.)

7 When you have finished experimenting, click the selection tool in the toolbox.

8 Make sure that the text block is selected.

Note: A question mark in the Fill box indicates that more than one filled object is selected. Since the different objects have different fills, the question mark is displayed.

9 Click the Fill box in the Paint Style palette, click the second gray swatch in the second row to paint the selected type with 50% black.

Creating type on a path

With the path type tool, you can create type that follows a path. The path can be an open path or a closed path. In this part of the lesson, you'll design the address by creating circles and then adding type that follows the circles.

To create type on a path:

1 Click the oval tool in the toolbox.

2 Scroll to find an empty space to work in. Move the pointer to the empty space, and click the mouse button.

3 Enter 127 for the Width.

4 Click the word Height to enter 127 for Height automatically. Then click OK.

The circle is filled with the same color as the last object you painted, in this case, the type.

5 Select the path type tool in the toolbox. You can access this tool by positioning the pointer on the regular type tool, holding down the mouse button, and dragging to the right. Notice the status line reads *Path Type.*

6 Move the pointer to the drawing area. The pointer has a slanted crossbar, indicating that you can create type on a path.

7 Click the top edge of the circle. The circle disappears, and you see the blinking insertion point.

8 Type the following:

2000 Vista Drive

9 Click the type tool in the toolbox. This selects the type and the circle. Notice the type is entered at its default of a 100% black fill with no stroke. The circle is now unfilled and unstroked.

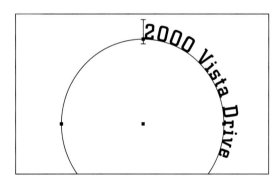

10 In the Paint Style palette, click the second gray swatch in the second row to paint the selected type with 50% black.

You can drag type to move it along a path. You can also drag it to the other side of the path. You use the large I-beam at the beginning of the type as a handle to drag.

Time out for a movie

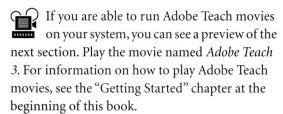 If you are able to run Adobe Teach movies on your system, you can see a preview of the next section. Play the movie named *Adobe Teach 3.* For information on how to play Adobe Teach movies, see the "Getting Started" chapter at the beginning of this book.

To move type on a path:

1 Click the selection tool in the toolbox.

2 Position the pointer on the I-beam at the beginning of the type.

3 Hold down the mouse button and begin dragging counterclockwise around the circle. Release the mouse button when the type is where you want it.

4 Experiment with repositioning the type on the inside of the circle. Position the pointer on the I-beam, and drag across the circle. The type is moved inside the circle, and the direction of the type is changed.

5 Move the type back outside the circle with this shortcut. Double-click the I-beam.

6 Drag the type by the I-beam until it is positioned so that the 2000 begins just below the nine o'clock position.

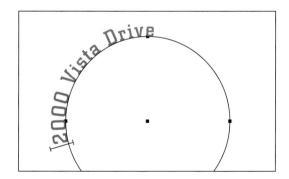

Next you create a smaller circle and add the next part of the address to it. In this case you'll copy and paste the type, rather than type it.

1 Click the oval tool in the toolbox.

2 Position the pointer on the center point of the existing circle. Hold down the Option key, and click the mouse button.

3 Enter 75 for Width and 75 for Height and click OK.

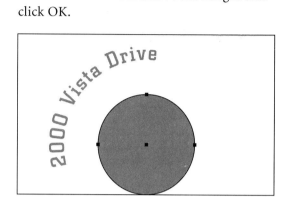

4 Click the path type tool in the toolbox.

5 Triple-click to select *San Francisco, CA* in the rectangle you typed earlier. Notice that the path type tool icon changes to a regular I-beam when it is over existing type.

6 Choose Copy from the Edit menu (Command-C).

7 Click the path type tool in the toolbox.

8 Click the top of the inner circle. You see the blinking insertion point.

9 Choose Paste from the Edit menu (Command-V). The type is pasted onto the path. The existing type color is retained, and the circle is converted to an unstroked, unfilled path.

10 Click the selection tool in the toolbox.

11 Drag the I-beam on the inner type circle to position the type so that the *S* in San Francisco is beneath the last *0* in 2000.

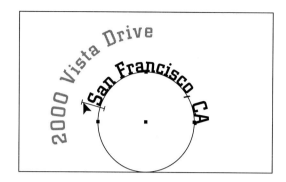

12 Click the path type tool in the toolbox.

You can use any of the different type tools when you want to edit type. Each of them displays the I-beam pointer over existing type.

13 Drag to select *San Francisco, CA.*

14 Choose Size from the Type menu and 12 from the submenu to change the size.

Adding the zip code

The final line of type, the zip code, will be created on a gray background circle. Then you'll scale the type to fit the circle. To complete the project, you'll copy and scale the type to the other pieces of stationery.

First you'll switch to Artwork view. Working in Artwork view can be faster because it takes less time to redraw the screen each time you add artwork.

1 Choose Artwork from the View menu (Command-E).

2 Click the oval tool in the toolbox.

3 Hold down the Option key and click the center point of the two existing circles.

4 Enter 40 for the Width, click Height to enter 40, and click OK.

5 Select the regular type tool in the toolbox. You will have to drag to select this type tool.

6 Click the center anchor point of the circles.

7 Type the zip code, *94111*.

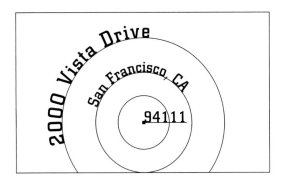

8 Click the selection tool in the toolbox.

9 Use the Paint Style palette to fill the selected type with white. (You won't see the change because you are in Artwork view.)

10 Zoom in on the zip code until the title bar zoom factor is 300%.

11 Use the selection tool to center the type inside the circles.

12 Click the scale tool in the toolbox.

13 Click the bottom of the 9.

14 Move the pointer to the top of the last 1. Drag slightly upward and left to make the type taller and narrower.

15 Choose Preview from the View menu (Command-Y).

16 Use the arrow keys to fine-tune the position of the zip code.

Copying and scaling the address

Now that you've finished designing the zip code, you'll make copies for the stationery.

1 Use the selection tool to drag a marquee to select the three circles and the type.

Note: You don't have to enclose the entire circle with the marquee; just drag across any part of the circles and the type baselines.

TIP: USE THE HIDE EDGES COMMAND TO HIDE SELECTION EDGES AND ANCHOR POINTS FOR A BETTER VIEW. SELECT THE OBJECT BEFORE YOU CHOOSE THE COMMAND.

2 Choose Group from the Arrange menu (Command-G).

3 Choose Fit In Window from the View menu (Command-M) so you can see the different pieces of stationery.

4 Use the selection tool to drag the address to the lower right corner of the letterhead.

5 Make a copy of the grouped address by holding down the Option key and dragging. Drag the copy over the business card.

6 With the business card address selected, double-click the scale tool, and make a uniform scale of 44%.

7 Click the zoom tool in the toolbox.

8 Drag a marquee around the business card to enlarge it.

9 Use the selection tool (or the arrow keys) to position the address on the card.

10 Choose Fit In Window from the View menu (Command-M).

11 Click the selection tool in the toolbox.

12 Select the address on the letterhead.

13 Begin dragging; hold down the Option key, and drag another copy from the letterhead to the envelope.

14 Double-click the scale tool in the toolbox.

15 Scale the envelope address to a uniform scale of 60%.

16 Choose Hide Edges from the View menu (Command-Shift-H).

When you choose the Hide Edges command, all selection edges and anchor points are made invisible. You may want to do this to get a better view of the actual object. The selected object can still be moved and manipulated with the selection tool or the arrow keys.

17 Use the selection tool or arrow keys to reposition the artwork under the logo on the envelope. Zoom in on the envelope if you need to.

18 Choose Show Edges from the View menu (Command-Shift-H).

Making final touch-ups

The file you began with contained rectangle borders with drop shadows. In some cases, the gradient airplane may overlap the rectangles.

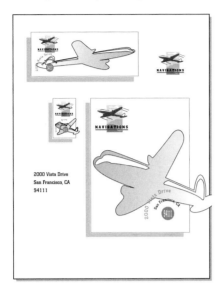

As a final touch-up, you'll move the rectangles in front of the airplanes to enhance the presentation. The rectangles were locked to prevent you from accidentally selecting them during the lesson.

1 Choose Fit In Window from the View menu (Command-M) to see the entire drawing.

2 Choose Unlock All from the Arrange menu (Command-2).

All locked objects are now unlocked and selected.

3 Choose Select None from the Edit menu (Command-Shift-A).

4 Click the selection tool in the toolbox.

5 Click the edge of the rectangle around the letterhead to select it.

6 Hold down the Shift key and select the rectangle around the business card and the rectangle around the envelope.

7 Choose Bring to Front from the Arrange menu (Command-Equal).

8 Choose Select None from the Edit menu (Command-Shift-A).

The rectangles are now in front of the airplane.

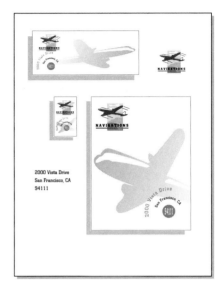

9 Choose Save from the File menu (Command-S) to save your work.

10 If you would like to print your work, choose Print from the File menu and click Print.

11 Close any open files.

You've done a great job adapting the Navigations logo to the stationery. Without doing much drawing at all, you've scaled and modified the airplane. You've also explored the type features of the Adobe Illustrator program. Let's hope Navigations likes it. If they do, you might get a more interesting assignment next time. In fact, you might even get to go to the beach with all expenses paid.

Lesson

5

Lesson 5: Let's Go to the Beach

Success! Now that you've established a corporate identity for Navigations, it's time to kick back and relax. The company has decided you can work off-site on your next project. Their only requirement is that you return with images and thoughts for future advertising.

Be sure to take your camera and shoot plenty of photos. And record some relaxing thoughts on your laptop computer. You can scan in the visuals and import the text for future projects. A full-color advertisement touting life at the beach just might work. In this lesson, you'll give it a try.

While creating the advertisement, you'll

- learn how to use guides to make layout easier
- convert type into artwork outlines that you can paint with a gradient fill
- import other files into your Adobe Illustrator files
- learn how to make masks
- import text
- paint with a pattern

Completing this lesson may take anywhere from 1 to 2 hours.

In this lesson, you will create this advertisement.

Because Navigations is a worldwide company, this advertisement will be translated into many different languages. You'll work on the Spanish version.

The final file contains placed art from two imported files. Both were saved in the EPS (Encapsulated PostScript) language format.

There is also a text file you can use when you import the text into the document.

PLANNING THE PROJECT

Begin by taking a look at the complete advertisement.

1 Open the Lesson 5 folder and the file named *05Final*.

This file contains the finished artwork.

Now that you've been working with the Adobe Illustrator program, you can recognize how some of the artwork was created. There's a drop shadow in the headline type, and there's some type and a picture that have been rotated.

Notice the crop marks at the four corners of the document. Crop marks define where the printed artwork will be trimmed.

Take a look at the photo with the umbrellas in the top of the picture. This photo is a separate EPS file that has been placed into the artwork.

2 Use the selection tool and click the beach photo with the umbrellas to select it.

When you click the photo, you see three selected rectangles. The large rectangle with diagonal lines represents the placed image of the beach photo. The smaller rectangle that outlines the photo in

the document is a *mask*. A third rectangle to the right is a text rectangle that was grouped with the other two.

When you mask an object, you cover part of an image so that only a portion of the image appears through the shape you create. In this case, the smaller rectangle masks the larger area of the photo. Although the beach photo is the size of the larger rectangle, you see only the portion that shows through the smaller rectangle that is the mask.

3 Choose Attributes from the Object menu.

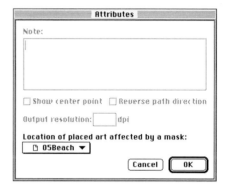

At the bottom of the dialog box, you see "Location of placed art affected by a mask." This tells you that the file is masked. You can also find the location of the placed file.

4 Position the pointer on the triangle next to the file name, and hold down the mouse button. The pop-up menu shows where the file is located.

5 Click OK to close the dialog box.

6 Use the selection tool to click the edge of the circle that is filled with type.

The palm tree photo in the circle is also masked. The circle is a mask that blocks out part of the photo. The photo was scanned with a color scanner. Then it was opened in Adobe Photoshop, screened back (lightened), and saved as an EPS file. After that, it was brought into the Adobe Illustrator file.

A second circle was created, and the text was imported into that circle.

Notice that a pattern has been painted on the left side of the document. And finally, the Navigations logo has been copied and pasted from another file.

7 Choose Artwork from the View menu (Command-E). Take a look at the artwork.

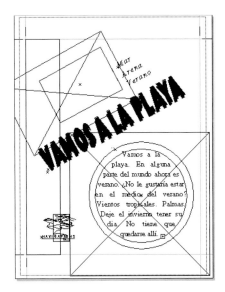

8 Choose Preview from the View menu (Command-Y).

9 Choose Select None from the Edit menu (Command-Shift-A) to deselect everything in the final artwork file.

10 Resize the window so that it is about the size of one-fourth of your screen. Drag the window to the top right corner of your screen.

11 Choose Fit In Window from the View menu (Command-M).

To create the working file:

1 Choose New from the File menu.

2 Choose Save As from the File menu, name the file *05Work*, and save it in the Project folder.

SETTING UP RULER UNITS AND ORIGIN

In the first part of the lesson, you'll change the measurement units to inches and reset the ruler origin.

Changing the ruler units

1 Choose Show Rulers from the View menu (Command-R). The rulers show measurements in points and picas by default.

2 Choose Preferences from the File menu and General from the submenu. You see the General Preferences dialog box.

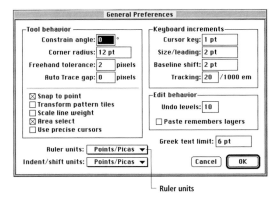

Ruler units

3 Locate the Ruler Units field.

4 Change the Ruler Units to inches by positioning the pointer on the triangle and dragging down to select Inches. *Do not change* the Indent/Shift units.

5 Click OK to close the dialog box.

The rulers now show inches instead of points and picas. You can see that the page rectangle is 8.5 inches wide. Since the zoom factor is 50%, each major mark on the ruler represents two inches instead of one. These marks change when you zoom in and out.

Also notice that as you move the pointer around in the window, a dotted line moves in each ruler to help you know the exact position of the pointer.

6 If necessary, scroll so that the bottom left corner of the page rectangle is on your screen.

Notice that the bottom left corner of the page is represented on each ruler as zero. This point is known as the *ruler origin.* You'll change the ruler origin so that the zero-zero point is at the top left, instead of the bottom left.

7 Position the pointer in the lower right corner at the box where the rulers intersect.

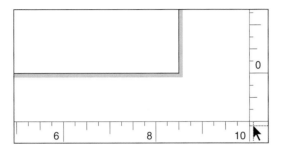

8 Hold down the mouse button and drag the pointer to the upper left corner of the page. As you drag, dotted lines indicate your position on the page. Drag until the origin matches the top of the page. (The screen will scroll automatically.) Then release the mouse button.

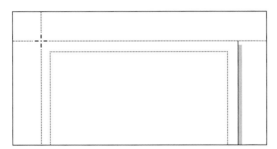

If you released the mouse button in the wrong place, you can move the pointer back to the ruler intersection box and drag again.

CREATING GUIDES

Guide objects are dashed lines that are usually locked in place. You can use them to help you align graphics and text. Any object can be turned into a guide object. You can also create horizontal and vertical ruler guides.

Creating ruler guides

You create ruler guides by dragging from the ruler.

1 Position the pointer inside the bottom ruler.

2 Hold down the mouse button and drag upward toward the top of the page. Continue dragging until the guide is positioned at the 1-inch mark on the right ruler. (This mark will be halfway between the 0 and the 2 on the ruler, and probably will not be marked with a 1.)

If you make a mistake and release the mouse button in the wrong place, choose Undo from the Edit menu to undo the guide. Then drag a new one.

3 Move the pointer back to the bottom ruler; hold down the mouse button, and drag a ruler guide up to the 10-inch mark on the right ruler.

4 Move the pointer to the right ruler, and drag a guide from the ruler to the left. Put the guide at the ½ inch mark on the bottom ruler.

5 Drag another guide from the right ruler to the left to the 8-inch mark on the bottom ruler.

The guides should look something like this.

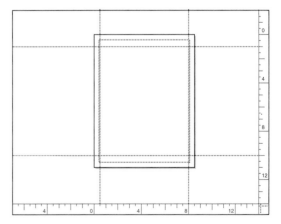

Your page rectangles may look different from the above figure due to differences between printers.

The corner points where the four guides intersect define the size of the final artwork, which is 7.5 inches wide and 9 inches tall.

Next you'll use the ruler guides you just drew to create a rectangle that precisely defines your working area. You'll paint the rectangle with no fill and a black stroke, and then you'll lock it so it can't be moved.

Making a locked rectangle

1 Click the rectangle tool in the toolbox.

2 Position the pointer on the intersection of the upper and left guides. Drag diagonally to draw a rectangle from this point to the bottom right intersection of the guides.

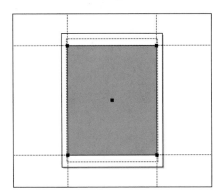

3 With the rectangle selected, choose Paint Style from the Object menu (Command-I).

4 In the Paint Style palette, click the Fill box, and click the None swatch.

5 In the Paint Style palette, click the Stroke box, click the Black swatch, and set the Stroke Weight to 2 points. Press Return.

The border rectangle defines the 7.5 by 9-inch working area for the advertisement.

6 With the rectangle selected, choose Lock from the Arrange menu (Command-1). The anchor points disappear from the rectangle.

7 Click the selection tool in the toolbox.

8 Try to select the rectangle.

Because the rectangle is locked, you are unable to select it. This makes it easy to work with as a border; you won't select it by mistake.

9 Drag a ruler guide from the right ruler to the 2-inch mark on the bottom ruler. This guide will be used for positioning the pattern later in the lesson.

10 Choose Save from the File menu (Command-S) to save your work.

WORKING WITH TYPE

The main headline of the advertisement (VAMOS A LA PLAYA) consists of three copies of type. One layer provides the drop shadow, one provides the stroke, and one has been turned into artwork outlines and filled with a gradient. All copies have been rotated. Take a look at the headline in the final artwork.

Entering the type

1 Click the type tool in the toolbox. Make sure that you click the type tool and not the path type or area type tool.

2 Click somewhere near the left side of the bottom of the page. (You will move the type to its final position later.)

3 Type the following in all capital letters:

VAMOS A LA PLAYA

The type may appear as gray lines. This is known as *greeked* type. When type is smaller than a certain size, the type is replaced on-screen with non-letterforms that act as placeholders. In the General Preferences dialog box you can specify a size below which type will be greeked. Zooming out may also reduce the type to its greeked appearance.

Although you *could* zoom in to see the type, you won't do it now, because you will set the type to a larger size in a few steps.

4 Click the type tool in the toolbox.

5 Choose Character from the Type menu (Command-T).

6 Select a font by choosing Gill Sans from the Font pop-up menu and Extra Bold from the submenu.

7 Set the size to 102 points and press Return.

8 Set the Horizontal Scale to 40. (If you don't see the Horizontal Scale option in the Character palette, click the lever at the bottom right of the window.)

9 Set the Tracking to 25 and press Return.

Now that you can see the type, check to see if you spelled everything correctly. If you need to make corrections, drag to select the type and correct any errors.

10 Close the Character palette.

11 Click the Fill box in the Paint Style palette, and fill the type with 50% black. (You can click the second swatch in the second row if you want.)

12 Click the Stroke box in the Paint Style palette, and click the None swatch.

The type you have just created will be the headline shadow.

Copying the type and creating outlines

Next you make a copy for the stroke. In general, it is not a good idea to stroke type, because you distort the font from its true shape. When you want to create a stroked effect for type, you make a copy of the type and stroke it. Then you paste the stroked copy behind another copy.

That portion of the stroke that is outside the center of the path remains visible, and the type is not distorted. Because you see only one-half of the stroke (the part outside the regular outline), you should make the stroke larger than you normally would.

To copy the type:

1 Click the selection tool in the toolbox.

2 Position the pointer on the baseline of the selected type, hold down the Option key, and drag upward and to the right about one-eighth inch to offset the copy.

You can use the arrow keys to position the selected type if you need to.

3 Click the Stroke box in the Paint Style palette, and stroke this copy of the type with a 75% black stroke. (You can click the third swatch in the second row if you want.)

4 Set the Stroke Weight to 3 points and press Return.

5 Choose Copy from the Edit menu (Command-C).

6 Choose Paste In Front from the Edit menu (Command-F).

The Paste In Front command pastes the copy of the type exactly in front of the type you copied. You now have three copies of the type, and the third copy is selected.

Next you will convert the top copy of the type to outlines so you can paint the type with a gradient fill.

To create type outlines:

1 Choose Create Outlines from the Type menu.

The type is converted to a set of paths that you can edit and manipulate just as you would a graphic object. All of the paths are currently selected. Note that once you have created type outlines, you cannot turn the outlines back to type.

2 Choose Group from the Arrange menu (Command-G).

3 In the Paint Style palette, click the Stroke box and the None swatch. The top (third) copy of the type is now a filled outline with no stroke.

Painting the type outlines with a gradient

Next you'll create a new gradient and paint the type outlines.

To create a gradient:

1 Choose Gradient from the Object menu, or double-click the gradient vector tool in the toolbox.

2 The Gradient palette appears.

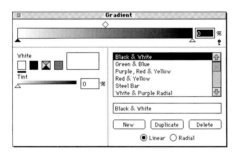

3 Click New.

4 In the text box beneath the list, change the name of the gradient to Playa. Press Return.

The left triangle below the gradient bar should be selected. This triangle represents the starting color.

5 Click the Process box in the Gradient palette.

6 Set the values for the starting color as follows:

Cyan............. 0 %
Magenta....90 %
Yellow........75 %
Black .... 10 %

7 Click the right triangle below the gradient bar to set the ending color.

8 Click the Process box in the Gradient palette.

9 Set the values for the ending color as follows:

Cyan ....0 %
Magenta ......0 %
Yellow........53 %
Black............0 %

10 Press Return.

11 Close the Gradient palette.

To paint the type outlines:

1 In the Paint Style palette, click the Fill box and then click the Gradient box.

2 Choose Playa from the gradient list.

3 Click the gradient vector tool in the toolbox.

4 Drag from the top to the bottom of the type outlines.

To group the type and outlines:

1 Click the selection tool in the toolbox.

2 Use the selection tool to select all three copies of the type: the drop shadow, the stroked version, and the gradient-filled outlines.

Note: You don't have to drag a marquee around the outside of all of the type. You only have to drag across any part of the outlines as well as the baselines.

When the group outlines are selected, you see the anchor points around the path. When the other two versions are selected, you see one baseline because these two versions are exactly on top of one another.

3 Choose Group from the Arrange menu (Command-G) to group the three copies of the type.

4 Choose Save from the File menu (Command-S) to save your work.

IMPORTING AND MASKING A PHOTO

The photo you took while working at the beach has been scanned and converted to an EPS file in the Adobe Photoshop program. You'll import the entire photo into the Adobe Illustrator program. Then you'll create a mask to hide parts of the photo.

Importing an EPS file

1 Choose Place Art from the File menu.

The Place Art dialog box appears. You use this dialog box to locate the art that you want to import.

2 Locate the Lesson 5 folder, and select the file named *05Beach*. Click Place.

The photo is imported into your document. The box with diagonal lines from corner to corner defines the photo's dimensions. The imported file is placed in front of any other artwork in the document, and the imported file is selected.

3 If necessary, use the selection tool to drag the imported file away from the type.

Making a mask

A *masking object* is an artwork object placed on top of other objects and made into a mask. Once the masking object is defined, only the artwork inside the mask is visible. You'll create a small rectangle, position it on the imported photo, and make a mask to hide part of the photo. Keep in mind that a mask should always be on top of the other objects.

1 Click the rectangle tool in the toolbox.

2 Click the center of the imported photo.

3 Enter 3 for Width and 2 for Height, and click OK.

4 Click the Fill box in the Paint Style palette, and set the fill to none.

5 Click the selection tool in the toolbox.

6 Drag the smaller rectangle until it is positioned over the two umbrellas on the right side of the photo. Center the umbrellas in the rectangle you are dragging.

7 Hold down the Shift key and click the photo somewhere outside of the rectangle you just created so that both the rectangle and the photo are selected.

When you make a mask, both the background object and the masking object must be selected.

8 Choose Masks from the Object menu and Make from the submenu.

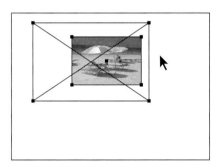

Only the part of the photo that is inside the mask shows through. If the original masking object had any fill or stroke, those characteristics are removed.

9 Choose Group from the Arrange menu (Command-G) to group the photo with the mask.

10 Use the selection tool to position the photograph so that the left edge lines up with the *M* in *VAMOS* and the photo is about three quarters of an inch above the type.

11 If you haven't saved the file in a while, now would be a good time to do so.

Adding type

Next you add the type to the right of the photo.

1 Choose Select None from the Edit menu (Command-Shift-A).

2 Click the type tool in the toolbox.

3 Choose Character from the Type menu (Command-T) to open the Character palette.

4 Set the font to Times-Italic.

5 Set the size to 23 and the leading to 30, and press Return.

6 Click *Horizontal Scale* to return the value to its default of 100%.

7 Click *Tracking* to return the value to its default of 0.

8 Close the Character palette.

9 Click to the right of the photo to set an insertion point.

10 Type **Mar** and press Return.

11 Type **Arena** and press Return.

12 Type **Verano** and press Return.

13 Click the selection tool in the toolbox. The type is automatically selected.

14 Position the type about one quarter of an inch from the right edge of the photo. Line up the bottom of the type with the bottom of the photo.

Next you group all three objects and rotate them.

1 Use the selection tool and the Shift key to select the type you just created, the headline type (VAMOS A LA PLAYA), and the masked photo.

2 Choose Group from the Arrange menu (Command-G).

3 Double-click the rotate tool in the toolbox.

4 Enter 28 for Angle and click OK.

The objects are rotated.

5 Use the selection tool and drag the grouped objects by the bottom of the *V* in *VAMOS*. Position the bottom of the *V* at the 2-inch mark on the bottom ruler and the 6-inch mark on the right ruler.

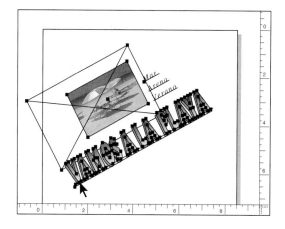

6 Choose Save from the File menu (Command-S) to save your work.

ADDING ANOTHER MASKED PHOTO

Now you'll import the other photo and mask it.

1 Choose Place Art from the File menu.

2 Select the file named *05Palm* and click Place.

3 Use the selection tool to drag the photo below the headline type and to the side so that it doesn't overlap any existing artwork.

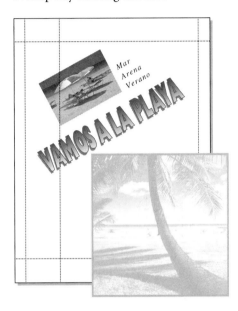

4 Click the oval tool in the toolbox.

5 Hold down the Option key and click the center of the photo.

6 Enter 4.5 for Width.

7 Click the word *Height* to enter 4.5 for the Height. Click OK.

The circle is filled, but it will be unfilled when you make the mask.

8 Click the selection tool in the toolbox.

9 With the circle selected, hold down the Shift key and select the photo so that both objects are selected.

10 Choose Masks from the Object menu and Make from the submenu.

To position the mask over the photo:

1 Click away from the artwork to deselect everything.

2 With the selection tool, click the edge of the circle to select the circle. If you don't click exactly on the edge, you'll select the photo instead.

3 Try dragging the circle by its edge to different locations on the photo. When you release the mouse button, you see different parts of the photo through the mask.

4 Click just outside the circle to select the photo rectangle with the diagonal lines.

5 Drag the rectangle to position the masking circle over the photo, as shown below.

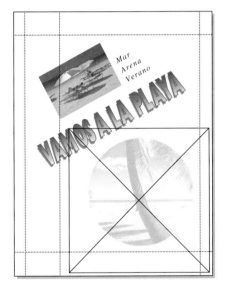

6 Use the Shift key and select both the circle and the photo.

7 Choose Group from the Arrange menu (Command-G).

8 Use the selection tool to position the circle in the lower right corner of the drawing.

9 Choose Save from the File menu (Command-S) to save your work.

CREATING AREA TYPE

Now you'll create a circular type area and add text inside it. Then you'll set the specifications for the imported text.

To create area type:

1 Click the oval tool in the toolbox.

2 Move the pointer to the center of the masked circle, hold down the Option key, and click the mouse button.

3 Enter 4 for Width and 4 for Height, and click OK.

 When you want to create type in an area, you use the area type tool.

4 Select the area type tool from the toolbox. (You'll have to drag from the type tool.)

5 Click the edge of the circle you just created.

You see the blinking insertion point.

6 Choose Import Text from the File menu.

7 Locate the file named *05 Text*, and click Import.

The type is imported into the circle. If you are at a low zoom factor, the type may be greeked, that is, you see only gray bars.

To set the type specifications:

1 Click the zoom tool in the toolbox, and zoom in on the circle.

2 Click the area type tool in the toolbox, and triple-click in the text to select it all.

3 If the Character palette is not open, choose Character from the Type menu.

4 Choose Times-Roman for the font.

5 Enter 22 for the Size and press Return.

6 Enter 30 for Leading and press Return.

7 Close the Character palette.

8 Choose Alignment from the Type menu and Justify from the submenu.

9 Click the selection tool in the toolbox. The type and circle are automatically selected.

10 Hold down the Shift key and click near the edge of the masking circle to select the grouped mask and photo.

11 Choose Group from the Arrange menu (Command-G) to group the objects.

12 Choose Save from the File menu (Command-S) to save your work.

PAINTING WITH A PATTERN

The green pattern on the left side of the drawing is a rectangle that has been filled.

1 Choose Fit In Window from the View menu (Command-M).

2 Click the rectangle tool in the toolbox.

3 Move the pointer to the top left corner of the rectangle.

4 Drag down to the bottom of the guide rectangle and right to the 2-inch mark on the bottom ruler.

5 In the Paint Style palette, set the Stroke to none, and click the Fill box.

6 Click the Pattern box. (The Pattern box is the next to last in the row of boxes on the top right of the palette. You see *Pattern* above the boxes when you have chosen the correct box.)

7 Choose any pattern in the pattern list. Just for fun, try out the different patterns.

8 Choose Waves-Transparent from the pattern list.

9 Choose Send to Back from the Arrange menu (Command-Hyphen).

10 Choose Save from the File menu (Command-S) to save your work.

ADDING THE LOGO

To complete the advertisement, you'll add a copy of the Navigations logo.

1 Drag a ruler guide up from the bottom ruler to the 9½ inch mark on the right ruler.

2 Open the Lesson 5 folder and the file named *Logo*.

3 Use the selection tool to select the logo in the upper right corner of the page.

4 Choose Copy from the Edit menu (Command-C).

5 Choose *05Work* from the Window menu to display the file.

6 Choose Paste from the Edit menu.

The logo is pasted into the file and is selected.

7 Double-click the scale tool in the toolbox.

8 Scale the file to a uniform scale of 120%. Make sure that Scale Line Weights is checked. Click OK.

9 Use the selection tool to position the center of the logo on the right edge of the pattern, with the bottom of the logo on the 9½ inch guide.

10 Close the *Logo* file.

11 Choose Save from the File menu (Command-S) to save your work.

SETTING CROP MARKS

Crop marks define where printed artwork will be trimmed. You can set crop marks by drawing a rectangle to define the boundaries where you want the crop marks to appear. In this file, you drew the rectangle earlier and locked it. You will use that rectangle to define the position of the crop marks.

1 Choose Unlock All from the Arrange menu.

The rectangle you locked earlier is now unlocked and is selected.

2 Choose Cropmarks from the Object menu and Make from the submenu.

You see the crop marks at the corners of the drawing.

3 Choose Save from the File menu (Command-S) to save your work.

4 If you want to print your file, choose Print from the File menu and click Print.

5 Close all the files.

Finally

It's not every day that going to the beach can produce such great payoffs. A few vacation photos, some imported area type, outlines with gradient fills, a pattern, and of course the ubiquitous Navigations logo—put them all together, and you've got a great advertisement. If the accountants report enough scheduled beach vacations, you'll really be on your way. Next stop: Europe.

Lesson

6

LESSON 6: THREE-FOLD ART BROCHURE

This lesson provides a project that you can use to practice the techniques that you have learned in previous lessons. You'll create this brochure for Navigations.

Source file (06ArtA)   *Source file (06Art1)*

Source file (06Art2)

Source file (06Art3)

THE TASK

Once again, Navigations is looking for business. This time the focus is on world travelers who take lengthy vacations. The target audience is upscale and adventurous. Instead of pure leisure, this audience expects to get something for its money.

The brochure should be slick and upscale, and it should emphasize the benefits of travel while it provides some eye-catching reasons to take a trip now.

This lesson provides step-by-step instructions for creating the brochure. If you find you need more explanation than a step provides, refer back to the more detailed information in previous lessons.

The brochure contains several pieces of placed art: sculpture, painting, crafts, and architecture. Here are the source files for the images in the brochure.

If time is limited

Completing all the tasks in this project may take between 3 and 4 hours. For this review project we have provided interim files. These are files that have been saved at key points during the lesson. If you should lose your working file, or if you would like to focus on just a particular part of the lesson, you can open an interim files and all the steps up until that point will already be completed.

The interim files are named *06Int1, 06Int2, 06Int3,* and *06Int4*, and they are stored in a folder named *Extras.* The points in the lesson where the files have been saved are identified in the lesson.

PLANNING THE PROJECT

You'll have two documents open on the screen. One is the finished artwork that you can use as a reference. The other is the file you will be working with.

You'll begin by opening the final artwork.

To open the reference file:

1 Open the Lesson 6 folder and the file named *06Final.*

Take a look at the brochure to see what the components of the drawing are. The brochure consists of three different panels.

For the final presentation, the panels are sheared slightly to give the "folded" impression. A drop shadow has also been added.

To make the reference file easier to use, we've included an unsheared version for you to look at while you are working. Each version of the final artwork is on a separate layer.

2 Choose Show Layers from the Window menu (Command-Control-L).

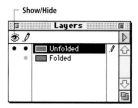

There are two layers—Folded and Unfolded. The Folded version is currently displayed, and the Unfolded layer is hidden. You can change the display by clicking the dots below the eye icon.

3 In the Layers palette, click the dot below the eye icon to the left of the Folded layer. The dot disappears, the Folded layer is hidden, and everything on the screen disappears.

4 Click below the eye icon to the left of the Unfolded layer. This layer is now displayed.

You can see two gradients on the first panel, one for the entire panel and one in the word *Art.* You see some type on a circular path in the second panel, and there is imported type in the second and third panels.

5 Close the Layers palette.

6 Choose Artwork from the View menu (Command-E), and take a look at the artwork.

7 Choose Preview from the View menu (Command-Y) to return to Preview view.

8 To ensure that nothing in the final file is selected, choose Select None from the Edit menu (Command-Shift-A). If nothing is selected, the command will be grayed out.

9 Resize your window so that it is about the size of one-fourth of your screen.

10 Choose Fit In Window from the View menu (Command-M).

11 Drag the drawing to a convenient location on your screen.

To create the working file:

1 Choose New from the File menu (Command-N).

2 Choose Save As from the File menu, name the file *06Work*, and save it in the Project folder.

SETTING UP THE DOCUMENT

To set up the document, you choose a page size and orientation, set the ruler origin, and create some guides.

1 Choose Document Setup from the File menu (Command-Shift-D). The Document Setup dialog box appears.

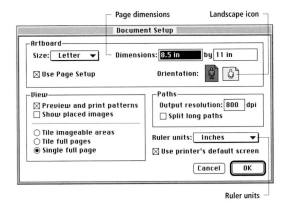

If you have just completed the previous lesson, the Ruler Units will be set to Inches. Notice that the Dimensions are 8.5 by 11 inches.

2 Change the Ruler Units to Points/Picas. Notice that the Dimensions are automatically changed to points and picas.

3 Make sure that Use Page Setup is checked. When this option is checked, the Artboard size will match the page size set in the Page Setup dialog box.

4 Click OK to close the dialog box.

5 Choose Page Setup from the File menu.

6 Change the Orientation from portrait to landscape, and click OK.

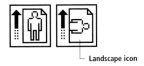

Landscape icon

7 Choose Show Rulers from the View menu (Command-R).

8 Position the pointer in the box where the rulers intersect, and drag a new ruler origin to the lower left corner of the page.

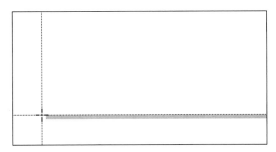

As a final step in page setup, you'll add two guides that divide the page into the three panels.

9 Position the pointer in the right ruler, hold down the mouse button, and drag to the left until the guide is at 22 picas.

10 Drag a second guide to the left to a position of 44 picas.

11 Choose Save from the File menu (Command-S) to save your work.

CREATING A GRADIENT

Next you create a rectangle for the left panel, fill it with a gradient, and stroke it.

To create a rectangle:

1 Click the rectangle tool in the toolbox.

2 Position the pointer at the upper left corner of the page boundary. Drag down to the bottom of the page boundary and right to the 22-pica guide. Release the mouse button.

To create a gradient:

1 Choose Gradient from the Object menu.

2 Click New.

3 Name the gradient *Background*, and press Return.

4 Click the Process box in the Gradient palette. The starting color defaults to process white, which is the color you want.

5 Click the right triangle below the gradient bar to select the triangle and set the ending color.

6 Click the Process box in the Gradient palette.

7 Set the ending colors as follows:

Cyan...........52 %
Magenta......0 %
Yellow........47 %
Black.........40 %

Remember that you can use the Tab key to move between the color fields.

8 Press Return when you have finished.

9 Close the Gradient palette.

To paint the rectangle:

1 Choose Paint Style from the Object menu (Command-I).

2 Make sure that the rectangle is selected.

3 In the Paint Style palette, click the Fill box, then click the Gradient box.

4 Choose Background from the gradient list.

5 Click the Stroke box, click the Black swatch, and set the Stroke Weight to 1 point.

6 Choose Save from the File menu (Command-S) to save your work.

PLACING AND MASKING THE SCULPTURE

The sculpture art is a rectangle. After you place the art, you draw a rough outline of the sculpture itself and make a mask.

To place the art:

1 Choose Place Art from the File menu.

2 Locate the Lesson 6 folder and the file named *06ArtA*. Click Place.

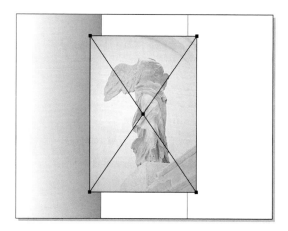

3 Click the zoom tool in the toolbox.

4 Click the center of the sculpture photo and zoom to a factor of 100%.

5 Choose Select None from the Edit menu (Command-Shift-A) to deselect everything.

To create the masking path:

1 Click the pen tool in the toolbox.

2 In the Paint Style palette, click Fill and click the None swatch.

3 In the Paint Style palette, click the Stroke box, click the Black swatch, and set the Stroke Weight to 1 point.

TIP: ASSIGN A STROKE VALUE WHEN YOU WORK IN PREVIEW. IF YOU DESELECT THE PATH, YOU'LL STILL BE ABLE TO SEE THAT PATH. YOU CAN CHANGE THE STROKE WHEN YOU HAVE FINISHED.

4 Use the pen tool to trace a rough outline of the sculpture. Trace around the edge of the sculpture.

Your goal is to trace only the sculpture and separate it from the background. You do not need to trace the stone base.

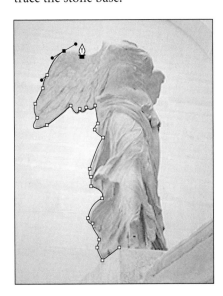

Here are some tips you can use if it's been a while since you've used the pen tool.

• To draw straight lines, you click the mouse button, move the pointer, and click at the end of the line.

• To draw a curve, you first drag to create a direction line. Then you move the pointer to the other side of the curve, and drag again.

• To switch from lines to curves, or vice versa, you go back to the last anchor point and click or drag to make a corner point.

Review Lesson 1 if you need more pen tool practice.

5 Trace all the way around the sculpture before you go back and edit any curves or anchor points. Be sure to close the path. You should see the circle next to the pen tool when you are about to close the path.

6 Use the direct selection tool to edit the path.

Note: *If you click anywhere except the sculpture path, you will select the rectangle of the photo instead of the sculpture path. Click directly on the path to select it.*

To make the mask:

1 Click the selection tool in the toolbox.

2 Click the edge of the sculpture path to select it.

3 Hold down the Shift key and click outside the sculpture, but within the rectangle, to select the rectangle for the photo. The sculpture path and the photo should both be selected.

4 Choose Masks from the Object menu and Make from the submenu.

The path masks the photo, and you see only the sculpture. The stroke is removed from the masking path.

5 Choose Group from the Arrange menu (Command-G).

6 Choose Fit In Window from the View menu. (Command-M).

TIP: CHANGE THE SIZE
OF A LARGE BLINKING
INSERTION POINT
BY CHOOSING SIZE
FROM THE TYPE MENU
AND A SMALLER SIZE
FROM THE SUBMENU.

7 Use the selection tool to position the sculpture on the left panel, near the top of the brochure. Use the final file as a reference for placement.

8 Choose Select None from the Edit menu (Command-Shift-A) to deselect everything.

9 Choose Save from the File menu (Command-S) to save your work.

CREATING TYPE FOR THE LEFT PANEL

Take a look at the type of the left panel in the final file. The word *Art* is made of type outlines that are filled with a gradient. Because only an entire text object can be converted to outlines, you must first create the text, and then copy the word *Art* to convert only that word.

You begin by creating the text box and entering the type.

To create the type:

1 Click the type tool in the toolbox. (Make sure you have the type tool, and not the area type or path type tool.)

2 Move the pointer to the left edge of the left brochure panel. Do not press the mouse button. Notice that when the pointer is exactly over the left edge, the pointer is surrounded by a dotted circle, and the status line reads *Area Type*. If you were to click now, the existing rectangle would

be converted to a text rectangle. Now move the pointer to the right just slightly inside the rectangle. The pointer changes to a dotted square, and the status line reads *Type*. With this pointer, you can drag to create a new text rectangle.

3 Drag to create a text rectangle just inside the bottom half of the left panel. Make the width of the rectangle a little less than the width of the panel. Don't worry about the exact dimensions. You will position the type later.

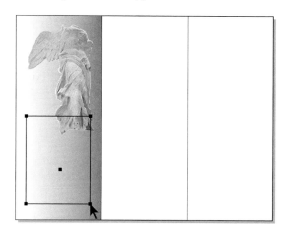

Note: If you have a very large blinking insertion point, you can change it to a smaller one by choosing Size from the Type menu and a smaller size from the submenu.

4 Type the following words. Put a Return after each word. Be sure to type *TRAVEL* in all capital letters.

The
Art
of
TRAVEL

5 Click the type tool in the toolbox to select the entire text rectangle and the type.

6 Click the zoom tool in the toolbox, and zoom in on the type to 100%.

To fine-tune the type:

1 Choose Character from the Type menu (Command-T).

2 Choose AGaramond Semibold from the font pop-up menu.

3 Click the Size field and set the size to 42 points.

4 Make sure that Auto Leading is selected. Press Return.

5 Click the type tool in the toolbox.

6 Double-click the word *The* to select it.

7 Change the font to AGaramond Semibold Italic.

8 Double-click the word *of* to select it.

9 Change the font to AGaramond Semibold Italic.

10 Double-click the word *Art* and change the size to 116 points.

11 Deselect Auto Leading so that the leading will remain at 50.5.

The size of the word *Art* is enlarged, and the word now overlaps the word above it.

12 Double-click the word *The* to select it.

13 Click Baseline Shift and change the value to 45. (You may need to click the lever to expand the palette.) Press Return.

14 Click the selection tool in the toolbox to deselect the words and select the rectangle.

15 Choose Save from the File menu (Command-S) to save your work.

To create guides:

1 Move the pointer inside the bottom ruler.

2 Hold down the mouse button and drag upward, and position the guide on the 15-pica mark on the right ruler.

3 Move the pointer inside the right ruler.

4 Hold down the mouse button and drag left to the 4-pica mark on the bottom ruler.

5 Make sure that the text rectangle is selected.

6 Position the type so that the baseline of the word *TRAVEL* is on the 15-pica guide. Then move the type so that the *T* is flush left with the 4-pica guide.

You can use the arrow keys for fine-tuning the position of the type.

7 Position the pointer in the bottom ruler, and drag upward to place a guide that is aligned with the baseline of the word *Art*.

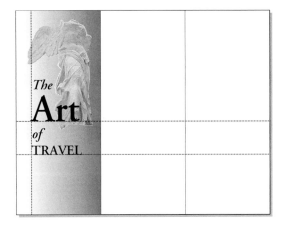

To create the type outlines:

1 Click the type tool in the toolbox.

2 Click at the end of the word *Art*.

3 Type a space.

The space will act as a place holder when you cut the type.

4 Drag to select the word *Art*. Do *not* select the space after the word.

TIP: GROUP A WORD
THAT YOU CONVERT
TO TYPE OUTLINES SO
YOU CAN EASILY MOVE
THE ENTIRE WORD.

5 Choose Cut from the Edit menu (Command-X).

6 Click the type tool in the toolbox.

7 Click in the drawing area, outside the original text rectangle.

8 Choose Paste from the Edit menu (Command-V).

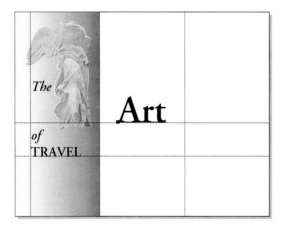

9 Click the selection tool in the toolbox. The word *Art* is selected.

10 Choose Create Outlines from the Type menu.

11 Choose Group from the Arrange menu (Command-G).

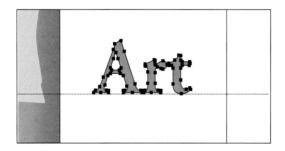

12 Choose Save from the File menu (Command-S) to save your work.

To create a gradient:

1 Choose Gradient from the Object menu.

2 Click New.

3 Name the gradient *Art*, and press Return.

4 Click the Process box in the Gradient palette. The starting color triangle is selected.

5 Set the starting colors as follows:

Cyan ....0 %
Magenta ......0 %
Yellow ....36 %
Black............0 %

6 Click the right triangle below the gradient bar to select the triangle.

7 Click the Process box in the Gradient palette.

8 Set the ending colors as follows:

Cyan ....76 %
Magenta ......0 %
Yellow ....68 %
Black..........51 %

9 Close the Gradient palette.

10 Choose Save from the File menu (Command-S) to save your work.

To paint the type:

1 Make sure that the *Art* type outlines are selected.

2 In the Paint Style palette, click the Fill box; then click the Gradient box.

3 Choose Art from the gradient list.

4 Click the Stroke box, click the Black swatch, set the Stroke Weight to 3 points, and press Return.

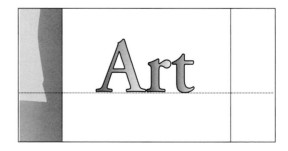

5 Click the gradient vector tool in the toolbox.

6 Drag from right to left across the word *Art.*

You will paste an additional unstroked copy of the type on top of the stroked version.

7 Choose Copy from the Edit menu (Command-C).

8 Choose Paste In Front from the Edit menu (Command-F).

9 In the Paint Style palette, click the Stroke box, then click the None swatch.

10 Click the selection tool in the toolbox.

11 Drag a marquee across the type to select both versions of the type. (Make sure you do *not* select the masked rectangle.)

12 Choose Group from the Arrange menu (Command-G).

13 Choose Fit In Window from the View menu (Command-M).

14 Drag the *Art* type and position it so that the baseline is lined up with the guide you created earlier for the word. Align the left side of the word with the vertical guide so that it is aligned with the rest of the type.

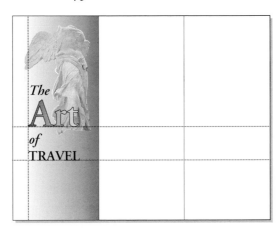

CREATING AN ACCENT LINE

Take a look at the final file, and notice the line that has been added around *The Art of TRAVEL.* In this part of the lesson, you will create this line and the circle at the end of the line.

To draw the accent line:

1 Choose Select None from the Edit menu (Command-Shift-A).

2 In the Paint Style palette, click the Fill box and the None swatch.

3 In the Paint Style palette, click the Stroke box, click the Black swatch, and set the Stroke Weight to 1 point.

4 Click the zoom tool in the toolbox, and zoom to 100%.

5 Click the pen tool in the toolbox.

Note: If you see a cross-hair pointer instead of the pen tool pointer, press the Caps Lock key to return to the regular pointer.

6 Use the pen tool and click to draw the accent line. Use the final file as a reference. Use the Shift key to constrain the line.

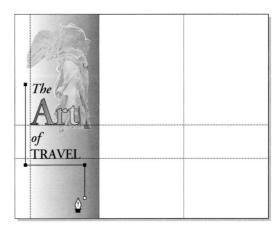

Remember to click the pen tool in the toolbox when you have finished.

7 Click the oval tool in the toolbox.

8 Position the pointer on the end of the accent line, hold down the Option key, and click the mouse button.

9 Enter 33 for Width, 33 for Height, and click OK.

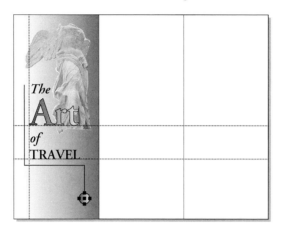

10 In the Paint Style palette, click the Fill box; then click the Process box. Set the colors as follows:

Cyan.......... 50 %
Magenta.... 25 %
Yellow.......... 0 %
Black .... 0 %

11 Make sure the Stroke is set to None.

12 Choose Save from the File menu (Command-S) to save your work.

Note: Interim file 06Int1 was saved at this point.

PLACING AND MASKING ART FILES

The center and right panels contain three placed files. In this part of the lesson, you'll place the files, make a mask for each of them, and position them in the brochure panels.

Placing and masking the painting file

The painting art is a rectangle. After you place the art, you draw a rough outline of the painting itself and make a mask.

To place the art:

1 Choose Place Art from the File menu.

2 Locate the Lesson 6 folder and the file named *06Art1*. Click Place.

3 Choose Select None from the Edit menu (Command-Shift-A) to deselect everything.

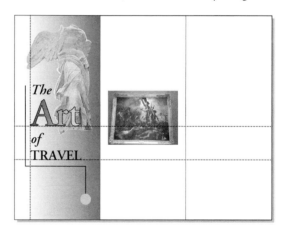

To create the masking path:

1 Click the pen tool in the toolbox.

2 In the Paint Style palette, click the Fill box, and click the None swatch.

3 In the Paint Style palette, click the Stroke box, click the Black swatch, and set the Stroke Weight to 1 point.

4 Use the pen tool to trace a rough outline of the painting, just as you did earlier for the sculpture.

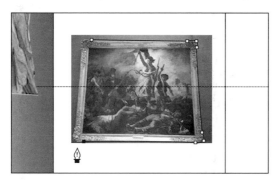

5 Drag all the way around the painting before you go back and edit any curves or anchor points. Be sure to close the path.

6 Use the direct selection tool to edit the path.

Note: If you click anywhere except the painting path, you will select the rectangle of the photo instead of the path. Click directly on the path to select it.

To make the mask:

1 Click the selection tool in the toolbox.

2 Click the edge of the path around the painting to select it.

3 Hold down the Shift key and click away from the path, but within the photo rectangle, to select that rectangle. (You see the diagonal lines when it is selected.) The painting path and the photo should both be selected.

4 Choose Masks from the Object menu and Make from the submenu.

The path masks the photo, and you see only the painting inside the path you traced. The stroke is removed from the masking path.

5 Choose Group from the Arrange menu (Command-G).

6 Choose Fit In Window from the View menu (Command-M).

7 Use the selection tool to position the painting on the center panel with the top edge of the painting on the 15-pica guide. Center the painting between the left and right edges of the panel.

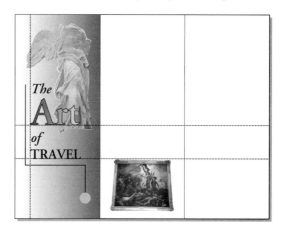

8 Choose Save from the File menu (Command-S) to save your work.

Placing and masking the building file

The building art is a also rectangle. You'll use the same procedure you used for the painting file to create a mask.

To place the art:

1 Choose Select None from the Edit menu (Command-Shift-A) to deselect everything.

2 Choose Place Art from the File menu.

3 Locate the Lesson 6 folder and the file named *06Art3*. Click Place.

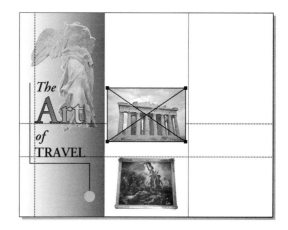

4 Click the zoom tool in the toolbox.

5 Click the center of the photo and zoom to a factor of 100%.

6 Choose Select None from the Edit menu (Command-Shift-A) to deselect everything.

To create the masking path:

1 Click the pen tool in the toolbox.

2 In the Paint Style palette, click the Fill box, and click the None swatch.

3 In the Paint Style palette, click the Stroke box, click the Black swatch, and set the Stroke Weight to 1 point.

4 Use the pen tool to trace a rough outline of the building, just as you did earlier for the earlier photo.

5 Drag all the way around the building before you go back and edit any curves or anchor points. Be sure to close the path.

6 Use the direct selection tool to edit the path.

Note: If you click anywhere except the building path, you will select the rectangle of the photo instead of the path. Click directly on the path to select it.

To make the mask:

1 Click the selection tool in the toolbox.

2 Click the edge of the building path to select it.

3 Hold down the Shift key and click away from the path, but within the right side of picture, to select the rectangle for the photo. The path and the photo should both be selected.

4 Choose Masks from the Object menu and Make from the submenu.

The path masks the photo, and you see only the building inside the path you traced. The stroke is removed from the masking path.

5 Choose Group from the Arrange menu (Command-G).

6 Choose Fit In Window from the View menu (Command-M).

7 Position the pointer in the bottom ruler, and drag upward to create a new guide at the 12-pica mark on the right ruler.

8 Use the selection tool to position the building on the right panel, with the bottom edge of the building on the 12-pica guide. Center the building between the left and right sides of the panel.

9 Choose Save from the File menu (Command-S) to save your work.

Placing and masking the crafts file

The crafts painting will be masked with a rectangle. This time you won't have to trace anything.

To place the art:

1 Choose Select None from the Edit menu (Command-Shift-A) to deselect everything.

2 Choose Place Art from the File menu.

3 Locate the Lesson 6 folder and the file named *06Art2*. Click Place.

4 Use the selection tool to drag the photo to the upper right corner of the page.

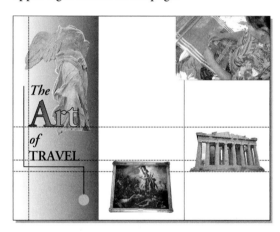

5 Use the zoom tool to zoom to a factor of 100%.

6 Position the pointer in the bottom ruler, and drag upward to create a new guide at the 36-pica mark on the right ruler.

To create the masking path:

1 Click the rectangle tool in the toolbox.

2 Drag to create a rectangle from the upper right corner of the panel. Drag down to the 36-pica mark, and drag left to the guide at the edge of the right panel.

To make the mask:

1 Click the selection tool in the toolbox.

2 The rectangle you just drew should still be selected. Hold down the Shift key and click outside the rectangle, but within the crafts photo rectangle, to select both rectangles.

3 Choose Masks from the Object menu and Make from the submenu.

The path masks the photo, and you see only the painting inside the path you traced. The stroke is removed from the masking path.

4 Choose Group from the Arrange menu (Command-G).

5 Choose Fit In Window from the View menu (Command-M).

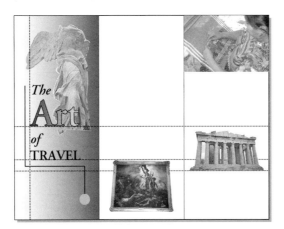

6 Choose Save from the File menu (Command-S) to save your work.

Note: Interim file 06Int2 was saved at this point.

ADDING TEXT AND ACCENTS

Take a look at the center panel of the final file. In the bottom half of the panel you see some title type (*Painting*), an accent line with a number in a circle, and some imported text.

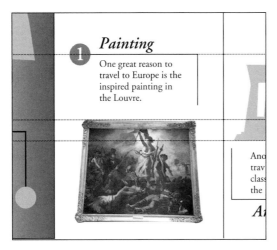

In this part of the lesson you will create these elements of the drawing.

Importing the text

Before you import the text, you use the rectangle tool to draw a precisely defined rectangle. Then you convert the rectangle into a text rectangle.

1 Click the rectangle tool in the toolbox.

2 Choose a location to the left of the drawing, and click the mouse button. (If necessary, scroll to choose a location.) Where you click is not important. You'll position the text into the brochure panel after you've imported it.

3 Enter 130 for Width, 84 for Height, and click OK.

4 Click the area type tool in the toolbox. You can check the status line to make sure that you have the area type tool.

5 Click the top edge of the rectangle.

The rectangle disappears and you see the blinking insertion point. (If the insertion point is very large, choose a smaller size from the Type menu.)

6 Choose Import Text from the File menu.

7 Locate the Lesson 6 folder, and click the file named *06Text1*. Click Import.

8 Click the area type tool in the toolbox to select all the type.

9 Choose Character from the Type menu (Command-T).

10 Set the font to AGaramond Regular.

11 Set the size to 15 points and the leading to 17 points, and press Return.

12 Click the zoom tool in the toolbox.

13 Zoom in on the type to proofread it for errors.

14 Choose Save from the File menu (Command-S) to save your work.

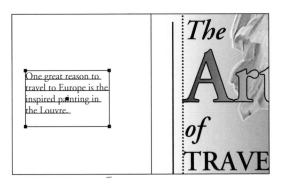

Creating the accent line

The accent line is created by drawing a rectangle and cutting part of it. First you'll drag some ruler guides to help you position the rectangle.

To create guides and a rectangle:

1 Use the zoom tool and click just above the painting to zoom to a level of 150%.

2 Position the pointer in the bottom ruler, and drag upward to create a guide at the 23-pica mark on the right ruler.

3 Position the pointer in the right ruler and drag left to create a vertical guide at the left edge of the top of the painting.

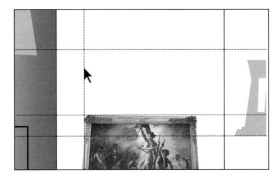

4 Click the rectangle tool in the toolbox.

5 Position the pointer on the intersection of the two guides you just created and click the mouse button.

6 Enter 180 for Width, 72 for Height, and click OK.

7 In the Paint Style palette, click the Fill box and the None swatch.

8 In the Paint Style palette, click the Stroke box, click the Black swatch, and set the Stroke Weight to 1 point.

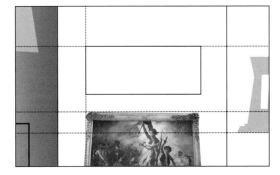

To modify the rectangle:

1 Click the direct selection tool in the toolbox.

2 Click away from the artwork to deselect everything.

3 Click the bottom line of the rectangle.

4 Press the Delete key to delete the line.

5 Choose Select None from the Edit menu (Command-Shift-A).

6 Click the left edge of the rectangle. Be sure to click directly on the edge of the rectangle. If you click away from the edge, you may select the masked photo instead of the rectangle path.

7 Press the Delete key to delete the line.

Notice that an anchor point remains in the drawing when you deleted the left line.

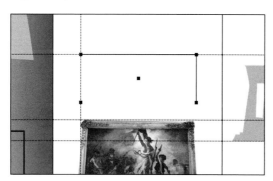

In general, it is not a good idea to leave stray anchor points in your files. In this case, it is difficult to select only the anchor point because it is behind the sculpture photo. You can use a special filter to delete the point.

8 Choose Select from the Filter menu and Select Stray Points from the submenu.

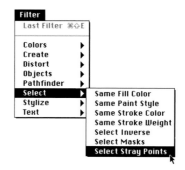

Any stray points in the drawing are selected.

9 Choose Cut from the Edit menu (or press the Delete key) to remove the points.

You will learn more about filters in another lesson.

10 Position the pointer in the right ruler and drag a guide to the 28-pica mark on the bottom ruler.

11 Click the selection tool in the toolbox.

12 Scroll so you can see the text rectangle with the imported text that you created earlier.

13 Select the text rectangle and position it so that the left edge is aligned with the 28-pica guide you just drew. The top of the text rectangle should be just below the accent line. Scroll if you need to.

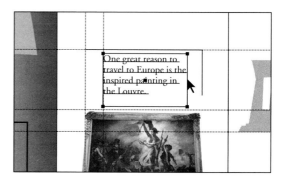

14 Choose Save from the File menu (Command-S) to save your work.

Adding the title type

Next you add the title type above the accent line.

1 Click the regular type tool in the toolbox.

2 Click above the accent line to set an insertion point at the 28-pica guide. You are aligning this text with the imported text.

3 Type **Painting**.

4 Click the type tool in the toolbox.

5 In the Character palette, set the font to AGaramond Semibold Italic.

6 In the Character palette, set the size to 25 points, and press Return.

7 Click the selection tool in the toolbox.

8 Use the arrow keys to fine-tune the position of the type above the accent line and aligned left with the 28-pica guide.

Adding the accent circle

To add the accent circle, you'll copy the circle from the left panel. Then you'll add the number.

To copy the circle:

1 Choose Fit In Window from the View menu (Command-M) so you can see all three panels of the drawing.

2 Click the selection tool in the toolbox.

3 Click to select the blue circle near the bottom of the left panel.

4 Hold down the Option key and drag a copy of the circle over the end of the top line in the center panel.

5 Use the arrow keys to position the copy of the circle so that it is centered over the end of the line.

6 With the circle selected, choose Bring To Front from the Arrange menu (Command-Equal) to move the circle in front of the line.

To add the number:

1 Click the zoom tool in the toolbox, and zoom in on the circle to a zoom level of 400%

2 Click the regular type tool in the toolbox.

3 Click just above the circle away from other artwork.

4 Type **1**.

5 Click the type tool in the toolbox.

6 In the Character palette, set the font to AGaramond Semibold.

7 In the Character palette, set the size to 30 points and press Return.

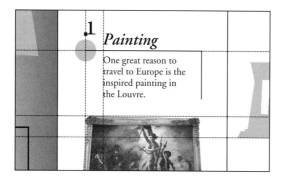

8 Click the selection tool in the toolbox.

9 Drag the *1* over the circle.

You can use the arrow keys to refine the position of the number in the circle.

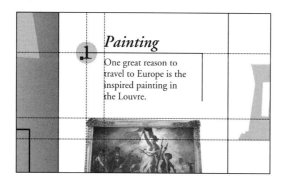

10 In the Paint Style palette, click the Fill box and click the White swatch. Click the Stroke box and click the None swatch.

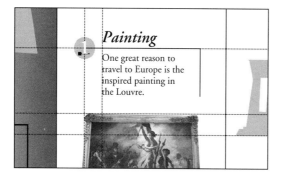

11 Choose Save from the File menu (Command-S) to save your work.

ADDING ADDITIONAL TEXT AND ACCENTS

Take a look at the right panel of the final file. As you can see, this panel contains modified versions of the type elements you just created.

To create these objects, you'll copy the originals from the center panel, move them to the right panel, and modify them for the other versions.

To copy the type elements:

1 Use the zoom tool to zoom out to a level of 150%. (Remember to hold down the Option key to zoom out.)

2 Choose Artwork from the View menu (Command-E).

3 Use the selection tool and the Shift key to select the following objects from the center panel: the *Painting* title, the circle, the *1* inside the circle, the accent line, and the text rectangle.

4 Choose Group from the Arrange menu (Command-G).

5 Choose Fit In Window from the View menu (Command-M).

6 Choose Preview from the View menu (Command-Y).

7 Drag the grouped elements to the right panel. Hold down the Option key while you drag to make a copy. Center the copy between the left and right sides of the panel, between the two photographs.

To edit the type:

1 Click the zoom tool in the toolbox.

2 Click the selected type element in the right panel until you have zoomed to a level of 100%

3 Choose Select None from the Edit menu (Command-Shift-A).

4 Click the type tool in the toolbox.

5 Drag across the *1* to select it.

6 Type **2**.

7 Double-click the word *Painting* to select the word.

8 Type **Crafts**.

Note that the new word has the same font and size as the one you replaced.

9 Drag across the imported text to select it.

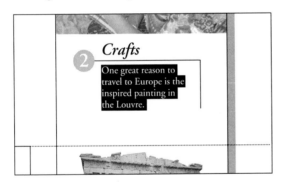

10 Choose Import Text from the File menu.

11 Locate the file named *06Text2*, and click Import.

12 Drag to select all of the imported type.

13 In the Character palette, set the font to AGaramond Regular. Set the size to 15 and the leading to 17, and press Return.

14 Choose Save from the File menu (Command-S) to save your work.

To create an additional copy

1 Position the pointer in the right ruler, and drag left to create a guide at the 48-pica mark on the bottom ruler.

2 Click the selection tool in the toolbox.

3 Click the edge of the circle to select the grouped type and accent line.

4 Hold down the Option key and drag a copy of the grouped type to the bottom of the right panel.

5 Position the type so that the text is aligned with the 48-pica guide you just drew, and the word Crafts is just below the building.

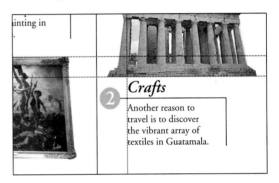

6 Choose Save from the File menu (Command-S) to save your work.

Modifying the accent line and number

To modify the accent line for the bottom right corner, you'll reflect it vertically and horizontally. Then you'll add the number in the circle. You'll also reposition the title type and import new text.

To modify the line:

1 Choose Ungroup from the Arrange menu (Command-U). All of the objects are selected.

2 Click away from the artwork to deselect everything.

3 Click the accent line to select it.

4 Hold down the Shift key and click the edge of the circle to add it to the selection. Do not select the number *2*.

You don't reflect the number because it would be backwards and upside down after you reflected it.

5 Double-click the reflect tool in the toolbox.

6 Click Horizontal in the Reflect dialog box, and click OK.

7 Double-click the reflect tool in the toolbox.

8 Click Vertical in the dialog box, and click OK.

9 The line and circle have been repositioned.

10 Use the Down Arrow key to move the accent line and circle down below the imported text. The line should be about one and one-half picas below the text.

11 Check the position of the left side of the accent line. The line should be aligned with the left side of the building. Use the arrow keys to make fine adjustments if necessary.

12 Choose Save from the File menu (Command-S) to save your work.

To modify the number:

1 Choose Artwork from the View menu (Command-E).

In Artwork view, you can see the *2*. You couldn't see it in Preview because it is painted white.

2 Click the selection tool in the toolbox.

3 Drag the *2* over the circle at the end of the accent line.

4 Click the type tool in the toolbox.

5 Drag to select the *2*, and change it to a *3*.

6 Click the type tool in the toolbox.

7 Choose Preview from the View menu (Command-Y).

8 Use the arrow keys to position the *3* in the circle.

To modify the title type:

1 Click the selection tool in the toolbox.

2 Click the baseline to select the word *Crafts*.

3 Drag the word *Crafts* by its alignment point below the bottom of the accent line. Align the left side with the 48-pica mark. Don't worry if the word is on the bottom of the page. You'll move it later.

4 Click the type tool in the toolbox.

5 Drag to select *Crafts*.

6 Type **Architecture**.

7 Click the type tool in the toolbox.

8 Drag to select all of the imported text.

9 Choose Import Text from the File menu.

10 Locate the file named *06Text3*, and click Import.

11 Triple-click to select all of the imported type.

12 In the Character palette, set the font to AGaramond Regular. Set the size to 15 and the leading to 17, and press Return.

13 Click the selection tool in the toolbox, and drag a marquee to select the text, accent line, title type, and circle.

14 Choose Group from the Arrange menu (Command-G).

15 Use the arrow keys to fine-tune the position of the grouped type. The baseline of the first line should be on the 10-pica mark on the right ruler.

16 Choose Save from the File menu (Command-S) to save your work.

Note: Interim file 06Int3 was saved at this point.

CREATING THE CIRCULAR TYPE EFFECTS

Take a look at the center panel of the final file. The top half of the panel contains the phrase *Three Reasons To Travel*, on a circular path superimposed over a large three.

In this part of the lesson, you'll create these effects. Before you begin, you'll lock the other objects in the drawing so that you won't accidentally select them while you are working.

To lock the existing art:

1 Click the selection tool in the toolbox.

2 Choose Select All from the Edit menu (Command-A).

3 Choose Lock from the Arrange menu (Command-1).

4 Scroll until the top part of the center panel is in the middle of your screen.

To create the large background *3*:

1 Click the regular type tool in the toolbox.

2 Click in the middle of the panel, and type **3**.

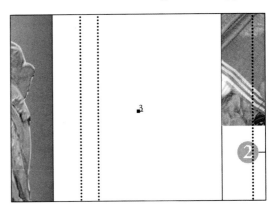

3 Click the selection tool in the toolbox.

4 In the Character palette, set the font to AGaramond Semibold. Set the size to 220 points, and press Return.

5 In the Paint Style palette, click the Fill box, click the Process box, and set the color as follows:

Cyan ....0 %
Magenta ....25 %
Yellow ....25 %
Black............0 %

6 Press Return when you have finished.

7 Make sure that the Stroke box is set to None.

8 Center the *3* in the top part of the panel.

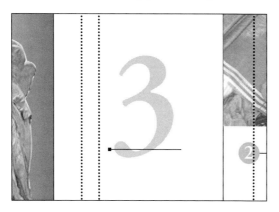

Creating type on a circle

You'll create the type on a circle by making two different circles, one for the type at the top and one for the type at the bottom.

To create the first circle and type:

1 Click the oval tool in the toolbox.

2 Hold down the Option key and click in the middle of the *3*.

3 Enter 190 for Width and 190 for Height, and click OK. Notice the circle is filled.

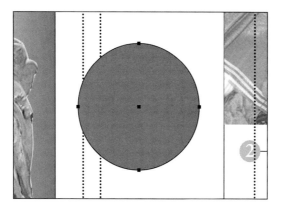

4 Select the path type tool in the toolbox. (You may have to drag across the other type tools.) Check the status line at the bottom of the window to make sure that you have the path type tool.

5 In the Character palette, set the size to 25 points, and press Return.

You change the size before you click the path, because the last type you created was a very large 220 points. Setting the size before you click lets you avoid the giant blinking cursor.

6 Click the top of the circle.

The circle disappears, and you see the blinking insertion point.

7 Type **THREE** in all capital letters.

8 In the Character palette, set the font to AGaramond Semibold.

9 Click the type tool in the toolbox.

10 Choose Alignment from the Type menu and Center from the submenu.

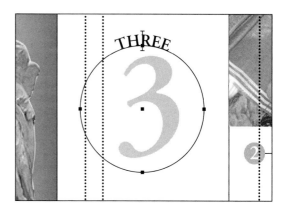

The word is centered on the alignment where you first clicked.

Next you create the second circle. The type you create for the second circle will be below the circle.

To create the second circle and type:

1 Choose Artwork from the View menu (Command-E).

2 Click the selection tool in the toolbox.

3 Hold down the Option key and drag to create a copy of the type and circle about three-fourths of an inch below the original circle.

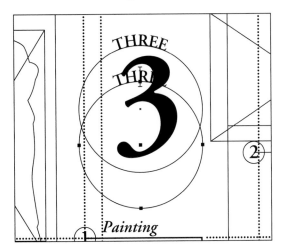

4 Click the type tool in the toolbox.

5 Drag to select the word *Three* on the lower circle.

6 Type in all capital letters **TO TRAVEL**.

7 Click the selection tool in the toolbox.

8 Drag the type by the type handle until it is positioned at the bottom center of the circle. The pointer turns hollow when you are over the bottom anchor point of the circle.

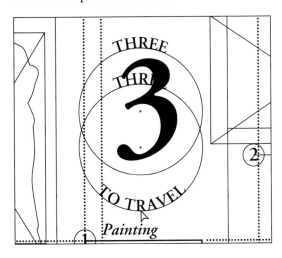

9 In the Character palette, set the Baseline Shift to -20 (minus 20), and press Return.

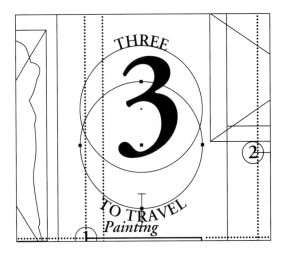

10 Position the pointer on the center anchor point of the lower circle.

11 Drag upward until the pointer is over the center anchor point of the upper circle. Again, the pointer turns hollow when you are exactly over the anchor point.

12 Choose Save from the File menu (Command-S) to save your work.

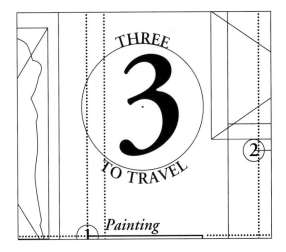

To add the REASONS type:

1 Select the regular type tool in the toolbox. (You may have to drag across the other type tools.)

2 Click just outside the left side of the circle.

3 Type **REASONS** in all capital letters.

4 Click the selection tool in the toolbox.

5 In the Character palette, set the font to AGaramond Semibold. Set the size to 40 points. Set the tracking to 100. Click Baseline Shift to set the value back to its default of 0.

6 Use the selection tool to center the word *REASONS* over the large *3*.

7 Choose Preview from the View menu (Command-Y).

8 Choose Save from the File menu (Command-S) to save your work.

ADDING THE LOGO

To complete the advertisement, you'll add a copy of the Navigations logo.

1 Choose Fit In Window from the View menu (Command-M).

2 Open the Lesson 6 folder and the file named *Logo*.

3 Use the selection tool to select the logo in the upper right corner of the page.

4 Choose Copy from the Edit menu (Command-C).

5 Choose *06Work* from the Window menu to display the file.

6 Choose Paste from the Edit menu.

The logo is pasted into the file and is selected.

7 Use the selection tool to position the logo in the lower left corner of the left panel.

8 Choose Save from the File menu (Command-S) to save your work.

9 Choose Logo from the Window menu.

10 Close the file named *Logo*.

Note: Interim file 06Int4 was saved at this point.

USING A FOLDED DISPLAY TECHNIQUE

You have now completed all the artwork for the brochure. What's left is to resize the entire drawing, shear the panels to create the "folded" effect, and add the drop shadows

1 Choose Select None from the Edit menu (Command-Shift-A).

2 In the Paint Style palette, set the Fill to white. Set the Stroke to black with a 1-point Stroke Weight.

3 Choose Fit In Window from the View menu (Command-M).

4 Click the rectangle tool in the toolbox.

5 Drag to draw a rectangle over the center panel.

6 Choose Send to Back from the Arrange menu (Command-Hyphen).

7 Drag to draw a rectangle over the right panel.

8 Choose Send to Back from the Arrange menu (Command-Hyphen).

9 Choose Unlock All from the Arrange Menu (Command-2).

10 Choose Select All from the Edit menu (Command-A).

11 Double-click the scale tool in the toolbox.

12 Click Uniform Scale, enter 80, make sure Scale Line Weight is selected, and click OK.

13 Click the selection tool in the toolbox.

14 Choose Hide Guides from the View menu.

15 Center the artwork inside the page rectangle.

16 Choose Save from the File menu (Command-S) to save your work.

To shear the panels:

1 Choose Select None from the Edit menu (Command-Shift-A).

2 Use the selection tool to select every object in the left panel. You can drag a selection marquee across the entire panel.

3 Make sure that nothing in the center panel is selected.

4 Click the shear tool in the toolbox.

5 Hold down the Option key and click the right edge of the left panel.

6 Enter -5 (minus 5), click Vertical, and click OK.

7 Choose Select None from the Edit menu (Command-Shift-A).

8 Use the selection tool and drag a marquee to select everything in the center panel. Some objects from the other panels will also be selected.

Note: An easy way to select the objects in the center panel is to drag a long narrow selection marquee from top to bottom down the center of the panel. In this way, you avoid selecting the overlapping art from the other two panels.

9 Shift-click to deselect any objects that are part of the left or right panel. Make sure that nothing in the left or right panel is selected.

10 Click the shear tool in the toolbox.

11 Hold down the Option key and click the left edge of the center panel.

12 Enter 5, click Vertical, and click OK.

13 Drag a selection marquee to select all the objects in right panel. If you drag a long marquee from top to bottom across the right half of the panel, you can avoid selecting objects from the center panel. Make sure that nothing in the center panel is selected.

14 Click the shear tool in the toolbox.

15 Hold down the Option key and click the right edge of the right panel.

16 Enter -5 (minus 5), click Vertical, and click OK.

To make the drop shadows:

1 Choose Select None from the Edit menu (Command-Shift-A).

2 Click the selection tool in the toolbox.

3 Click the bottom edge of the left panel.

4 Hold down the Shift key and click the bottom edge of the center panel.

5 Hold down the Shift key and click the bottom of the right panel. The outside rectangle of all three panels should be selected.

6 Position the pointer on the top center of the panels. Hold down the Option key and drag upward and right (about one-fourth inch) to make a copy. Release the mouse button and then the Option key.

7 Choose Send to Back from the Arrange menu (Command-Hyphen).

8 In the Paint Style palette, click the Fill box. Click the first swatch in the second row to fill the background rectangles with 25% black. There should be no stroke.

9 Choose Select All from the Edit menu (Command-A), and drag the artwork so that it fits inside the inner page rectangle. You can then print the file on letter-size paper if you want.

10 Press Command-S to save your work. You've done so much, you wouldn't want to lose it now.

11 Print the file if you want.

12 Close the files.

Sit back and relax!

If you've completed this review project, you know an awful lot about using the Adobe Illustrator program. You know how to create a text rectangle and how to create type on a path, You know how to place art and make masks. And you can create guides to put things exactly where you want them. You've spent time selecting, deselecting, dragging, positioning, and repositioning with the arrow keys. Fine-tuning is your speciality.

Needless to say, it's time for another trip. While Navigations patrons are busy touring the Louvre in response to your excellent brochure, you're going to the French countryside to sample the local wines and design a full-size poster especially for wine lovers. You can eat, drink, be merry, and learn about the exciting new filters that are included with Adobe Illustrator. If you've never used filters before, you're in for a treat. You'll love them because *they* do more of the work than you do.

LESSON 7: DESIGNING A POSTER OF THE FRENCH WINE COUNTRY

A respected worldwide travel service knows the value of good will and gifts. Navigations likes to send its regular customers occasional rewards for doing business with them. In this case, they would like a full-size poster they can present to all of their European travelers—perhaps something to do with wine.

The work must be of an exceptionally high quality. (Your work, of course, fits this category.) Second, they have asked for a poster that is decidedly unique. They want a look and feel that set it apart from all the other wine posters.

Once again, the Adobe Illustrator program comes to the rescue. You can use the plug-in filters that come with the program to create easily a variety of unique effects. You'll explore just some of these filters in this lesson.

While creating the poster, you'll

• learn how to use layers to make working with complex drawings easier

• explore some of the interesting design effects you can create with filters

• draw with the freehand tool

• use the blend tool to blend colors and shapes

• create dashed lines

Completing this lesson may take anywhere from 3 to 4 hours.

If your system or your time is limited

The Pathfinder filters used in this lesson require a math coprocessor. If no math coprocessor is detected, the Pathfinder filters will not load. If your system does not include a math coprocessor, you can do the other parts of this lesson by using the interim file named *07Int1* that is included in the Extras folder.

You can also use this file if you should lose your working file, or if you would like to focus on the latter parts of the lesson.

To use the interim file, open the Extras Folder and the file named *07Int1*, and turn to the section named "Creating a Contour Map." All the steps up until that point have been completed in the file.

PLANNING THE PROJECT

First we'll take a look at the finished poster.

1 Open the Lesson 7 folder and the file named *07Final*. This file contains the finished artwork.

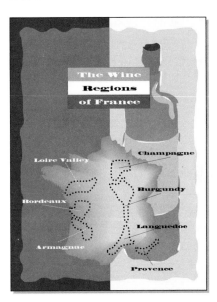

As the seasoned Adobe Illustrator user that you've become, you're undoubtedly seeing lots of curves, both the ones around the inner background and the ones around the bottle. In fact, not one of these curves was drawn with the pen tool; they are all special effects created with filters. The only objects drawn with the pen tool are the straight lines.

A second feature of this drawing is that it was created on several different layers. Although this doesn't make any difference in the final presentation, it can make life easier while you are doing the work.

Examining layers

You'll learn how to create different layers in this lesson. But first, let's take a look to see how they work.

1 Choose Show Layers from the Window menu (Command-Control-L).

You may remember that the preceding lesson contained the folded and unfolded versions of the final drawing on two different layers. In this lesson you'll create three different layers.

2 Click the dot beneath the eye icon to the left of *Regions* to hide the Regions layer.

3 Click the dot beneath the eye icon to the left of *Background* to hide the Background layer.

Take a look at the green shape that represents France. Notice the contoured effect as the colors blend from a darker green on the outside to the lighter green of the contour shape.

4 Choose Artwork from the View menu (Command-E) to see the map artwork.

When you look at the artwork, you can see the intermediate shapes between the two objects. The effect was created with the blend tool.

5 Position the pointer on the right triangle at the top right of the palette, and hold down the mouse button to see the Layers palette pop-up menu.

6 Drag to choose Show All from the Layers palette pop-up menu. All of the layers are shown.

Notice in the Layers palette that the dots below the eye icon are hollow, indicating that all the layers are in Artwork view.

7 Drag to choose Preview All from the Layers palette pop-up menu. Everything is returned to Preview view. The dots below the eye icon are solid, indicating Preview view.

8 Close the Layers palette.

Setting up the windows

Next you'll resize the window and reposition it so you can access it while you are working on the artwork in the working file.

1 Use the size box in the lower right corner of the window to resize the window so that it's about one-fourth the size of your screen.

2 Choose Fit In Window from the View menu (Command-M).

3 Drag the window to the upper right corner of your screen.

4 Open the Lesson 7 folder and the file named *07Begin*.

5 Choose Save As from the File menu, and name the file *07Work*. Save the file in the Project folder.

SETTING UP THE DOCUMENT

First you'll set up the document and explore some different page options. The actual size of the poster is 18 inches by 24 inches.

1 Choose Document Setup from the File menu (Command-Shift-D). The Document Setup dialog box appears. Notice that the Ruler Units are set to Inches.

2 Change the dimensions by typing 18 in the first Dimensions field, pressing the Tab key, and entering 24 in the second Dimensions field.

3 Make sure that the Use Page Setup option is *not* selected. Click OK.

4 Choose Fit In Window from the View menu (Command-M).

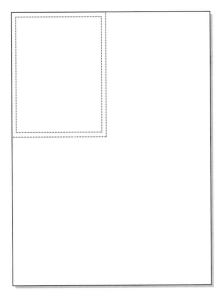

Notice that the imageable area is in the upper left corner of the window. It appears smaller than usual because your document size is larger (18 inches by 24 inches). The imageable area is still at the standard paper size of 8.5 by 11 inches.

Changing the page tiling

Most people don't have access to imagesetters that can handle large paper sizes. One way to print the document for proofing is to print different pieces of it.

You can use the page tool to move the imageable area of the drawing from one place to another.

1 Click the page tool in the toolbox.

2 Move the pointer into the drawing area and hold down the mouse button. You can now drag the page rectangle to a different location. The page rectangle is positioned when you release the mouse button.

3 To reposition the page rectangle, hold down the mouse button and drag again. Position the page rectangle somewhere near the center of the page boundary.

If you want to print the entire document in pieces, you can have the document *tiled* (divided) into letter-sized sections.

4 Choose Document Setup from the File menu (Command-Shift-D).

5 Under View, click Tile Imageable Areas, and click OK.

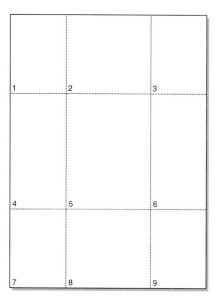

As you can see, the document is tiled into different pages, and you could choose to print any of the different pages by choosing the page number in the Print Dialog box when you print.

Reducing the size in the Page Setup dialog box

Another way to handle large documents is to reduce the size of the printed version in the Page Setup dialog box.

By reducing the size of the printed drawing, you can print it on letter-sized paper for proofing purposes. When you want to print the document on larger paper, you can change the setting back. This is the technique you'll use while you are creating the wine poster. First you return the tiling to a single page.

1 Choose Document Setup from the File menu (Command-Shift-D).

2 Under View, choose Single Full Page and click OK.

3 Choose Page Setup from the File menu.

4 In the Reduce or Enlarge field, enter 40.

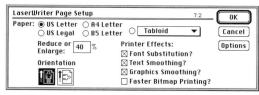

Page Setup dialog boxes will vary from printer to printer.

5 Click OK.

6 Click the page tool in the toolbox.

7 Hold down the mouse button and position the double rectangles around the page rectangle. The outer rectangles disappear when you release the mouse button.

You could, if you wanted, print the entire document on letter-sized paper.

8 Choose Show Rulers from the View menu (Command-R).

9 Position the pointer in the box where the rulers intersect and drag to move the ruler origin to the lower right corner of the page rectangle.

Now that you have reset the page origin, you can easily see that the document is 18 by 24 inches.

10 Choose Show Layers from the Window menu.

11 Click the word *Layer 1* to highlight that layer so you can work on it.

12 Position the pointer in the right ruler, and drag left to create a guide at the 9-inch mark on the bottom of the ruler. This divides the page in half.

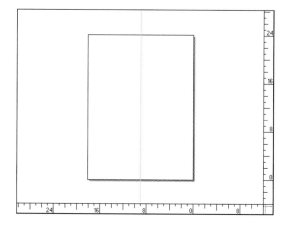

(Remember that you can delete a guide by choosing Guides from the Object menu and deselecting the Lock command. Then select the guide and delete it. Choose Guides from the Object menu and Lock from the submenu to lock future guides.)

13 Position the pointer in the bottom ruler, and drag upward to create a guide at the 12-inch mark on the right ruler. This divides the page into quarters.

14 Choose Save from the File menu (Command-S) to save your work.

CONSTRUCTING THE BOTTLE ELEMENTS

To create the wine bottle, you first create a rough shape using the oval and rectangle tools. Later you'll add the magic of filters.

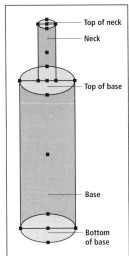

Bottle elements

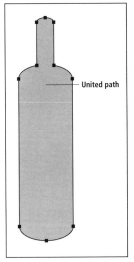

Bottle elements united into a single path with Unite filter

Creating the base and neck of the bottle

The base and the neck are made from rectangles.

1 Click the rectangle tool in the toolbox.

2 Hold down the Option key and click near the center of the right half of the drawing.

3 Enter 5 for Width, 13 for Height, and click OK.

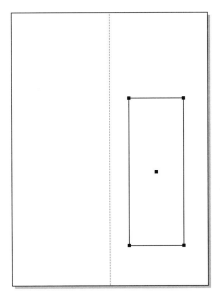

4 Choose Paint Style from the Object menu (Command-I).

5 Click the Fill box and the None swatch. Click the Stroke box and the Black swatch. Set the Stroke Weight to 1 point, and press Return.

6 To create the neck of the bottle, click near the top of the drawing.

7 Enter 1.6 for Width, 5 for Height, and click OK.

8 Click the selection tool in the toolbox.

9 Use the selection tool to position the neck so that it is centered on the top of the base.

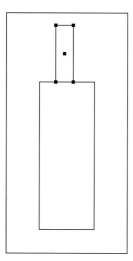

Creating the tops and bottoms of the base and the neck

The top and bottom of the base and the top of the neck are made from circles. Although you will roughly position the elements, you don't need to precisely position them now. In fact, you can be somewhat sloppy about lining up the objects from left to right, because you'll be using a filter to align them horizontally.

1 Click the oval tool in the toolbox.

2 Position the pointer on the top of the neck rectangle, and click the mouse button.

3 Enter 1.6 for Width, and .8 (eight-tenths) for Height, and click OK.

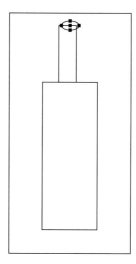

4 If necessary, scroll to see the bottom of the base rectangle.

5 Position the pointer on the center of the bottom of the base rectangle; hold down the Option key, and click the mouse button.

6 Enter 5 for Width, 2.5 for Height, and click OK.

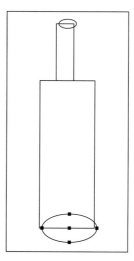

7 Click the selection tool in the toolbox.

8 Hold down the Option key, and drag a copy of the bottom circle to the top of the base. Release the mouse button before you release the Option key.

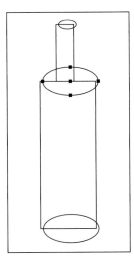

9 Choose Save from the File menu (Command-S) to save your work.

USING FILTERS TO MODIFY THE SHAPES

Plug-in filters allow you to apply special effects such as distortions, color manipulations, aligning objects, calligraphic effects, and many others. A number of filters are included with the program. You can also purchase filters from third-party vendors. For a complete overview of the different filters that are included with the Adobe Illustrator program, refer to the *Adobe Illustrator User Guide.*

You've already used the Select Stray Points filter in a previous lesson. Now you'll try the Align Objects and the Unite filters.

Using the Align Objects filter

The Align Objects filter is one of many Objects filters. (Other Objects filters let you create copies of paths a specified distance from the original paths or let you replace a stroked path with a filled object.)

You'll use the Align Objects filters to align the elements of the bottle.

To align the objects:

1 Choose Select All from the Edit menu (Command-A).

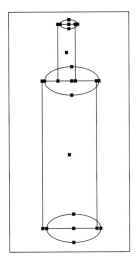

2 Choose Objects from the Filter menu and Align Objects from the submenu.

3 Under Horizontal, click Center.

Notice that the objects in the third panel move to display what you selected under Horizontal.

4 Under Vertical, click None, and click OK.

The selected objects are aligned with their center points along a straight axis.

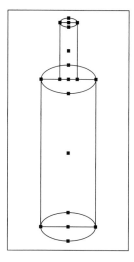

5 Click the selection tool in the toolbox.

6 Drag the bottle so that it is centered in the right half of the poster.

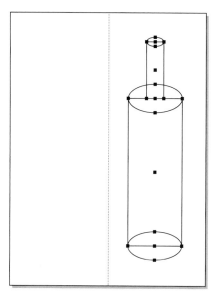

If you liked that filter, wait until you see the next one.

Using the Unite filter

The Pathfinder filters combine, isolate, and subdivide paths, and build new paths formed by the intersection of objects. The Mix Hard and Mix Soft filters blend overlapping colors. You'll use the Unite filter to change the path for the bottle.

Note: *If your computer does not have a math coprocessor, you cannot use the Unite or any other of the Pathfinder filters.*

To unite the paths:

1 Make sure that everything is still selected.

2 Choose Pathfinder from the Filter menu and Unite from the submenu.

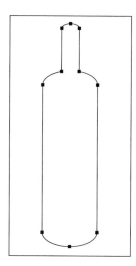

3 Choose Save from the File menu (Command-S) to save your work.

CREATING THE LABEL

Take a look at the wine bottle in the final file. There's a label on the bottle, a foil wrap on the neck, and a highlight on the bottle. Next you'll create the label. You won't draw the label. You'll copy parts of the bottle, paste them, and then use the Join command to create a path between them.

Time out for a shortcut:

In this part of the lesson you will be switching back and forth from the selection tool to the direct selection tool. This is a great time to practice using a keyboard shortcut to switch between the two different selection tools. Before you try the short-cut, check the toolbox to make sure that the direct selection tool is next to the selection tool in the toolbox.

1 Hold down the Command key and press and release the Tab key. The tool pointer changes from the regular selection tool (solid arrow) to the direct selection tool (hollow arrow).

2 Keep the Command key down and press and release the Tab key again. The pointer changes back to the regular selection tool pointer (solid arrow). Each time you press the Tab key with the Command key down, the selection tool changes.

To make the label:

1 Choose Artwork from the View menu (Command-E).

2 Hold down the Command key and press and release the Tab key until the direct selection tool is selected.

3 Click away from the bottle path to deselect everything.

4 Click the right edge of the bottle path to see the hollow anchor points.

5 Click the center point on the bottom curve of the bottle.

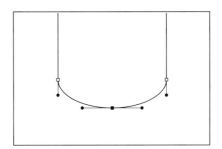

The segments on both sides of the anchor point you clicked are selected.

6 Choose Copy from the Edit menu (Command-C) to copy the bottom segment. The copy is pasted into the Clipboard.

7 Hold down the Command key and press and release the Tab key to access the selection tool.

8 Click the bottle path. The entire path is selected.

9 Choose Lock from the Arrange menu (Command-1).

10 Choose Paste from the Edit menu (Command-V). The bottom segment you copied is pasted into the drawing area.

You'll construct the label on the left side of the drawing and move it to the bottle later.

TIP: YOU CAN USE THE JOIN COMMAND TO CLOSE ANY OPEN PATH. SELECT THE ENTIRE PATH AND CHOOSE JOIN FROM THE OBJECT MENU TO DRAW A LINE BETWEEN THE ENDPOINTS.

11 Drag the curved shape you pasted, and position it in the left half of the drawing, about one-third of the way up the bottle.

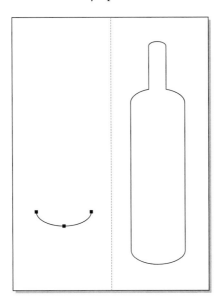

12 Choose Paste from the Edit menu (Command-V).

13 Drag the second copy of the curved line, and position it in the left half of the drawing, about two-thirds of the way up the bottle.

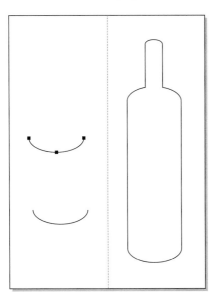

14 Choose Save from the File menu (Command-S) to save your work.

To align and join the two curved lines:

1 Drag a selection marquee to select both of the pasted curved lines.

2 Choose Objects from the Filter menu and Align Objects from the submenu.

3 Under Horizontal, click Center. Under Vertical, click None. Click OK.

4 Hold down the Command key and press and release the Tab key to switch to the direct selection tool.

5 Click away from the artwork to deselect everything.

6 Drag a marquee to select the anchor point on the right end of each curved line. Make sure that only those two points are selected.

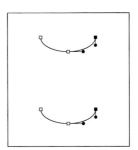

7 Choose Join from the Object menu (Command-J).

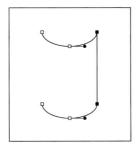

The Join command lets you connect any two path endpoints. A path is drawn between the two points.

You can also use the Join command to close an open path by selecting the entire path and choosing the command.

8 Hold down the Command key and press and release the Tab key to switch to the regular selection tool.

9 Click to select the entire path.

10 Choose Join from the Object menu (Command-J). The two endpoints are joined, and the path is closed.

11 Click the edge of the label path to select it all.

12 Drag the label onto the bottle.

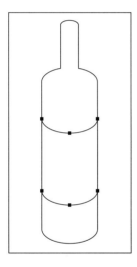

13 Choose Save from the File menu (Command-S) to save your work.

CREATING THE FOIL TOP AND WRAP

Next you'll construct the foil top and wrap. You'll use the same procedure you used for the label. You'll begin with a circle for the top, copy and paste parts of the circle, and then align and join them. This time it will be a snap.

1 Click the oval tool in the toolbox.

2 Hold down the Option key and click near the top of the neck.

3 Enter 1.6 for Width, and .8 for Height (eight-tenths), and click OK.

4 Click the selection tool in the toolbox.

5 Center the circle on the top of the bottle neck.

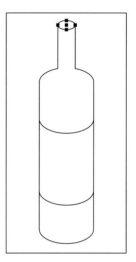

6 Click the zoom tool in the toolbox.

7 Drag a marquee around the neck of the bottle to zoom in on it.

8 If necessary, use the arrow keys to precisely position the circle.

9 Click the direct selection tool in the toolbox.

10 Click away from the artwork to deselect everything.

11 Click the edge of the circle path to see the hollow anchor points.

12 Click the center point on the bottom curve of the circle.

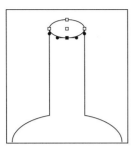

13 Choose Copy from the Edit menu (Command-C) to copy the bottom segment. The copy is pasted into the Clipboard.

14 Choose Paste from the Edit menu (Command-V).

15 Click the selection tool in the toolbox.

16 Drag the pasted curve onto the neck of the bottle, about one-fourth of the way down from the top.

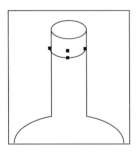

17 Choose Paste from the Edit menu (Command-V).

18 Drag the second copy of the curved line, and position it about one-fourth of the way up from the bottom of the neck.

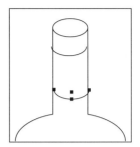

19 Choose Save from the File menu (Command-S) to save your work.

To align and join the two curved lines:

1 Drag a selection marquee to select both of the pasted curved lines.

2 Choose Align Objects from the Filter menu. Notice that the Align Objects command has moved to the top of the Filter menu commands because it was the last filter used. When you choose it, it repeats the same Horizontal and Vertical options you last chose.

3 Hold down the Command key and press and release the Tab key to switch to the direct selection tool.

4 Click away from the artwork to deselect everything.

5 Drag a marquee to select the anchor point on the right end of each curved line. Make sure that only those two points are selected.

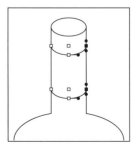

6 Choose Join from the Object menu (Command-J) to draw a path between the two points.

7 Hold down the Command key and press and release the Tab key to switch to the selection tool.

8 Click to select the entire path.

9 Choose Join from the Object menu (Command-J).

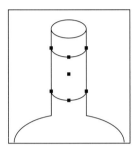

10 Choose Save from the File menu (Command-S) to save your work.

ADDING THE BOTTLE HIGHLIGHT

Take a look at the final file and notice the highlight on the top of the bottle. You'll use the freehand tool to draw the highlight. First, you'll practice using the freehand tool.

Using the freehand tool

The freehand tool lets you work as if you were drawing with a pencil on paper. You use the freehand tool when you want your artwork to have a more spontaneous look than you can achieve with the pen tool. When you use the freehand tool, anchor points are automatically set down; you do not determine where they occur.

1 Click the freehand tool in the toolbox.

You'll practice a little bit with the freehand tool before you draw the bottle highlight. Use any empty white area of the drawing.

2 Hold down the mouse button and drag to draw a path.

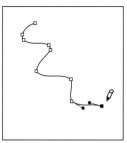

As you draw with the mouse button down, a dotted line follows the pointer. When you release the mouse button, the anchor points are added.

You can add to an existing path by starting to draw on an endpoint.

3 Position the pointer on an endpoint. Notice the eraser on the pencil turns black.

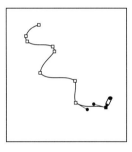

4 Hold down the mouse button and drag to add to the path.

You can erase while you are drawing a path. You can erase (in this way) only as long as the mouse button is held down.

5 Hold down the mouse button and begin drawing a path. Do not release the mouse button.

6 Hold down the Command key and drag back over the path without releasing the mouse button. The pointer changes to an eraser. The bottom tip of the eraser is the hot spot. Slowly drag the hot spot over the path while holding down the mouse button.

Note: One way to identify precisely the hot spot on any drawing tool pointer is to use the Caps Lock key. When you press this key, the drawing tool pointers become a crosshair with the hot spot in the center.

You can create both closed and open paths with the freehand tool, and the paths can be filled and stroked.

7 Try drawing several different paths. Draw a closed path by making the path end on the first anchor point of the path. You see the small circle when you are closing the path.

8 Click the selection tool in the toolbox. Drag to select your practice drawings. Press the Delete key.

Adding the bottle highlight

1 Scroll until you can see the top part of the bottle, above the label.

2 Click the freehand tool in the toolbox.

3 Use the freehand tool to draw the bottle highlight, using the figure below as a reference. Don't be afraid to be creative. Be sure to close the path.

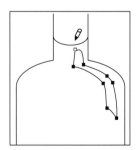

4 Choose Save from the File menu (Command-S) to save your work.

PAINTING THE BOTTLE

Next you'll paint everything you have drawn so far.

1 Choose Fit in Window from the View menu (Command-M).

2 Choose Unlock All from the Arrange menu (Command-2).

3 Choose Select None from the Edit menu (Command-Shift-A) to deselect everything.

4 Click the selection tool in the toolbox.

Next you'll use the Paint Style palette to fill each of the objects. Remember to press the Return key when you enter numbers.

5 Select the bottle, click the Fill box in the Paint Style palette, click the Process box, and fill as follows:

Cyan ....46 %
Magenta ..100 %
Yellow ....55 %
Black ....18 %

Note: There should be no stroke.

6 Select the label and the highlight. Click the Fill box, and click the White Swatch. Click the Stroke box, and click the Black swatch. Set the Stroke Weight to 1.

7 Select the circular foil top and paint it with 100% black and no stroke.

8 Select the foil wrap on the neck of the bottle, click the Fill box in the Paint Style palette, click the Process box, and fill as follows:

Cyan ....83 %
Magenta ....75 %
Yellow ....22 %
Black............9 %

Note: There should be no stroke.

9 Choose Preview from the View menu (Command-Y).

10 Choose Save from the File menu (Command-S) to save your work.

ADDING A BACKGROUND RECTANGLE

1 Click the rectangle tool in the toolbox.

2 Hold down the Option key and click near the center of the drawing.

3 Enter 16 for Width, 22 for Height, and click OK.

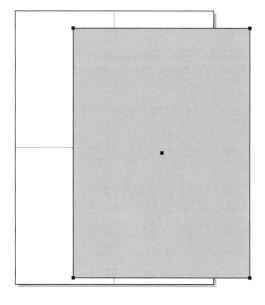

4 Click the selection tool in the toolbox.

5 Drag to center the rectangle on the page.

6 Choose Send To Back from the Arrange menu (Command-Hyphen).

7 Select the background rectangle, click the Fill box in the Paint Style palette, click the Process box, and fill as follows:

Cyan ....25 %
Magenta ....20 %
Yellow ....0 %
Black............0 %

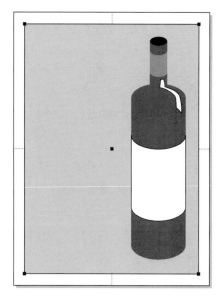

8 Choose Save from the File menu (Command-S) to save your work.

USING FILTERS TO MODIFY COLORS

Now you'll experiment with some interesting filters. First you'll modify all the artwork. Then you'll make some changes to the bottle.

To modify the entire drawing:

1 Choose Select All from the Edit menu (Command-A).

2 Choose Pathfinder from the Filter menu and Mix Soft from the submenu.

3 Leave the Rate at its default of 50% and click OK.

The Mix Soft filter creates a transparent effect on overlapping colors in the image. The selected items are now grouped.

4 Choose Colors from the Filter menu and Desaturate from the submenu.

The colors are lightened.

To modify everything but the background:

1 Choose Ungroup from the Arrange menu (Command-U).

2 The objects are ungrouped but are still selected.

3 Click the selection tool in the toolbox.

4 To deselect the background rectangle, hold down the Shift key and click inside the rectangle away from the other artwork. Everything else remains selected.

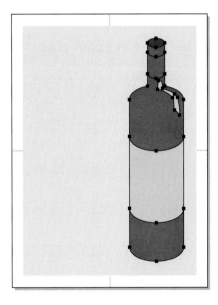

5 Choose Colors from the Filter menu and Adjust Colors from the submenu. The Adjust Colors dialog box appears.

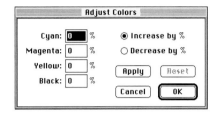

Before you make the final choices, you will try out several different settings. You can apply them to see what they look like. Then you can use the Reset button to return to the original colors.

The Adjust Colors filter changes the percentage of CMYK color for a selected object. You can either increase or decrease the percentage of each color by entering a positive value in the text box next to the color and then clicking the Increase By or Decrease By button.

When you click Apply, you see the results. When you click Reset, you are returned to the original. When you click OK, whatever values you have chosen become the values of the selected objects. Wait to click OK until you have examined different color choices.

6 Enter 50 for Cyan, and click Increase By.

7 Click Apply to see the results.

8 Click Reset.

9 Enter 40 for Magenta, and click Decrease By.

10 Click Apply to see the results.

11 Click Reset.

12 Set the values as follows:

Note: Make sure the Decrease By button is selected.

Cyan............ 5 %
Magenta.... 20 %
Yellow........ 15 %
Black .... 5 %

13 Click OK.

14 Choose Save from the File menu (Command-S) to save your work.

USING FILTERS TO DISTORT

You can create special effects with the Distort filters that change an object's shape and path directions.

1 Choose Select All from the Edit menu (Command-A).

2 Choose Distort from the Filter menu and Roughen from the submenu.

The Roughen filter moves anchor points in a jagged array from the original path, creating a rough edge on the object.

3 Enter 1 for Size.

4 Enter 1 for Detail.

5 Click to select Rounded.

6 Click OK.

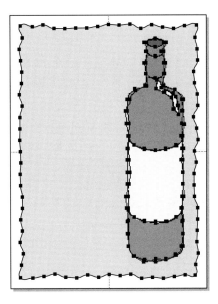

7 Choose Save from the File menu (Command-S) to save your work.

FINISHING THE BACKGROUND

To complete the background of the drawing, you'll create and paint the background rectangles.

Take a look at the final file. The background consists of a black and a yellow rectangle. You'll create these rectangles now.

Creating the rectangles

1 Click the rectangle tool in the toolbox.

2 Drag to draw a rectangle over the right half of the page. Use the guide in the center to help draw the rectangle.

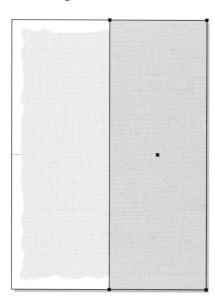

3 Use the Paint Style palette to fill the rectangle with 25% yellow. There should be no stroke.

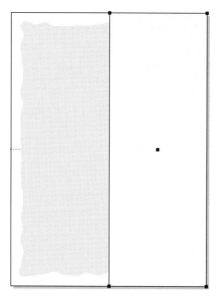

4 Choose Send to Back from the Arrange menu (Command-Hyphen).

5 Use the rectangle tool and drag to draw a rectangle over the left half of the page.

6 Use the Paint Style palette to fill the rectangle with 100% black. There should be no stroke.

7 Choose Send to Back from the Arrange menu (Command-Hyphen).

8 Choose Save from the File menu (Command-S) to save your work.

Dividing the jagged rectangle

Look at the final file again. Notice that the jagged inner rectangle is filled with a different color on the left than it is on the right. To divide the rectangle so that you can fill it with different colors, you'll use the Divide Fill filter.

1 Click the direct selection tool in the toolbox.

2 Drag to select the objects on the left half of the page. An easy way to do this is to drag a small selection marquee across the top left corner of the page so that a part of both rectangles (background and jagged) is selected.

3 Choose Pathfinder from the Filter menu and Divide Fill from the submenu.

The Divide Fill filter divides the purple rectangle into two filled faces. A *face* is an area undivided by a line segment. Now that the fill has been divided, you can paint the left half separately from the right half.

4 Choose Select None from the Edit menu (Command-Shift-A).

5 Click inside the jagged purple rectangle on the left side of the page. Notice that only the left half is selected.

6 In the Paint Style palette set the fill as follows:

Cyan............ 87 %
Magenta..... 75 %
Yellow......... 19 %
Black .... 16 %

7 Choose Save from the File menu (Command-S) to save your work.

SETTING UP LAYERS

The work you have done so far has all been on the first layer. Now you'll name that layer and create another layer.

1 If the Layers palette is not already open, choose Show Layers from the Window menu (Command-Control-L). (Notice there's a layer named *Regions*, which you haven't worked on yet.)

2 Double-click Layer 1 to see the Layer Options dialog box for Layer 1.

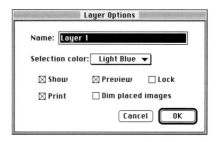

3 Change the name to *Background, an*d click OK.

4 Position the pointer on the right triangle at the top right of the palette, and hold down the mouse button to see the Layers palette pop-up menu.

5 Drag to select New Layer from the Layers palette pop-up menu.

6 In the New Layer dialog box, type **Map** for name.

7 Change the Selection Color to Black by dragging from the pop-up menu, and click OK.

8 Click the Show/Hide dot beneath the eye icon to the left of the Background layer to hide that layer. You'll leave it hidden while you work on the map. Make sure that the Map layer is the highlighted layer.

Note: Interim file 07Int1 was saved at this point.

CREATING A CONTOUR MAP

You took a look at the green map when you first looked at the final file. Recall that the map consists of a series of intermediate shapes between the outer edge and the highlight. You'll create the map by autotracing the outside, drawing the inner highlight, and blending between the two.

To autotrace and paint the map:

1 Choose Open from the File menu (Command-O).

2 Open the Lesson 7 folder and the file named *07Map.*

3 Access the auto trace tool in the toolbox. The auto trace tool is in the palette next to the brush tool. You will have to hold down the mouse button and drag across the freehand tool you used earlier.

4 Position the pointer on the edge of the gray map, and click the mouse button.

5 When the map has been traced, choose Select All from the Edit menu (Command-A).

6 Choose Copy from the Edit menu (Command-C).

7 Close the file named *07Map.* Do not save the changes.

8 Choose Paste from the Edit menu (Command-V).

9 Double-click the scale tool in the toolbox.

10 Enter 200, and click OK.

11 In the Paint Style palette, click the Fill box. Click Process Color, and set the fill as follows:

Cyan........ 100 %
Magenta...... 0 %
Yellow...... 100 %
Black .... 0 %

12 Click the selection tool in the toolbox.

13 Drag the map so that it is centered in the bottom half of the page.

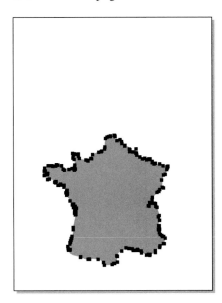

To draw the inner map contour:

1 Click the zoom tool in the toolbox.

2 Drag a marquee around the map to zoom in.

3 Access the freehand tool in the toolbox. You'll have to drag from the auto trace tool to access the freehand tool.

You'll draw a rough contour shape on the right side of the map.

4 Draw the contour shape within the right half of the map. The shape doesn't have to be precise. Just follow the outline on the right side of the map, about one-third of the way in. Then draw up the center. Be sure you see the circle next to the pencil when you finish drawing the path.

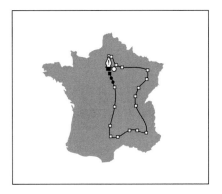

5 In the Paint Style palette, click the Fill box. Click Process Color, and set the fill as follows:

Cyan ....30 %
Magenta ......0 %
Yellow ....50 %
Black............0 %

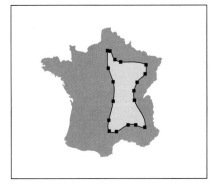

6 Choose Save from the File menu (Command-S) to save your work.

Blending shapes and colors

 You can use the blend tool to blend from one color to another and from one shape to another. Both processes are used to create the map. Before you blend the map, you'll practice using the blend tool to see how it works. First you'll blend shapes; then you'll blend both shapes and colors.

To practice blending shapes:

1 Use the scroll bars to scroll to some empty white space on the screen.

2 Choose Artwork from the View menu (Command-E).

3 Click the rectangle tool in the toolbox.

4 Click in the white space.

5 Enter 3.5 for Width, 5 for Height, and click OK.

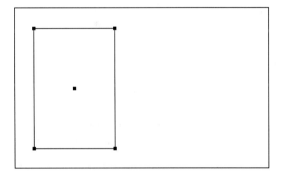

6 Click the oval tool in the toolbox.

7 Hold down the Option key and click to the right of the rectangle.

8 Enter 2 for Width, 2 for Height, and click OK.

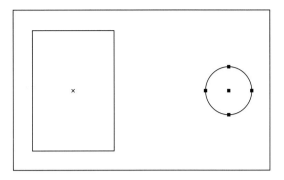

9 Click the selection tool in the toolbox.

10 Drag a marquee to select both objects.

When you use the blend tool, you must blend between two *selected* points, one on each path. It's all right if all the points on the path are selected. You'll use the blend tool to choose the points to blend to and from.

11 Click the blend tool in the toolbox.

12 Click the top right anchor point of the rectangle.

13 Click the top anchor point of the circle. The blend dialog box appears.

```
┌─────────── Blend ───────────┐
│                              │
│   Steps: [1      ]           │
│   First: [50    ] %          │
│   Last:  [50    ] %          │
│                              │
│   [ Cancel ]    [   OK   ]   │
└──────────────────────────────┘
```

14 Enter 12 for Steps and click OK.

15 The objects that are part of the blend are grouped.

16 Choose Select None from the Edit menu (Command-Shift-A) so the anchor points won't be displayed.

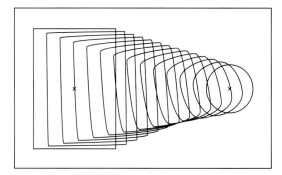

17 Hold down the Command key to access the current selection tool. Drag a marquee around the blend and the original shapes, and press the Delete key to delete them.

Next you'll try blending a shape that is on top of another shape. The shapes are different colors.

To practice blending shapes with colors:

1 Draw a square about 3 inches by 3 inches. Use a purple swatch in the Paint Style palette to fill it with purple. Set the stroke to none.

2 Draw a small circle in the center of the square. Paint the circle light blue by clicking a swatch in the Paint Style palette. Set the Stroke to None.

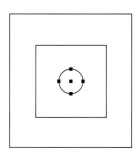

3 Click the selection tool in the toolbox.

4 Drag a selection marquee around the objects.

5 Click the blend tool in the toolbox.

6 Click one of the corner anchor points of the rectangle.

7 Click one of the outside anchor points of the circle.

8 Enter 50 for Steps, and click OK.

9 Choose Select None from the Edit menu (Command-Shift-A).

10 Choose Preview from the View menu (Command-Y) to see the results.

11 Click the selection tool in the toolbox.

12 Drag a selection marquee around the blend you just drew, and press the Delete key to delete it.

13 Now that you're a pro at blending, you'll go back to the contour map.

To blend the map:

1 Scroll so that the map is in the center of your screen.

2 Choose Artwork from the View menu (Command-E).

3 Click the direct selection tool in the toolbox.

4 Click the edge of the outer map path. Hold down the Shift key and click the inner contour path. You should be able to see the open anchor points on both paths.

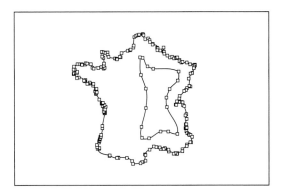

Recall that when you blend, you need to have at least one selected point on each of the two paths.

5 Hold down the Shift key and click an anchor point at the upper right corner of the inner contour path. The selected anchor point will be solid.

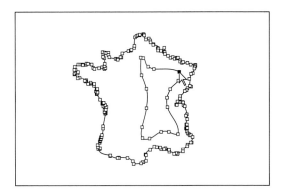

6 Hold down the Shift key and click an anchor point at the upper right corner of the outer map path. This anchor point will be solid.

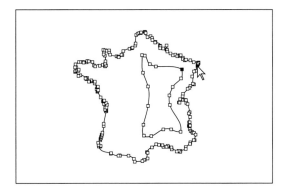

7 Click the blend tool in the toolbox.

8 Click the selected anchor point on the inner contour path.

9 Click the selected anchor point on the outer map path.

10 Enter 25 for Steps, and click OK.

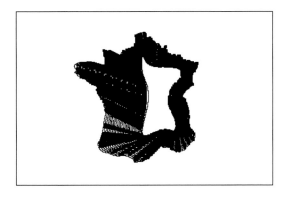

11 Click the selection tool in the toolbox.

The blend is selected, but the inner and outer shapes are not. You'll select them and group them with the blend.

12 Hold down the Shift key and click on the outermost path of the map to add it to the selection.

13 Hold down the Shift key and click on the innermost path to select it. The first path, the blend, and the last path should all be selected.

14 Choose Group from the Arrange menu (Command-G).

15 Click away from the artwork to deselect everything.

16 Choose Preview from the View menu (Command-Y).

17 Choose Fit In Window from the View menu (Command-M).

18 Choose Save from the File menu (Command-S) to save your work.

ADDING THE REGIONS

Once again, take a look at the final file. The dotted paths for the regions, the region names, and the lines are all created on yet another layer. This is the Regions layer that was already created in this file. You'll switch to that layer to add the rest of the artwork.

Setting up the layers

You'll turn off the background layer, lock the Map layer, and work on the Regions layer.

1 Open the Layers palette, if it is not open.

2 In the Layers palette, click the dot to the left of Map below the pencil icon to lock the Map layer.

3 Click the pen tool in the toolbox, and move the pointer to the drawing area.

Notice that the pointer changes to a pencil with a line through it, indicating that the layer is locked and that you cannot draw on it.

4 Click to the left of Regions beneath both the eye icon and the pencil icon. The flag title and the region names become visible in the window.

Rearranging layer order

Take a look at the order of the layers in the Layers palette. The Map layer was created last, and it is currently the top layer. You'll rearrange the layers so that the Regions layer is the top and the Map is the middle layer.

1 In the Layers palette, move the pointer to the word *Map*.

2 Hold down the mouse button and drag the word *Map* down until it is over *Regions*. Then release the mouse button.

3 Click the word Regions so that layer is highlighted.

You can now see both the Regions and Map layers, and you can write to the Regions layer.

Setting up your screen and windows

The regions drawn on the map are meant to be a general representation rather than a precise depiction of the actual regions. You can use the final file as a guideline to draw the regions. You may want to set up the final file and the working file side by side to make it easy to refer to the final file.

How you set up your windows will depend on your screen size. If possible, size the final file to the same zoom factor as the working file, and place the maps side by side.

Drawing the region shapes

First you'll set up the line options and draw a practice shape in the white space outside the drawing. Then you'll draw the shape for the Champagne region at the top of the map.

To set up the line options:

1 Click the freehand tool in the toolbox.

2 Choose Select None from the Edit menu (Command-Shift-A).

3 In the Paint Style palette, click the Fill box and the None swatch.

4 In the Paint Style palette, click the Stroke box, and click the Black swatch.

5 Set the Stroke Weight to 8, and press Return.

If you cannot see the line options at the bottom of the Paint Style palette, use the pop-up menu on the right to expand the palette.

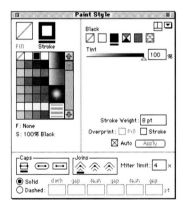

6 Click Dashed at the bottom of the window.

7 Enter 8 in the first Dash field and press the Tab key.

8 Enter 12 in the first Gap field, and press Return.

You have now set up the line options so that your path will be a dashed line 8 points wide with an 8-point dash and a 12-point gap.

To draw the region shapes:

1 Use the zoom tool to zoom in on the map.

2 Use the freehand tool to draw a path for the Champagne region at the top right of the map. Be sure to close the path.

3 Choose Select None from the Edit menu (Command-Shift-A) to see how the path looks.

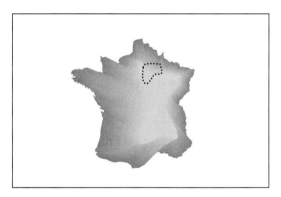

4 Draw shapes to represent the other six regions. Don't worry about being too precise.

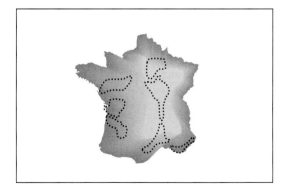

5 Use the selection tool if you want to reposition the paths on the map.

6 Choose Save from the File menu (Command-S) to save your work.

Repositioning the region names

The region names were included with that layer. Now that you've drawn the regions, you can reposition the region names. First you'll turn on the background so that you can see the white region names on the left.

1 In the Layers palette, click the dot to the left of Background, beneath the eye icon, to show the background layer.

2 Use the zoom tool and the Option key to zoom out to 25%

All three layers are now visible, and you see all of the region names.

3 Use the selection tool to drag the region names by their baselines and position them closer to the map, as shown below.

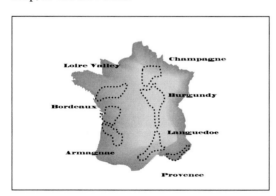

4 Choose Save from the File menu (Command-S) to save your work.

Adding and painting the region lines

1 Click the pen tool in the toolbox.

2 Click to draw a line from Champagne to the region representing Champagne.

Recall that you draw a line by clicking at the beginning and at the end of the line. Be sure to click the pen tool in the toolbox after you complete the line.

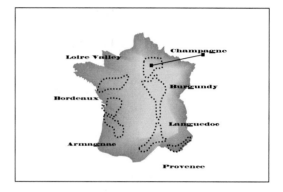

3 In the Paint Style palette, click the Fill box and click the None swatch. Click the Stroke box, and click the Black swatch. Set the Stroke Weight to 1 point.

4 Continue to add a line for each region. Click the pen tool in the toolbox after each line is complete.

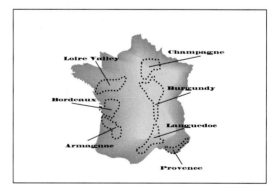

5 Choose Artwork from the View menu (Command-E).

6 Click the selection tool in the toolbox.

7 Select the region lines on the left side of the drawing. (You can hold down the Shift key and click to add additional lines to the selection.)

8 In the Paint Style palette, click the Stroke box, and click the White swatch. (The Stroke Weight should already be set to 1.)

9 Choose Preview from the View menu (Command-Y).

10 Choose Select None from the Edit menu (Command-Shift-A).

11 Choose Save from the File menu (Command-S) to save your work.

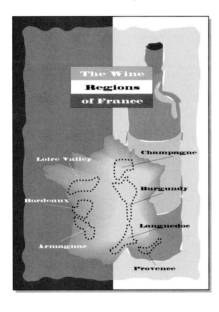

Preparing to print

1 Choose Actual Size from the View menu (Command-H). Remember that the poster size is 18 by 24 inches.

2 Choose Fit In Window from the View menu (Command-M) to see the entire poster.

3 Try turning different layers on and off by clicking under the eye icon in the Layers palette.

4 If you want to print the file, you can print it on letter-sized paper since you have changed the Page Setup to a 40% reduction.

You can print individual layers of a file if you want. Open the Layers palette by choosing Layer Options for "Layer name" from the Layers pop-up menu or by double-clicking the layer name in the Layers palette. In the Layer Options dialog box, select the print option to print a layer, or deselect the print option to keep that layer from printing. Because printing all layers is the default, you must deselect the print option for any layers you do not want to print.

5 Close the files.

Things to come

In this lesson you've practiced drawing with the free-hand tool as well as blending shapes and colors. The filters you've worked with are just a small selection of the ones that are available with the program. When you have some free time, try out the other filters to see what kinds of effects you can achieve.

As for Navigations, it's not quite time to say *au revoir* to France. In the next lesson you'll create some custom graphs, designed with that unique Navigations look. If you think graphs are boring, look ahead to see some interesting alternatives.

LESSON 8: DESIGNING CUSTOM GRAPHS

The wine poster was a big success. So big, in fact, that Navigations has decided to reprint it. This time they want to include a graph of wine production in France. Of course, the data is not available yet, but you can begin creating the graph with fictitious data.

While creating the graph, you'll

- learn the basics of creating a graph

- create and apply a custom graph design

Completing this lesson may take between 1 and 2 hours.

PLANNING THE PROJECT

First you'll take a look at the finished graph. Then you'll open the working file.

To examine the final file:

1 Open the Lesson 8 folder and the file named *08Final*. This file contains the finished artwork. The final file has been zoomed to 200%, so you can take a good look at the graph. In the background is the poster art.

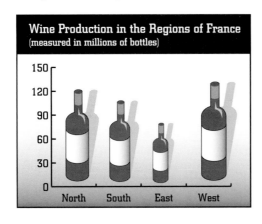

You can see the horizontal and vertical axes that you see in most graphs. Rather than using the typical bars or pie wedges, however, the data is represented with a custom design. The wine bottle from the preceding lesson is used to show the wine production. Bottle sizes are tied directly to the data.

You won't have to create the wine bottle all over again. You can just use a scaled copy.

Take a look at how the graph is used with the poster.

2 Choose Fit In Window from the View menu (Command-M).

Now that you've seen the final project, you'll take a look at the worksheet used to create the graphs.

3 Choose Show Layers from the Window menu (Command-Control-L).

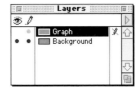

As you can see, the background layer is turned on, and the graph layer is turned off.

4 Click the dot beneath the eye icon to the left of *Background* to hide the Background layer. When you turn this layer off, there is nothing visible in the page rectangles.

5 Click beneath the eye icon to the left of *Graph* to show the working Graph layer.

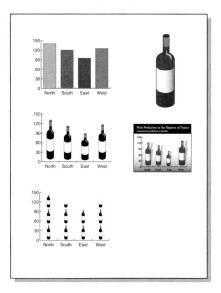

This layer was used as a working practice layer while the graphs were designed and created. The final design was then pasted onto the poster background layer.

6 Choose Hide Layers from the Window menu (Command-Control-L) to close the Layers palette.

7 Choose Artwork from the View menu (Command-E) to see the graph artwork.

8 Take a look at the bottle in the upper right corner. There's a rectangle around it that you don't see in the preview. This is part of the graph design.

For this lesson, you won't need to have the final file open.

9 Choose Close from the File menu, or click the Close box. Do not save changes.

To open the working file:

1 Choose Open from the File menu Command-O).

2 Open the Lesson 8 folder and the file named *08Begin.*

As you can see, we've provided the bottle for you. You can use the rest of the drawing area to create your graphs.

3 Choose Save As from the File menu, and name the file *08Work.* Save the file in the Projects folder.

CONSTRUCTING WORKING GRAPHS

In the first part of the lesson you'll create a graph and try out some different design styles.

You can use the graph tool and drag to draw a graph, or you can click and specify dimensions. The default graph style is a grouped column graph. Other graph styles include stacked column, line, pie, area, and scatter graphs.

To create a graph:

1 Click the graph tool in the toolbox.

You'll create your first practice graph next to the bottle.

2 Move the pointer to the white space to the left of the bottle, and click the mouse button.

3 Enter 3 for Width, 2 for Height, and click OK.

The Graph Data dialog box appears. This dialog box contains a worksheet into which you enter data.

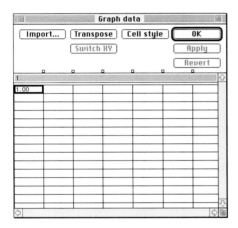

When you first open the dialog box, the first cell contains a default value of 1.00, and that cell is selected. A selected cell has a heavy black outline.

Entering labels and data

At the top of the worksheet is the *entry line* for entering information. When you create a graph, you enter labels and then data that corresponds to the labels. Each label or value is placed in a separate cell. A *cell* is the intersection of a row and a column.

To enter information:

1 Type **North** and press Return.

2 Type **South** and press Return.

3 Type **East** and press Return.

4 Type **West** and press Return.

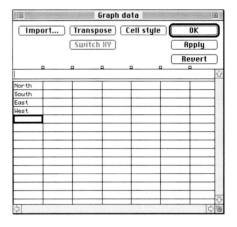

5 Move the pointer to the cell to the right of North, and click the cell to select it.

6 Type **140** and press Return.

7 Type **120** and press Return.

8 Type **95** and press Return.

9 Type **125** and click OK.

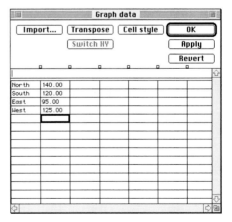

When you click OK, the graph is drawn on the screen.

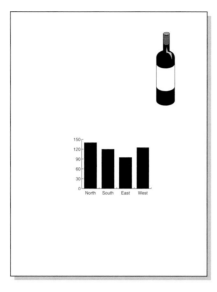

Notice that everything is selected.

Note: All graphs are created as grouped objects. It is important that you do not ungroup graphs because if you do, you will not be able to use the graph commands. If you want to ungroup a graph, wait until you have finalized the style and are certain the data is correct and won't be modified.

10 Click the selection tool in the toolbox.

11 Drag the graph and position it in the empty space to the left of the bottle.

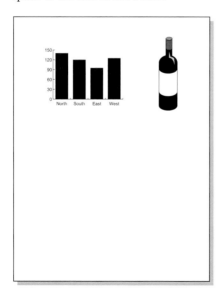

12 Click the zoom tool in the toolbox.

13 Drag a marquee around the graph to zoom in for a better look.

14 Choose Save from the File menu (Command-S) to save your work.

Painting the columns

Once you have created a graph, you can change the colors, change the typeface, and use any of the transformation tools to scale, rotate, reflect, and shear the graph. You'll paint the columns now.

To paint the columns:

1 Click the direct selection tool in the toolbox. (You need the direct selection tool because the graph is grouped.)

2 Click away from the artwork to deselect everything.

3 Click the left column to select it.

4 Choose Paint Style from the Object menu (Command-I).

5 Click the Fill box, and click any swatch of your choice to paint the column.

6 Click each of the columns with the direct selection tool. Then click a swatch to paint the columns.

USING CUSTOM GRAPH DESIGNS

As you saw in the final file, the wine bottle was used as a custom design to replace the columns. When you use a custom design, you first create the design. Then you apply it to the graph.

Creating a graph design

You can create a graph design from existing artwork. In this case, we've provided the bottle for you to use.

First, you'll create a background rectangle for the bottle art. Then you'll name and save the design.

To create the background rectangle:

1 Choose Actual Size from the View menu (Command-H).

2 Scroll until the bottle is in the middle of your screen.

3 Click the rectangle tool in the toolbox.

4 Drag to draw a rectangle around the bottle. Make the rectangle slightly larger than the bottle.

5 Choose Send To Back from the Arrange menu (Command-Hyphen). When you make a graph design, the backmost object must always be a rectangle.

6 In the Paint Style palette, set the Fill to none and the Stroke to none.

7 Click the selection tool in the toolbox.

8 Drag a marquee to select the background rectangle and the bottle.

9 Choose Group from the Arrange menu (Command-G) to group the objects.

10 Choose Save from the File menu (Command-S) to save your work.

To name and save the design:

1 Choose Graphs from the Object menu and Design from the submenu. The Design dialog box appears.

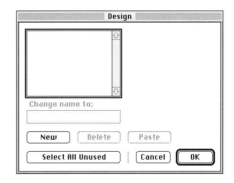

2 Click New.

A small preview of the design is displayed.

3 Type **Bottle** and click OK.

Applying a graph design

Next you'll apply the bottle design you just created to the graph. First you'll make a copy of the original graph, so you'll have the original to look at for comparison purposes. Then you'll apply the custom design in two different ways.

To apply a vertically scaled graph design:

1 Choose Fit In Window from the View menu (Command-M).

2 Use the selection tool and click the graph to select it.

3 Hold down the Option key and drag a copy of the graph below the original.

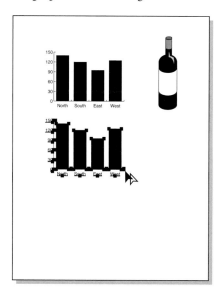

4 With the copy of the graph selected, choose Graphs from the Object menu and Column from the submenu. The Graph Column Design dialog box appears. Most of the options are grayed until you choose a design type.

5 Click Vertically Scaled.

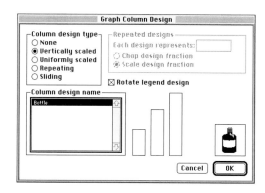

The Bottle custom design is highlighted.

6 Click OK.

7 Click away from the artwork to deselect everything.

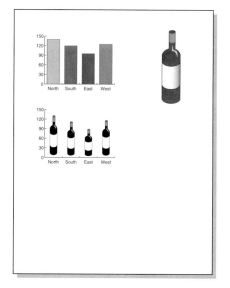

Notice that the bottles are proportional to the columns in the original graph.

8 Click the zoom tool in the toolbox.

9 Drag a marquee around the graph to zoom in for a better look.

10 Choose Save from the File menu (Command-S) to save your work.

To apply a repeating graph design:

1 Choose Fit In Window from the View menu (Command-M).

2 Click the selection tool in the toolbox.

3 Click the graph (with the bottles) to select it.

4 Hold down the Option key and drag to make a copy just below the current version.

5 Choose Graphs from the Object menu and Column from the submenu.

6 In the Graph Column Design dialog box, click Repeating.

7 Enter 50 in the Each Design Represents field.

8 Click Chop Design Fraction.

9 Click OK.

10 Click away from the artwork to deselect everything.

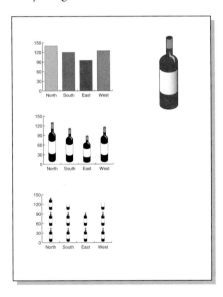

11 Click the zoom tool in the toolbox.

12 Drag a marquee around the graph to zoom in for a better look.

In this repeating design, the bottles are stacked to fill the columns. Each bottle represents 50, as you specified earlier. The Chop Design Fraction option cuts off a fraction of the top design as necessary to represent the data.

13 Choose Fit In Window from the View menu (Command-M).

14 Choose Save from the File menu (Command-S) to save your work.

Modifying a graph design

In this part of the lesson, you'll color the bottle in the graph design you've already created.

1 Use the zoom tool and drag a marquee around the bottle to zoom in on it.

2 Click the direct selection tool in the toolbox.

3 Choose Show Paint Style from the Window menu.

4 In the Paint Style Palette, scroll all the way down to the bottom of the swatches to locate the special swatches for this project.

5 Click the bottle. Click the Fill box and the burgundy swatch. Click the Stroke box and the Black swatch. Set the Stroke Weight to 1 point.

6 Click the label. Click the Fill box and the gradient in the lower right corner of the swatches. Click the Stroke box and the Black swatch. Set the Stroke Weight to 1 point.

7 Click the bottle highlight. Click the Fill box and the light gray swatch. Click the Stroke box and the None swatch.

8 Click the foil wrap. Click the Fill box and the purple swatch. Click the Stroke box and the None swatch.

9 Click the top of the foil wrap. Click the Fill box and the dark gray swatch. Click the Stroke box and the None swatch.

10 Drag a marquee to select the rectangle and all parts of the bottle.

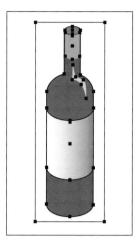

Recall that you have already made a graph design from the bottle. The background rectangle is already in place, so you do not have to recreate it.

11 Choose Graphs from the Object menu and Design from the submenu.

12 Click New.

13 Enter **Color Bottle** in the Change Name To field, and click OK.

14 Choose Save from the File menu (Command-S) to save your work.

COMPLETING A CUSTOM GRAPH

Now that you've made several working graphs, you'll use everything you've learned to make a complete graph for the wine poster.

First you make the background.

Creating the background

The background consists of a black rectangle. A second rectangle is filled with a yellow gradient.

1 Choose Fit In Window from the View menu (Command-M).

2 Click the rectangle tool in the toolbox.

3 Click below the bottle.

4 Enter 2.5 for Width, 2 for Height, and click OK.

5 Click the selection tool in the toolbox.

6 If necessary, drag the rectangle to position it on the page in the empty space below the bottle.

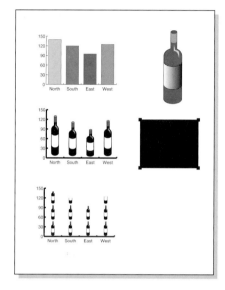

7 In the Paint Style palette, click the Fill box and the black swatch. Click the Stroke box and the black swatch. Set the Stroke Weight to 1 point.

8 Click the rectangle tool in the toolbox.

9 Hold down the Option key and click the center anchor point of the black rectangle.

10 Enter 2.5 for Width, 1.6 for Height, and click OK.

11 In the Paint Style palette, click the Fill box. Then click the yellow gradient near the bottom of the swatches.

12 Click the gradient vector tool in the toolbox.

13 Drag from the top to the bottom of the yellow rectangle to change the gradient direction.

14 Click the selection tool in the toolbox.

15 Position the pointer on the lower right anchor point of the yellow rectangle. Drag down until the pointer is over the lower right anchor point of the black rectangle and the pointer is hollow. Release the mouse button.

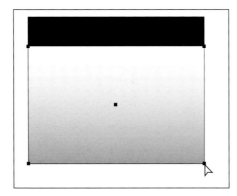

16 Choose Save from the File menu (Command-S) to save your work.

Drawing the graph and entering data

Now you'll draw the graph and enter the data. This time, you'll import the data rather than type it.

1 Click the zoom tool in the toolbox.

2 Drag a marquee around the background rectangles to zoom in.

3 Click the graph tool in the toolbox.

4 Position the pointer on the upper left corner of the yellow rectangle. Hold down the mouse button and drag diagonally to the lower right corner.

5 In the Graph Data dialog box, click Import.

6 Locate the Lesson 8 folder and the file named *08Data*. Click Import.

7 The data is automatically pasted into the worksheet.

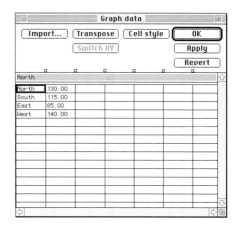

8 Click OK.

A column graph (the default style) is created. The graph may not be perfectly positioned on the other rectangles, but you'll position it later.

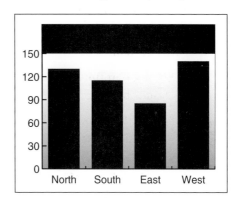

9 Choose Save from the File menu (Command-S) to save your work.

Adding a custom design

1 With the graph selected, choose Graphs from the Object menu and Column from the submenu.

2 In the Graph Column Design dialog box, click Uniformly Scaled.

3 Click Color Bottle in the list box, and click OK.

The columns are replaced with the bottles.

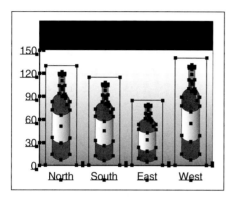

Now that the bottles are in the columns, you'll scale the graph and position it.

4 Double-click the scale tool in the toolbox.

5 Enter 75 for Uniform and click OK.

6 Click the selection tool in the toolbox.

7 Drag the selected graph to center it on the yellow rectangle.

8 Choose City from the Font menu and Medium from the submenu.

Because the entire graph is selected, all of the type for the numbers and labels is changed to City Medium. If you wanted to change an individual word or number, you would have to select it with the direct selection tool.

9 Choose Save from the File menu (Command-S) to save your work.

Adding shadows to the bottles

Next you'll add the shadows to the bottles in the graph.

1 Click the direct selection tool in the toolbox.

2 Click away from the artwork to deselect everything.

3 Click inside the left bottle, below the label. Make sure nothing is selected except the bottle.

4 Choose Copy from the Edit menu (Command-C) to make a copy of the bottle.

5 Choose Paste In Back from the Edit menu (Command-B).

The copy is pasted directly behind the original bottle and is still selected.

6 Click the shear tool in the toolbox.

7 Position the pointer on the anchor point of the bottom of the selected bottle. Hold down the Option key and click the mouse button.

8 In the Shear dialog box, enter 10 for Angle.

9 Click Horizontal, and click OK.

The bottle is sheared behind the original.

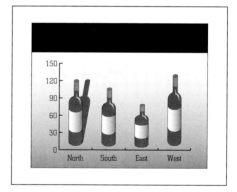

You'll repeat that process for the other three bottles.

10 Repeat steps 1 through 9 for each of the other bottles. When you have finished, your screen should look like this.

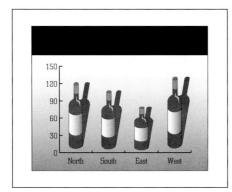

Next you will select all of the sheared bottles and paint them gray.

11 Use the direct selection tool and click inside the neck of one of the sheared bottles to select it.

12 Hold down the Shift key and click inside the other sheared bottles until all four of them are selected.

13 Use the Paint Style palette to fill the sheared bottles with 25% gray and no stroke. You can use the light gray swatch in the bottom row of swatches.

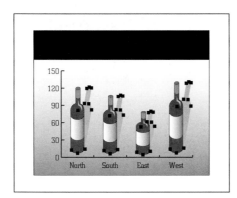

14 Choose Save from the File menu (Command-S) to save your work.

Adding the title text

Before you add the type, you'll lock the rest of the graph so you won't select it by mistake.

1 Drag a marquee around the outside rectangle to select the background rectangles and the entire graph.

2 Choose Lock from the Arrange menu (Command-1).

3 Click the type tool in the toolbox.

4 Drag to create a text rectangle over the black part of the background rectangle. (Make sure the rectangle is not over the yellow gradient-filled rectangle.)

5 In the Paint Style palette, click the Fill box and the white swatch. Make sure the stroke is set to none.

6 Type the following two lines. Put a Return between the two lines.

> **Wine Production in the Regions of France (measured in millions of bottles)**

7 Click the type tool in the toolbox to select the text rectangle.

8 Use the Character palette to set the type as specified below. Remember to press Return when you have finished.

> Font: City-Medium
> Size: 10 points
> Leading: 12 points

9 Drag the I-beam pointer across the bottom line of text to select it.

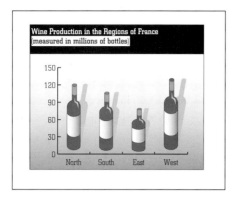

10 In the Character palette, change the font size to 8 points, and press Return.

11 Click the selection tool in the toolbox.

12 Drag the text box so that the upper line of text is centered between the left and right sides of the black rectangle. Then center the type between the top and bottom of the black rectangle.

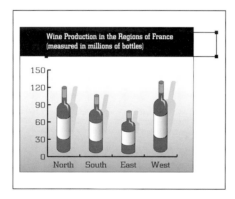

13 Choose Unlock All from the Arrange menu (Command-2).

14 Drag a selection marquee around the completed graph, title, and background rectangles to select everything.

15 Choose Group from the Arrange menu (Command-G).

Moving the graph to a different layer

Now that the graph is complete, you'll move it to the background layer and turn off the practice graph layer.

Although you could copy and paste the graph from one layer to another, in this case, you'll use the Layers palette to do the job.

1 Choose Fit In Window from the View menu (Command-M).

2 Choose Show Layers from the Window menu (Command-Control-L).

3 Click below the eye icon next to the background layer to view that layer.

4 Click below the pencil icon next to the background layer so you can write to that layer.

At this point you see both layers, one on top of the other. All your practice graphs are shown on top of the background layer. The final graph should still be selected, and the selection color is red.

5 Look at the Layers palette. Notice the red colored dot in the column to the right of the Graph layer. The dot indicates which layer the current selection is on.

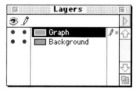

6 Position the pointer on the colored dot, and drag it down until it is next to the Background layer. The dot turns blue when it is placed next to the Background layer. The selection color of the graph itself also becomes blue.

7 Click the dot beneath the eye icon to the left of *Graph* to hide the graph layer.

The graph you just moved is now seen on the background layer and is still selected.

8 Use the selection tool to position the graph in the lower left corner of the poster.

9 Choose Select None from the Edit menu (Command-Shift-A) to review your work.

10 Choose Save from the File menu (Command-S) to save your work.

11 If you want to print the poster, remember to deselect the Print option for the Graph layer in the Layer Options dialog box.

Sit back, relax, and enjoy yourself

There's a slight possibility that you won't be drawing a lot of graphs in your work. But, now you're prepared, just in case you need to know. As a reward for learning about graphs, here's a trick to try.

1 Position the pointer on the status line at the bottom of the window on the left side. (It probably says *Selection*, to indicate the current tool.)

2 Hold down the Option key and hold down the mouse button.

3 Check out the shopping days 'til Christmas, the phase of the moon, or the national debt.

4 Close all the files.

The Art of TRAVEL

THREE 3 REASONS TO TRAVEL

① Painting
One great reason to travel to Europe is the inspired painting in the Louvre.

② Crafts
Another great reason to travel to Europe is the vibrant textiles you may find.

Another reason to travel is to explore the classic architecture in the city of Athens. ③

Architecture

NAVIGATIONS

150
120
90
60
30
0

North   South   East   West

Lesson

9

LESSON 9: TRAVEL TRENDS IN JAPAN CHART

This lesson provides a challenging project that you can use to practice the techniques you learned in Lessons 7 and 8 and in other previous lessons. In this project you will create a chart that will go inside the 1994 Annual report for Navigations.

Navigations started out as a small entrepreneurial travel company and over the last 10 years the leisure travel industry has grown substantially in particular with exciting trips to Europe and the Pacific Rim countries especially Japan.

In this lesson you'll

- apply pen tool skills
- create layers
- explore filters in more detail
- learn more advanced gradient techniques
- use the graph tool to create data
- create new custom gradients

Completing this lesson may take between one and two hours.

THE TASK

The artwork you will create is a chart whose purpose is to focus on travel in Japan. You will start from scratch to draw background art of a traditional oriental fan. Then you will create a blended version of the continent of Japan and incorporate Japanese characters. Navigations has gathered customer data from 1980 to 1990. A graph you create will represent this data. To complete this chart, you will add text and drop the Navigations logo into position. This chart will be a nice addition to the annual report Navigations is doing.

This lesson provides step-by-step instructions for creating the chart. If you find you need more explanation than a step provides, refer to the more detailed information in Lessons 7 and 8.

Note: The Pathfinder Filters used in this lesson require a math coprocessor. If no math coprocessor is detected, the Pathfinder Filters will not load.

PLANNING THE PROJECT

You'll have two documents open on the screen. One is the finished artwork that you can use as a reference. The other is the file you will be working with.

To open the reference file:

1 Open the Lesson 9 folder and the file named *09Final*. The document opens in Preview view.

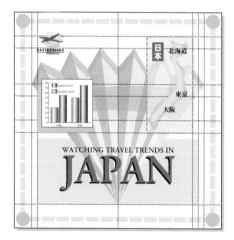

Take a look at the chart file to see what the components of the drawing are. In this lesson you will be working on three layers in which you will draw the artwork for your chart. The first will be the *Background layer*, the second will be the *Map and Graph layer*, and the third will be the *Type and Logo layer*.

2 Choose Show Layers from the Window menu (Command-Control-L).

3 Turn off the layers one at a time by clicking in the visible column of each layer.

TIP: TO DELETE GUIDES,

PRESS THE CONTROL-

SHIFT AND COMMAND

KEYS AND DOUBLE-

CLICK ON THE GUIDE

TO TURN IT INTO

A LINE. THEN PRESS

THE DELETE KEY

TO DELETE IT.

4 Turn on the layers one at a time by clicking in the visible column of each layer, until all layers are on.

Background layer

Map and Graph layer

Type and Logo layer

5 Use the size box in the lower right corner of the window to resize the window so that it's about one-forth the size of your screen.

6 Choose Fit In Window from the View menu (Command-M).

7 Drag the window to a convenient location on your screen.

PREPARING THE PAGE

You'll begin by creating a new file and making adjustments for the custom page size.

To open a new file:

1 Choose New from the File menu.

2 Choose Document Setup from the File menu (Command-Shift-D). The Document Setup dialog box appears.

3 Type 9 next to Dimensions, press the Tab key and type 9. Notice that *Custom* appears next to Page size, and the dimensions of the page are 9 by 9 inches.

4 Make sure Ruler units is set to Inches and click OK.

5 Choose Zoom out from the View menu if needed.

6 Choose Page Setup from the File menu, type 80 next to percent(%) to reduce the size, and click OK.

7 Click the page tool in the toolbox.

8 Position the pointer outside the page in the bottom left of your screen. Drag the page tool marquee until it is centered around the 9 by 9 inch square. The page guides disappear.

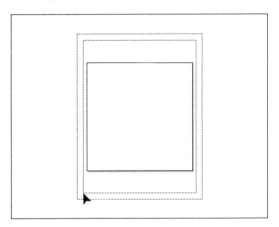

9 Choose Save As from the File menu, name the file *09Work*. Save the file in the Project folder.

CREATING THE FAN BACK

The oriental fan will be the first object you will draw using the pen tool.

Setting up ruler guides

1 Choose Show Rulers from the View menu (Command-R).

2 Drag the ruler origin from the corner ruler guide of the page to the bottom left corner of the page.

3 Position the pointer in the bottom ruler and drag upward to create a guide at the 1 inch mark on the right ruler.

4 Position the pointer in the bottom ruler and drag upward to create a guide at the 6 inch mark on the right ruler.

5 Position the pointer in the bottom ruler and drag upward to create a guide at the 7½ inch mark on the right ruler.

6 Position the pointer in the right ruler and drag left to create a guide at the ¾ inch mark on the bottom ruler.

7 Repeat Step 6 for the following two measurements: 4½ (center of the page) and 8¼.

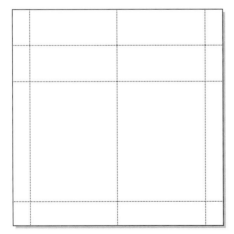

Drawing the shape of the fan

1 Choose Artwork from the View menu (Command-E).

2 Click the pen tool in the toolbox.

3 Position the pointer at the intersection of the 6 inch vertical ruler guide and the ¾ inch horizontal guide, and click the mouse button.

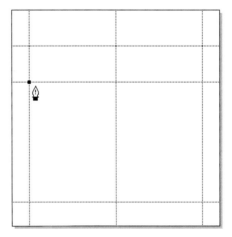

4 Position the pointer at the intersection of the center guide and the 1 inch right ruler guide. Click to continue the line segment.

5 Position the pointer at the 6 and 8¼ guides, and click the mouse button. You have created the bottom portion of the fan that looks like a large V.

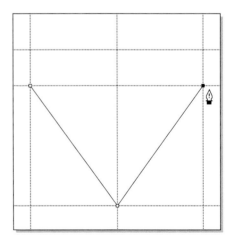

Drawing the top zigzag of the fan

1 Move the pointer left and up about ¾ of an inch, and click the mouse button.

2 Move the pointer left and down about ½ of an inch and click the mouse button. You have created one of three zigzags on the right half of the fan.

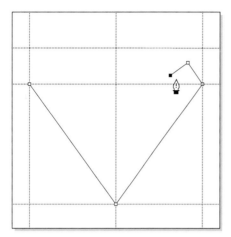

The next two zigzags will go to the center guide line with the down (valley) of the zigzag at the center guide. The next two zigzags will curve up slightly.

Note: You are just estimating the zigzags, They do not have to be perfect. Use the final file as a reference.

3 Draw two more zig zags spaced evenly to the left of the first zig zag. Use the final drawing or the illustration below as a guide. The second to last anchor point should touch the 7½ right ruler guide, and the last anchor point should touch the 4½ bottom ruler guide at approximately the 6¾ ruler measure.

Note: You may want to try the three zig zags a few times until you get them the way you want them. If you need to try again, select the zig zag path and delete it, or just delete one of the line segments. You can also use the Undo command to get to the point you want to redo. Make sure the last anchor point is selected. Click the last anchor point to continue the path and begin drawing again.

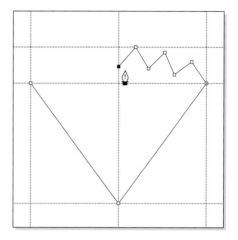

4 Choose Save from the File menu (Command-S) to save your work.

5 Continue to the left of the center guide, and create three more zigzags. Make sure that you close the path.

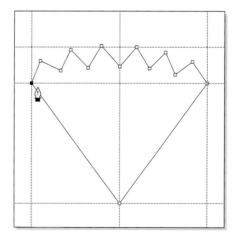

6 Click the direct selection tool in the toolbox.

7 Edit the zigzag lines by moving the anchor points to even out the spacing and shape of the curve of the fan, if needed.

8 Choose Paint Style from the Object menu (Command-I).

9 Make sure that the fan shape is selected.

10 In the Paint Style palette, click the Fill box. Then click the Process box, and fill as follows:

> Cyan........... 25%
> Magenta..... 12%
> Yellow........... 0%
> Black 0%

Note: You can use the Tab key to move between the fields.

11 Make sure the Stroke box reads None, and press Return.

12 Choose Preview from the View menu (Command-Y).

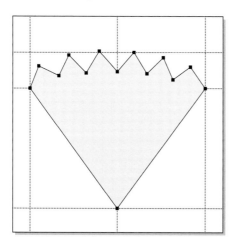

13 Choose Save from the File menu (Command-S) to save your work.

Copying a second zigzag of the fan

1 With the direct selection tool selected, drag a marquee around the top of the fan to select all the top points. Use the horizontal 6-inch guide as a reference.

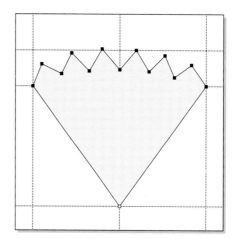

2 Hold down the Shift key and click the left corner point and then the right corner point to deselect them.

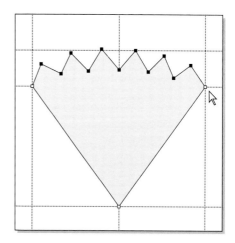

TIP: TO MOVE
THROUGH THE FIELDS
IN THE PAINT STYLE
PALETTE, PRESS THE
TAB KEY, TYPE THE
NUMBER YOU WANT
AND, PRESS THE
TAB KEY AGAIN.

3 Choose Copy from the Edit menu (Command-C).

4 Choose Select All from the Edit menu (Command-A).

5 Choose Lock from the Arrange menu (Command-1), to lock the shape of the fan.

6 Choose Paste In Front from the Edit menu to paste the zigzag (Command-F).

7 Click the selection tool in the toolbox.

8 Begin to drag the selected zigzag down about ¼ inch; then hold down the Option and Shift keys.

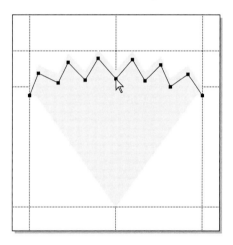

9 Release the mouse button and the keys.

10 Choose Artwork from the View menu (Command-E).

11 Choose Select None from the Edit menu (Command-Shift-A) to deselect everything.

12 Choose Save from the File menu (Command-S) to save your work.

Editing the pasted shapes

1 Click the zoom tool in the toolbox.

2 Drag a marquee around the top left edge of the fan to zoom in.

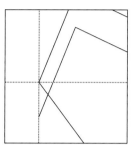

3 Select the add anchor point tool in the toolbox. (You'll have to drag out from the scissors tool.)

4 Hold down the Command key (the selection tool appears), and click the bottom zigzag anchor point to select the path. Release the Command key.

5 With the add anchor point tool, click the intersection of the bottom zigzag path and the shape of the fan to add 1 anchor point.

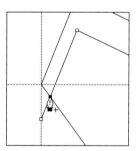

6 Click the direct selection tool in the toolbox.

7 Drag the endpoint up and right, and align it on the corner zig zag line.

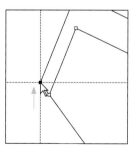

8 Drag a selection marquee over the selected point to add the point underneath it to the selection.

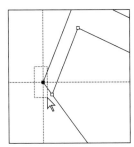

Note: Although you see only one anchor point selected, the one below the top anchor point is also selected.

9 Choose Join from the Object menu. The Join dialog box appears.

10 Click Corner and click OK.

11 Choose Save from the File menu (Command-S) to save your work.

12 Hold down the Space bar (the hand tool appears), position the hand toward the right of the screen, and drag left until the right side of the fan appears.

13 Repeat Steps 3 through 11 for the right side of the fan.

14 Choose Fit In Window from the View menu (Command-M).

Applying a fill to the zigzag shape

1 Make sure the zigzag path is selected. (The anchor points may be hollow when you want to apply a fill.)

2 In the Paint Style palette, click the Fill box. Then click the Process box and fill as follows:

Cyan...........70%
Magenta.....25%
Yellow...........0%
Black 0%

3 Make sure the Stroke box reads None, and press Return.

4 Choose Preview from the View menu (Command-Y).

5 With the direct selection tool, click outside the fan to deselect it.

6 Choose Save from the File menu (Command-S) to save your work.

CREATING THE CURVED BAND OF THE FAN

Now you will create the curved band of the fan. You will begin by adding some placement guides and then proceed to create the shape.

1 Position the pointer on the bottom ruler and drag upward to create a guide at the 4½ inch mark on the right ruler.

2 Position the pointer on the bottom ruler and drag upward to create a guide at the 5½ inch mark on the right ruler.

3 Click the pen tool in the toolbox.

4 Position the pointer on the left edge of the fan on the 5½ inch guide, and click the mouse button.

5 Position the pointer on the right edge of the fan at the 5½ inch guide, and drag a direction line to the right about 2 inches and down 1 inch.

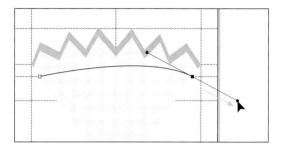

6 Move back to the last anchor point (on the right edge of the fan), and click the anchor point to create a corner point.

7 Move the pointer down the right edge of the fan to the 4½ inch guide, and click.

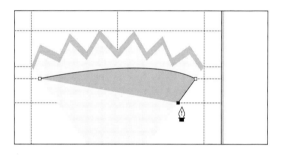

Note: Try to match the arch of the curve from above.

8 Move the pointer to the left edge of the fan on the 4½ inch guide. Drag a direction line left 2 inches and down about 1 inch.

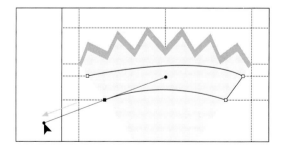

9 Move back to the last point, and click to create a corner point.

10 Close the path by clicking the original point.

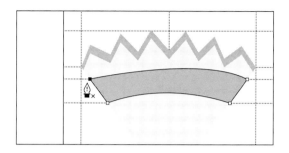

11 Edit the path, if needed, using the direct selection tool.

Note: If you prefer to edit in Artwork view, change to Artwork view to edit. Then return to Preview.

12 In the Paint Style palette, click the Fill box; then click the Process box, and fill as follows:

Cyan 25%
Magenta 50%
Yellow 0%
Black.............0%

13 Make sure the Stroke box reads None, and press Return.

14 Choose Save from the File menu (Command-S) to save your work.

CREATING THE FLOWER SHAPE

The flower shape in the middle of the fan is created by drawing an oval and modifying it to make a petal shape. The petal shape is then rotated and copied to create the flower shape.

Creating an oval

1 Click the oval tool in the toolbox.

2 Position the pointer about 1 inch above the bottom tip of the fan. Hold down the Option key and click.

3 Type .7 for Width and click the word Height (the setting changes to .7) and click OK.

4 If needed, use the arrow keys to reposition the bottom edge of the small oval about ½ inch from the bottom center tip of the fan art.

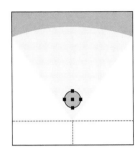

5 In the Paint Style palette, click the Fill box; then click the Process box, and fill as follows:

Cyan........... 50%
Magenta..... 25%
Yellow........... 0%
Black 0%

6 Make sure the Stroke box reads None.

7 Choose Save from the File menu (Command-S) to save your work.

8 Click the oval tool in the toolbox.

9 Hold down the Option key and click about 1½ inches above the top edge of the small oval. The Oval dialog box appears.

10 Type .7 for Width and 2.2 for Height and click OK.

11 In the Paint Style palette, click the Fill box; then click the Process box, and fill as follows:

Cyan............. 0%
Magenta....... 0%
Yellow......... 15%
Black 0%

12 Make sure the Stroke box reads None and press Return.

Converting the oval to a petal shape

1 Click the zoom tool in the toolbox.

2 Marquee zoom in on the bottom half of the fan.

3 Click the selection tool in the toolbox.

4 Center the bottom of the oval about ⅛ of an inch above the top of the small circle.

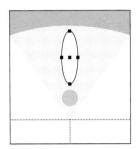

Note: Use the arrow keys to move in 1-point increments.

5 If necessary, scroll to see the top and bottom of the oval on the screen.

6 Select the convert direction point tool in the toolbox. (You'll have to drag from the add anchor point tool.)

7 Click the top and bottom of the oval to convert the anchor points to corner points. Notice now the shape takes on the petal characteristic.

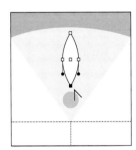

8 Choose Save from the File menu (Command-S) to save your work.

Repeating the petal shape for the right side

1 Choose Artwork from the View menu (Command-E).

2 Click the selection tool in the toolbox.

3 Select the petal shape.

4 Click the rotate tool in the toolbox.

5 Position the pointer on the *X* in the center of the small circle. Hold down the Option key and click the mouse button. The Rotate dialog box appears.

6 Type -10 (minus 10) next to Angle, and click Copy.

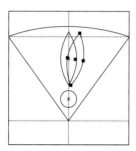

7 Choose Repeat Transform from the Arrange menu (Command-D), 3 times to make additional rotated copies. You now have 4 copies on the right side of the original center petal.

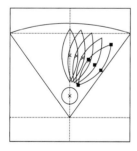

8 Choose Save from the File menu (Command-S) to save your work.

Repeating the petal shape for the left side

1 Click the selection tool in the toolbox.

2 Select the original petal.

3 Select the rotate tool in the toolbox.

4 Position the pointer on the *X* in the center of the small circle. Hold down the Option key and click. The Rotate dialog box appears.

5 Type 10 next to Angle, and click Copy.

6 Repeat step 7 from above for the petal copies on the left.

7 Choose Select None from the Edit menu (Command-Shift-A) to deselect everything.

8 Choose Fit In Window from the View menu (Command-M).

9 Choose Preview from the View menu (Command-Y) to preview the drawing.

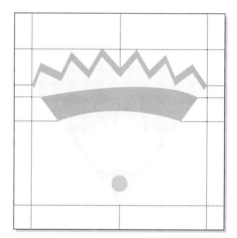

10 Choose Save from the File menu (Command-S) to save your work.

CREATING THE FOLDS OF THE FAN

The folds of the fan are triangular in shape. You will draw each fold of the fan with the pen tool. To begin, you will draw the leftmost fold.

Drawing the first fold

1 Click the pen tool in the toolbox.

2 Position the pointer on the intersection of the 6 inch ruler guide (the left corner of the fan), and the ¾ inch ruler guide and click the mouse button.

3 Move the pointer to the top point of the first fold of the fan, and click.

4 Move the pointer down to the bottom tip of the fan (very bottom center guide of fan), and click.

5 Move the pointer up and left to the starting point of the path and click to close the path.

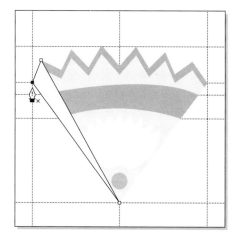

Note: Be sure to close the path.

6 Choose Save from the File menu (Command-S) to save your work.

7 In the Paint Style palette, click the Fill box; then click the Process box, and fill as follows:

Cyan 84%
Magenta 40%
Yellow 0%
Black.............0%

8 Make sure the Stroke box reads None and press Return.

9 Repeat Steps 2 through 6 to create five additional folds.

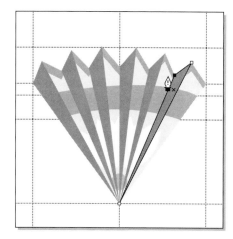

Note: Step 2 ruler locations will differ for each fold so refer to the final art and your curves. It is helpful to always begin the fold at the bottom of the v of the fan.

10 Choose Save from the File menu (Command-S).

Applying filters

1 Choose Select All from the Edit menu.

2 Choose Pathfinder from the Filter menu and Mix Soft from the submenu. The Mix Soft dialog box appears.

3 Use the default setting of 50, and click OK.

Note: The mix soft calculates every time a color overlaps and averages the colors.

4 Choose Hide Edges from the View menu (Command-Shift-H) to hide the selection. Hiding the edges is a neat trick so you can view the filter without being distracted by the edges being selected.

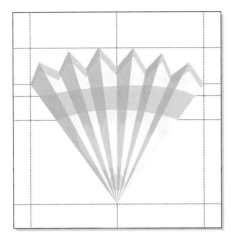

5 Choose Colors from the Filter menu and Desaturate from the submenu.

Note: Desaturate takes even amounts out of all colors.

6 Choose Undo from the Edit menu (Command-Z) to undo the last step. This shows you the "before" effect.

7 Choose Redo from the Edit menu (Command-Shift-Z) to redo the last step. This shows you the "after" effect.

8 Choose Colors from the Filter menu and Adjust Colors from the submenu. The Adjust Colors dialog box appears.

9 Click to select *Decrease by %*, enter the following settings. Then click OK:

    Cyan............ 10%
    Magenta....... 5%
    Yellow........... 0%
    Black 0%

10 Repeat steps 6 and 7 if you want to do a before-and-after preview.

11 Choose Show Edges from the View menu (Command-Shift-H).

12 Choose Save from the File menu (Command-S) to save your work. Notice the image is a little lighter.

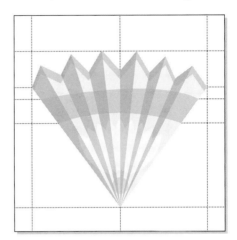

Creating the Map background rectangle:

1 Click the rectangle tool in the toolbox.

2 Click once above the fan in a white area. The Rectangle dialog box appears.

3 Type 2 for Width and 4 for Height and click OK.

4 In the Paint Style palette, click the Fill box; then click the Process box, and fill as follows:

    Cyan 20%
    Magenta 5%
    Yellow...........0%
    Black.............0%

5 Make sure the Stroke box reads None and press Return.

6 Position the pointer on the right ruler and drag left to create a guide at the 7¾ inch mark on the bottom ruler.

7 Position the pointer on the bottom ruler and drag upward to create a guide at the 8 inch mark on the right ruler.

8 Click the selection tool in the toolbox.

9 Select the rectangle and drag it to the intersection of the two guides you just created. The right and top sides of the rectangle should be touching the guides.

Note: Make sure the top of the rectangle lines up on the 8 inch horizontal guide.

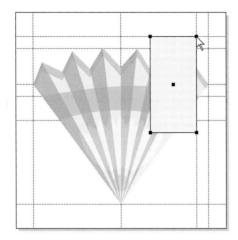

10 Choose Select All from the Edit menu (Command-A).

11 Choose Pathfinder from the Filter menu and Mix Soft from the submenu. The Mix Soft dialog box appears.

12 Make sure the setting reads 50, and click OK.

13 Choose Select None from the Edit menu (Command-Shift-A) to deselect everything.

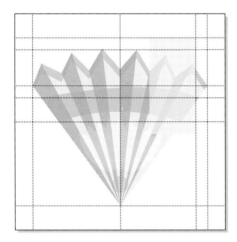

14 Choose Save from the File menu (Command-S) to save your work.

Creating a rectangle for the word *Japan*

1 Position the pointer on the right ruler and drag left to create a guide at the 1 inch mark on the bottom ruler.

2 Position the pointer on the right ruler and drag left to create a guide at the 8 inch mark on the bottom ruler.

3 Click the rectangle tool in the toolbox.

4 Click in a white area outside the drawing. The rectangle dialog box appears.

5 Type 7 for Width. Press the Tab key and type 2.75 for Height, and click OK.

6 In the Paint Style palette, click the Fill box; then click the Process box, and fill as follows:

Cyan 12%
Magenta 12%
Yellow 25%
Black.............0%

7 Make sure the Stroke box reads None and press Return.

8 Click the selection tool in the toolbox.

9 Drag the brown rectangle by the bottom edge so that the base of the rectangle is at the 1 inch right ruler guide. Center it between the 1 and 8¼ ruler guides.

10 Choose Send To Back from the Arrange menu (Command-hyphen or Command-minus).

11 Choose Save from the File menu (Command-S) to save your work.

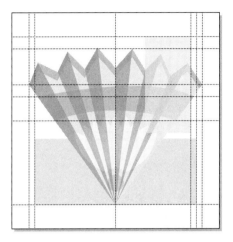

Creating the large background rectangle

1 With the rectangle tool selected, click in a white area outside the drawing. The Rectangle dialog box appears.

2 Type 8.25 for Width, click on the word Height, and click OK.

3 In the Paint Style palette, click the Fill box; then click the Process box, and fill as follows:

Cyan.............. 0%
Magenta........ 0%
Yellow......... 15%
Black 0%

4 Make sure the Stroke box reads None and press Return.

5 Click the selection tool in the toolbox.

6 Drag the rectangle by the top left corner, to center the rectangle inside the page.

7 Choose Send To Back from the Arrange menu (Command-hyphen or Command-minus).

Setting the stroke of the rectangle

1 In the Paint Style palette, click the Stroke box; then click the Process box, and set the stroke as follows:

Cyan 25%
Magenta 12%
Yellow 25%
Black.............0%

2 Type 15 for Stroke Weight.

3 Click Dashed, type 40 under Dash and 6 under Gap, and press Return.

4 Choose Save from the File menu (Command-S) to save your work.

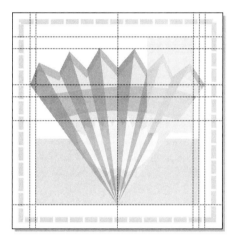

Creating the corner dots

1 Click the oval tool in the toolbox.

2 Click in the white area outside the drawing area. The Oval dialog box appears.

3 Type .6 for Width, click the word Height and click OK.

TIP: HOLD DOWN THE COMMAND KEY TO ACCESS THE ERASER AND ERASE BACK ALONG A FREEHAND PATH. YOU CAN DO THIS ONLY IF THE MOUSE BUTTON IS HELD DOWN.

4 In the Paint Style palette, click the Fill box; then click the Process box, and fill as follows:

Cyan........... 50%
Magenta..... .25%
Yellow......... 25%
Black 0%

5 Make sure the Stroke box reads None and press Return.

6 Click the selection tool in the toolbox.

7 Drag the oval to the top left corner.

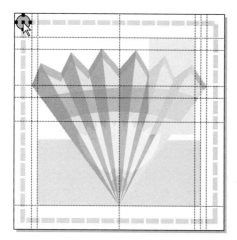

8 Begin to drag the corner dot (in the top left corner). Then hold down the Option and Shift keys.

9 Drag the first dot to the bottom left corner of the background rectangle, then release the mouse button and the Option key.

10 While holding down the Shift key, click to add the top corner dot to the selection.

11 Begin to drag the two corner dots right, then hold down the Option and Shift keys.

12 Position the dots on the right hand corners of the dashed line. Release the mouse button and keys.

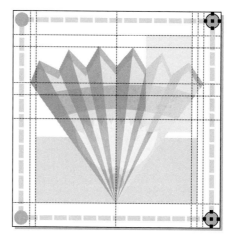

13 Choose Save from the File menu (Command-S) to save your work.

Naming and creating layers

1 Choose Show Layers from the Window menu.

2 Double click Layer 1. The Layers dialog box appears.

3 Type *Background* for the layer name, and click OK.

Note: You have done some intricate work in the background. To protect the background shapes you have drawn you will create a new layer to work on. This will avoid accidentally moving objects in the bottom layer when you continue to create more complex shapes.

4 Hold down the triangle on the right of the Layers palette and drag to choose New Layer from the menu. The New Layers dialog box appears.

5 Type **Map+Graph** for the Layer name.

6 Position the pointer on *Light Blue,* hold down the mouse button, drag to select *Black,* and click OK. Notice the Map + Graph layer is added to the Layers palette.

7 In the Layers palette, turn off writing options in the Background layer by clicking in the pencil column next to Background to get remove the dot. The Background layer cannot be edited in this mode.

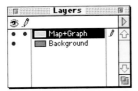

Note: Interim file 09Int1 was saved at this point.

DRAWING THE MAP OF JAPAN

In this next section you will draw the map of Japan on the new layer you just created.

Autotracing the map of Japan

1 Choose Open from the File menu.

2 Select *09Map* in the Lesson 9 folder, and click Open.

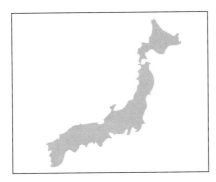

3 Select the auto trace tool in the toolbox. (You'll have to drag out from the freehand tool.)

4 Click the edge of the map. The auto trace tool traces the edge of the map and fills it with the last color selected.

5 Choose Select All from the Edit menu (Command-A).

6 Choose Copy from the Edit menu (Command-C) to copy the selection.

7 Close the *09Map* file, and do not save changes.

8 Choose Paste from the Edit menu (Command-V) to paste the selection into your working file.

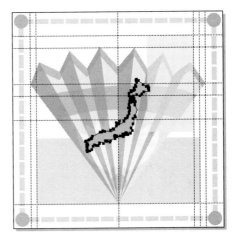

Note: Notice the black anchor points on the selection. Because the selection color for this layer is black, all the selections created or pasted into this layer will also be that color.

9 In the Paint Style palette, click the Fill box; then click the Process box, and fill as follows:

> Cyan 75%
> Magenta 0%
> Yellow 75%
> Black.............0%

10 Make sure the Stroke box reads None and press Return.

11 Click the selection tool in the toolbox.

12 Position the pointer over the bottom left corner of the selection, and drag over to the bottom inside edge of the blue box.

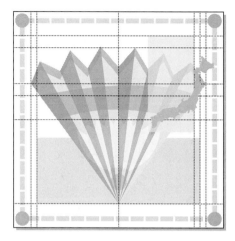

Rotating the map:

1 Click the rotate tool in the toolbox.

2 Click the bottom left corner of the map to set the point of origin so you can rotate visually.

3 Position the pointer on the top right corner of the map, and drag left until the map rotates and fits inside the light blue box.

4 You may want to use the arrow keys on the keyboard to adjust the placement of the map in the blue box.

5 Choose Save from the File menu (Command-S) to save your work.

Drawing the map highlights

1 Marquee zoom into the blue rectangle (use the zoom tool in the toolbox or Command-Spacebar).

2 Select the freehand tool in the toolbox. (You'll have to drag out from the auto trace tool.)

3 Draw a closed shape inside the map following the outer shape of the map. Start inside the top left edge, and drag down the left side and up the right inside of the map to the start point to close the path. Be sure to close the path.

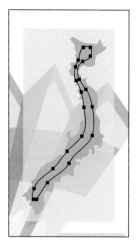

Note: The shape you draw inside the map doesn't have to be perfect. If you want to try it again, delete the shape you created inside the map and try again.

If you are able to run Adobe Teach movies on your system, play the movie named *Adobe Teach 4.* For information on how to play Adobe Teach movies, see the "Getting Started" chapter at the beginning of this book.

4 In the Paint Style palette, click the Fill box, then click Process box and fill as follows:

Cyan 30%
Magenta 0%
Yellow 50%
Black.............0%

5 Make sure the Stroke box reads None, and press Return.

6 Choose Select None from the Edit menu (Command-Shift-A).

7 Click the direct selection tool in the toolbox.

8 Using the keyboard commands (Command key and Space bar), marquee zoom in on the top of the map.

9 With the direct selection tool, click one anchor point on the inside shape to select it.

10 Hold down the Shift key and click one anchor point on the outside shape of the map to add it to the selection.

11 Click the blend tool in the toolbox.

12 Click the selected point of the inside shape. Then click the selected point of the outside shape. The Blend dialog box appears.

13 Type 25 for steps, and click OK.

Note: If you have lots of memory on your machine, you may want to increase number of steps of the blend to 100 for a smooth printed blend.

14 Choose Select None from the Edit menu (Command-Shift-A).

15 Choose Fit in Window from the View menu (Command-M).

ADDING JAPANESE CHARACTERS TO THE MAP

You will now add Japanese characters that have been translated from English and copy, paste, and position them into the map.

Creating a rectangle for the first text

1 Click the rectangle tool in the toolbox.

2 Position the pointer on the upper left corner of the blue map rectangle and click. The Rectangle dialog box appears.

3 Type .5 for Width and .78 for Height, and click OK.

4 In the Paint Style palette, click the Fill box; then click the Process box, and fill as follows:

Cyan 0%
Magenta .. 100%
Yellow 100%
Black.............0%

5 Make sure the Stroke box reads None and press Return.

6 Click the selection tool in the toolbox.

7 Move the red rectangle to the top left corner of the blue box. Position it about ¼ inch from the left corner and ¼ inch from the top of the blue box.

Copying the Japanese characters

1 Choose Open from the File menu.

2 Select the file named *09Type* in the Lesson 9 folder; and click Open.

Note: The Japanese Characters have been translated from English. The English version of what the characters represent is written in red to the right of or underneath the characters.

3 Click the selection tool in the toolbox.

4 Select the Japanese character to the left of the English word *Japan*.

5 Choose Copy from the Edit menu (Command-C).

6 Choose *09Work* from the Window menu.

7 Choose Paste from the Edit menu (Command-V) to paste the copy into your working file.

8 Move the text selection to the center of the red box.

9 In the Paint Style palette, click the Fill box: then click the White swatch.

10 Choose Save from the File menu (Command-S) to save your work.

Copying the other Japanese characters:

1 Choose *09Type* from the Window menu to view the Type file.

2 Click the selection tool in the toolbox.

3 Drag a marquee around the other three Japanese character sets to select them.

4 Choose Copy from the Edit menu (Command-C).

5 Choose Close from the File menu to close the *09Type* file.

6 Make sure the *09Work* file is selected and choose Paste from the Edit menu (Command-V).

7 Choose Select None from the Edit menu (Command-Shift-A) to deselect everything.

8 Select the top character, and drag it to the top portion of the map.

Note: You may want to refer to the final art for placement.

9 Drag the second and third characters to the following locations:

10 Choose Save from the File menu (Command-S) to save your work.

Creating the outside border of the map rectangle

1 Click the rectangle tool in the toolbox.

2 Drag directly over the light blue box by starting at the top left corner of the blue rectangle and dragging down to the bottom right corner.

3 In the Paint Style palette, click the Fill box; then click None.

4 In the Paint Style palette, click the Stroke box; then click Black.

5 Type 50 for Tint and set the Stroke Weight to 4.

6 Make sure the lower part of the Paint Style palette is open.

7 Click Dashed and type 12 for Dash. Press the Tab key and type 4 for Gap and press Return.

8 Choose Save from the File menu (Command-S) to save your work.

9 Choose Select None from the Edit menu (Command-Shift-A) to deselect everything.

10 Choose Fit In Window from the View menu (Command-M).

ADDING THE GRAPH TO THE LAYER

You will create a graph and add it to the layer on which the map was created.

Adding some guides for the graph

Position the pointer on the bottom ruler guide and drag upward to the bottom edge of the light blue dashed rectangle. Using the blue rectangle as the base for a guide will ensure that you will align the top of the graph on the same baseline.

Drawing the rectangle for the graph:

1 Click the rectangle tool in the toolbox.

2 Click in the white area outside the drawing area. The Rectangle dialog box appears.

3 Type 2.2 for Width. Press the Tab key and type 2 for Height and click OK.

Selecting the color for the shadow rectangle

1 Make sure the Caps Lock key is *up* and not *down*.

2 Click the eyedropper tool in the toolbox.

3 Click any corner dot to sample the fill color.

4 In the Paint Style palette, click the Fill box to select it. (It should fill with the color of the dot.) Click the Stroke box, click None, and press Return.

5 Click the selection tool in the toolbox.

6 Position the pointer on the bottom left edge of the rectangle and drag to the 1 inch bottom ruler guide and the 4 inch right ruler guide lined up with the blue rectangle.

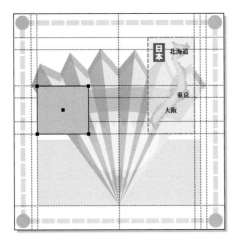

7 Choose Save from the File menu (Command-S) to save your work.

Creating the graph rectangle

1 Hold down the Option key and drag the graph rectangle ⅛ of an inch up and right to make a copy.

2 In the Paint Style palette, click the Fill box, then click White.

3 In the Paint Style palette, click the Stroke box, then click Black.

4 Set the Stroke Weight to .25, and press Return.

5 Choose Select None from the Edit menu (Command-Shift-A) to deselect everything.

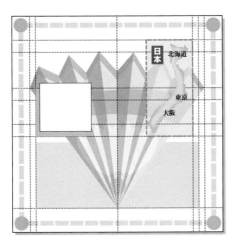

6 Choose Save from the File menu (Command-S) to save your work.

Creating the graph

1 Click the graph tool in the toolbox.

2 Position the pointer over the top left corner of the white rectangle, and drag down and right to create a graph rectangle over the entire white rectangle. The Graph data dialog box appears.

3 Press the Delete key to delete the default number in the first cell of the data entry box.

4 Press the Tab key to move one cell to the right.

5 Type **Group A** and press the Tab key.

6 Type **Group B** and press the Down Arrow key on the keyboard to go down one cell.

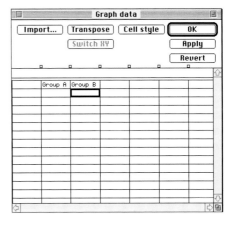

7 Type **55** and press the Left Arrow key to move one cell left.

8 Type **30** and press the Left Arrow key to move one cell left.

9 Type **"1980"** and press the down arrow key. Be sure to type the quote marks before and after the year.

10 Type "**1990**" and press the Right Arrow key to move one cell right.

11 Type **50** and press the Right Arrow key to move one cell right.

12 Type **75** and press the return key.

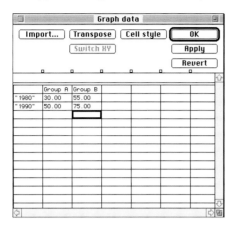

13 Click OK.

14 Choose Save from the File menu (Command-S) to save your work.

Modifying the graph data

1 Hold down the Command key and the Spacebar, drag a marquee around the graph so that you have about 2 inches around the graph on all sides.

2 Make sure the graph is selected.

3 Double-click the scale tool in the toolbox. The Scale dialog box appears.

4 Next to Uniform, type 80 and make sure the Scale line weight box is checked. Click OK.

5 Choose AGaramond from the Font menu and Semibold from the Submenu.

6 Click the selection tool in the toolbox.

7 Center the graph inside the box so that the legend hangs over the right hand edge.

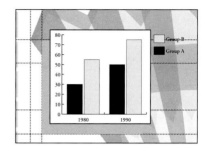

8 Choose Select None from the Edit menu (Command-Shift-A) to deselect everything.

9 Hold down the Command and Tab keys to toggle to the direct selection tool.

10 Drag a selection marquee around the two legends and names of the graph.

Note: Make sure that no other portion of the graph is selected. Only the two legends should be selected.

11 Drag the selected objects to the upper left corner to the right of the numbers in the graph and release.

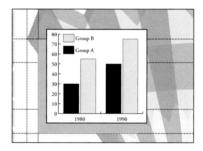

12 Choose Save from the File menu (Command-S) to save your work.

Editing the type next to the legends

1 Click the type tool in the toolbox.

2 Drag to select the text next to the legend reading Group A, and press the Delete key.

3 Type **European travel.**

4 Repeat steps 2 and 3 for the text reading Group B and replace it with **Japanese travel.**

5 Choose Select None from the Edit menu (Command-Shift-A) to deselect everything.

6 Choose Save from the File menu (Command-S) to save your work.

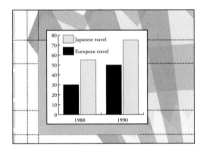

Creating the first gradient for the graph

1 Choose Gradient from the Object menu.

2 Click New.

3 Name the gradient *My Purple bar*, and press Return.

4 Click the Process box in the Gradient palette. The starting color defaults to process white.

5 Set the beginning colors as follows; then press Return:

Cyan........... 50%
Magenta... 100%
Yellow........... 0%
Black 0%

6 Position the pointer below the gradient bar and about one inch to the right and click to create another triangle.

7 Reposition the middle triangle by dragging the it to 37%.

8 Set the middle colors as follows, then press Return:

Cyan 0%
Magenta 0%
Yellow 40%
Black.............0%

9 Click the right triangle below the gradient bar to select the triangle.

10 Click the Process box in the Gradient palette.

11 Set the ending colors as follows; then press Return:

Cyan 50%
Magenta 78%
Yellow 0%
Black...........40%

Creating the second gradient for the graph

1 Click New.

2 Name the gradient *My Green bar*, and press Return.

3 Click the Process box in the Gradient palette. The starting color defaults to process white.

4 Set the beginning color as follows; then press Return.

Cyan 85%
Magenta 0%
Yellow 82%
Black...........29%

5 Position the pointer below the gradient bar and about one inch to the right, and click to create another triangle.

6 Reposition the middle triangle by dragging the it to 37%.

7 Set the middle colors as follows; then press Return:

Cyan.............. 0%
Magenta........ 0%
Yellow......... 30%
Black 0%

8 Click the right triangle below the gradient bar to select the triangle

9 Set the ending color as follows; then press Return.

Cyan........... 65%
Magenta....... 0%
Yellow......... 70%
Black 61%

10 Close the Gradient palette.

Using the group selection tool

The group selection tool is a selection tool located in the toolbox. You must drag right from the direct select tool to access the tool. This tool is particularly helpful while working with graphs. As you learned in a previous lesson, you should never ungroup graphs. To edit a graph, you select the parts you want to edit without ungrouping the graph, and this is easily done with the group selection tool.

Using the custom gradients

1 Make sure the Paint Style palette is open.

2 Click the group selection tool in the toolbox.

3 Double-click on the black legend to select the black legend and the black columns.

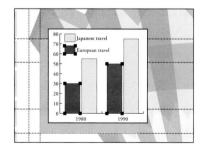

4 In the Paint Style palette, click the Fill box, and click Gradient in the right side of the palette.

5 Select My Green bar from the list.

6 In the Paint Style palette, click the Stroke box, set the Stroke to Black with a .4 stroke weight and press Return.

7 Use the group selection tool, and double-click the gray legend to select the gray legend and the columns.

8 In the Paint Style palette, click the Fill box; then click Gradient.

9 Select My Purple bar from the list.

10 In the Paint Style palette, click the Stroke box, set the Stroke to Black with a .4 Stroke Weight, and press Return.

11 Choose Select None from the Edit menu (Command-Shift-A) to deselect everything.

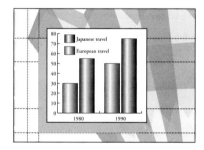

12 Choose Save from the File menu (Command-S) to save your work.

13 Choose Fit In Window from the View menu (Command-M).

Locking the Map and Graph layer

1 Make sure the Layers palette is open.

2 Double click on the *Map and Graph layer.*

3 Check the Lock box to lock this layer and click OK.

Note: Interim file 09Int2 was saved at this point.

WORKING ON THE FINAL LAYER

You will now work on creating the final text elements for this project. The final layer will include the text for the heading of the chart and the logo.

Creating the final layer

1 From the triangle on the right of the layers palette, drag to select New Layer. The New layer dialog box appears.

2 Type **Type + Logo** for the layer name.

3 Next to Selection color drag to select Red, and click OK.

Creating the heading

1 Select the type tool in the toolbox.

2 Position the I-Beam *outside and below* the top left corner of the brown text rectangle.

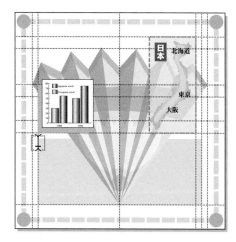

Note: Because you locked the Map and Graph layer earlier, you will not have to worry about accidentally selecting it as you create the art for this layer.

3 Drag the text I-beam past the right edge of the brown rectangle so that the text rectangle is a little bigger on all sides (except the top) of the rectangle. A blinking insertion point appears at the top left corner of the text rectangle.

4 Marquee zoom in on the bottom half of the page (zoom tool or Command-Space bar).

5 Type in all caps the following:

WATCHING TRAVEL TRENDS IN (return) **JAPAN** (no period).

6 Choose Select All from the Edit menu (Command-A). The text should be highlighted.

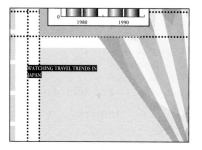

7 Open the Character palette (Command-T).

8 Make sure AGaramond Semibold is selected and set the Size to 23 points. Click Auto Leading and press Return.

9 Choose Alignment from the Type menu and Center from the submenu (Command-Shift-C).

10 With the type tool selected, drag to highlight just the word *Japan*.

11 With the Character palette open, set the Size to 120 points.

12 Click the lever to expand the Character palette. Set the Baseline Shift to 45, and press Return.

13 Click the selection tool in the toolbox.

14 Choose Fit In Window from the View menu (Command-M).

15 Choose Save from the File menu (Command-S) to save your work.

Creating a drop shadow for the heading

1 With the selection tool, drag a selection marquee over the type to select it.

2 Position the pointer on the bottom left corner of the selection, and hold down the Option key.

3 Drag the selection up and right approximately one-sixteenth of an inch to make a copy of the text.

4 In the Paint Style palette, click the Fill box; then click the Process box and fill as follows; then press Return.

Cyan............ 75%
Magenta...... 75%
Yellow........... 0%
Black 0%

5 Click the type tool in the toolbox.

6 Position the I-beam pointer on the first line of text and triple-click to select only the first line of text.

Note: If the word Japan is also selected repeat steps 5 and 6.

7 Press Return (not Delete) to remove just the text. The Black text, which was the original, is still showing.

8 Click the Selection tool in the toolbox.

9 Choose Select None from the Edit menu (Command-Shift-A) to deselect everything.

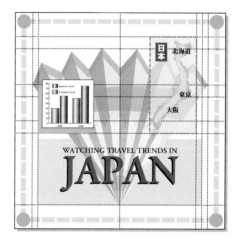

10 Choose Save from the File menu (Command-S) to save your work.

Copying, pasting, and positioning the logo

1 Choose Open from the File menu.

2 Select the file named *09Logo* in the Lesson 9 folder and click Open.

3 Click the logo in the upper right corner to select it.

4 Choose Copy from the Edit menu (Command-C) to copy the logo.

5 Close the *09Logo* file.

6 Choose Paste from the Edit menu (Command-V) to paste the logo in the working file.

7 Drag the logo by the bottom left corner to the upper left corner above the fan at the 1 inch ruler guide and about 1¾ inch from the top edge of the page. Use the final art as a reference

8 Choose Save from the File menu (Command-S) to save your work.

9 Choose Select None from the Edit menu (Command-Shift-A) to deselect everything.

10 Choose Print from the File menu and, click Print.

11 Choose Close from the File menu to close all the files.

You have completed the chart for Navigations' annual report. You have traveled through many techniques and have had plenty of time for practice on the previous skills. Congratulations, you are now ready to continue on to Lesson 10.

THREE
3
REASONS
TO TRAVEL

The
Art
of
TRAVEL

NAVIGATIONS

Painting
One great reason to
travel to Europe is the
inspired painting in
the Louvre.

Crafts
Another great reason
to travel to Europe is
the vibrant textiles
you may find .

Another reason to
travel is to explore the
classic architecture in
the city of Athens.

Architecture

150
120
90
60
30
0
North   South   East   West

Lesson

10

LESSON 10: PRODUCING AND PRINTING COLOR SEPARATIONS

Prior to this lesson, you've been assigning the four basic ink colors (or process colors) of cyan, magenta, yellow, and black to your artwork. With the Adobe Illustrator program you can also use custom colors (or premixed inks). After you learn how to use custom colors in your artwork, you'll make color separations. With that done, you'll then use the Adobe Separator™ program to prepare the artwork for your print shop.

While learning to produce and print color separations, you'll

• calibrate your color monitor

• use custom colors

• use the overprint technique

• learn how to use trapping

• work with layers

• place crop marks and add bleed to your artwork

• prepare your color artwork for separation

• set color separation options for your print shop using Adobe Separator

It should take you between 1 and 2 hours to complete this lesson.

Note: While working in this lesson, you may find it helpful to refer to Chapter 12, "Producing Color Separations," in the Adobe Illustrator User Guide, *because it contains many printed color examples of artwork similar to what you'll be producing.*

CALIBRATING YOUR COLOR MONITOR

Before beginning this lesson, you'll first *calibrate* your color monitor to simulate better the color output. Calibration is the process of adjusting your monitor and some Adobe Illustrator settings so that the colors you see when you display an Adobe Illustrator image match the colors you see in a final printed image.

Video monitors mix the three basic colors of light—red, green, and blue (or RGB). However, the printed page mixes the four basic ink colors of cyan, magenta, yellow, and black (or CMYK). Because of the differences in these two color models, matching the two perfectly is almost impossible.

You can best achieve the most accurate color calibration on a 24-bit monitor. On monitors that have a lower bit display, such as VGA, and Super VGA, color can only be approximated.

Calibration allows you to select a device-independent color model for converting RGB display colors to CMYK printing colors to compensate for factors affecting the monitor display, and to compensate for the ink and paper stock you plan to use to reproduce your image. If you use the Adobe Photoshop program with Adobe Illustrator, you can match artwork displayed in or printed from either program by using the same calibration settings.

To calibrate your color monitor:

1 Start the Adobe Illustrator program, if it is not already open.

2 Open the Lesson 10 folder and the file named *10Sample.*

3 Choose Preferences from the File menu and Color Matching from the submenu. The Color Matching dialog box appears.

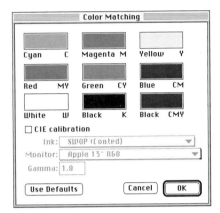

The dialog box shows the colors and color combinations that appear on a printed *progressive color bar*. The color bar displays all the possible combinations of cyan, magenta, and yellow. Additionally, it sometimes includes black and screen tints of the combinations. The color bars are printed on each sheet of a process-color printing job to ensure proper ink coverage and color. You can obtain a sample color bar from your print shop.

4 Click the CIE calibration check box if you use Adobe Illustrator with the Adobe Photoshop program. Please click it now.

This option improves the on-screen simulation of what colors will look like when printed, and instructs Adobe Illustrator to match the Adobe Photoshop settings used to convert RGB color to CMYK color.

Adobe Photoshop uses a color model developed by the Centre International d'Eclairage (CIE) to convert images between RGB and CMYK modes.

5 Under Ink, choose an ink from the pop-up menu that matches the printer you will use to print your artwork.

The Ink pop-up menu shows calibrations of some of the most commonly used ink sets and color printers.

6 Under Monitor, choose your monitor type from the pop-up menu.

This option controls how the monitor converts an RGB image to CMYK colors and how the CMYK colors are displayed on-screen by compensating for the different red, green, and blue phosphors used by monitors to display color.

7 Under Gamma, enter the same target gamma setting you used in Adobe Photoshop to calibrate your monitor.

If you have not used Adobe Photoshop, leave it at the default of 1.8. Or, if you are using a third-party monitor calibration utility, type in your gamma setting.

8 Click OK.

9 Choose Print from the File menu to print the sample file to the printer you are using.

10 Compare the on-screen *10Sample file* to the colors on the printed page. Also compare printed color bars on the output to the Color Matching dialog box when available.

Note: If a color bar sample is unavailable, you can use the sample color bar in the Adobe Illustrator Users guide on page 172. The color bar on this page may not match your printer's ink color exactly.

• If the colors displayed on the monitor closely match the colors on the printed sample, then no calibration is necessary.

• If the colors do not match, you need to adjust the colors using the Apple Color Picker to match the printed sample.

To adjust colors using the Apple Color Picker:

1 Choose Preferences from the File menu and Color Matching from the submenu.

2 In the Color Matching dialog box, click the CIE checkbox so that it is not selected.

Note: CIE must be unchecked to access the Color Picker.

3 Click the color swatch that does not match your printed color sample. The Color Picker appears.

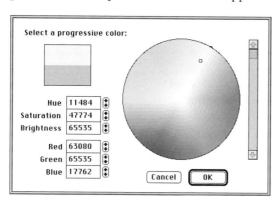

The color swatch in the upper left corner displays an ink simulation, or CMYK approximation, of the color. You'll want to match the swatch to your printed sample.

4 Adjust the screen color in one of the following ways:

• Drag the circle in the middle of the main color field to a new location.

• Drag the slider up or down on the luminosity bar that is to the right of the color display.

• Enter new values in the Hue, Saturation, and Brightness text boxes, or in the Red, Green, and Blue fields. You can type decimal percentages in these fields. You can also scroll through nondecimal percentages by clicking the scroll arrows to the right of the text boxes.

5 When the color in the swatch matches the printed sample, click OK.

6 Repeat this procedure for each of the colors in the Color Matching dialog box that do not match your printed sample.

Note: The colors you adjust in the Color Matching dialog box will change the affected color value display on the monitor.

7 Reprint your sample file to your output device.

8 Repeat steps 1 through 7 until your screen display represents the sample output.

9 Close the *10Sample* file.

BEGINNING THE LESSON

In this lesson you'll use the custom colors of the PANTONE MATCHING SYSTEM® to paint your artwork and then experiment with trapping as well as overprinting. Later you'll create color separations using Adobe Separator, and lastly, you'll prepare the separations for your print shop.

Note: It is strongly recommended that you work closely with your local print shop before beginning your print job and during the time that your job is being processed.

You'll begin by opening an artwork file, customized for this lesson, that lets you experiment with various techniques related to color separation. You'll recognize the modified plane in the artwork as the one that you created for the Navigations logo.

To open the reference file:

1 Locate the Lesson 10 folder and the file named *10Begin*.

2 Double-click the file named *10Begin* to open it.

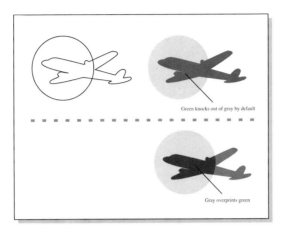

This file shows you some of the techniques you'll learn in this lesson. As you can see, three planes appear in various forms. In the top right corner is an example of a plane showing *knockout*. And the plane in the lower-right corner shows an example of *overprint*. Each of these techniques is discussed later in the lesson.

Before you work in this file, you'll become a little more familiar with custom colors.

USING CUSTOM COLORS

You can use the process colors of CMYK or custom colors to paint the artwork you create in Adobe Illustrator. Custom colors are premixed inks, such as those in the PANTONE MATCHING SYSTEM, FOCOLTONE COLOUR SYSTEM, TRUMATCH color swatching system, and TOYO Color Finder 1050.

Loading custom colors

You'll use the custom colors of the PANTONE MATCHING SYSTEM shortly.

Adobe Illustrator lets you select colors using other color systems. To load predefined custom colors into your palette, you choose Import Styles from the File menu and then open the file you want from the Color Systems folder.

To check the color list on the Paint Style palette:

1 Choose Paint Style from the Object menu (Command-I) to open the Paint Style palette. The Paint Style palette appears.

2 Click the Custom color box (fifth box from the left).

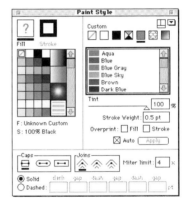

Notice the short list of general custom colors on the right side of the palette. Next you'll want to find out which PANTONE® custom colors are available. That's easy to do by importing the file named PANTONE Colors (coated). Coated stock is paper that has a light clay or plastic coating. A glossy or slick paper is coated. The color you want often depends on the type of stock on which you'll be printing.

To import the PANTONE Colors® *(coated)* file:

1 Choose Import Styles from the File menu.

2 Locate the Adobe Illustrator 5 folder, and double-click to open it.

3 Locate the Color Systems folder, and double-click to open it.

4 Double-click the file named *PANTONE Colors (coated).*

5 Click the Custom color swatch (fifth box from the left).

Information about more than 700 PANTONE colors appears showing what PANTONE colors are available and the color name abbreviations for specific colors.

6 Scroll down the color list on the right side of the palette to see the PANTONE colors, beginning with PANTONE 100 CV.

Note: The PANTONE colors are listed numerically.

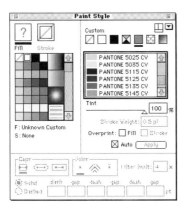

You can paint a selected object with any of the listed colors by clicking the Fill or Stroke box, then clicking the Custom box and clicking the color in the list. Because of the large number of available colors, you may want to create swatches for the PANTONE colors that you use in a particular file.

To create PANTONE custom color swatches:

1 Scroll down to the bottom of the color list on the right side of the Paint Style palette, and click to highlight PANTONE 5753 (green color).

2 On the left panel of the Paint Style palette, scroll all the way down to the bottom of the paint swatches so that the empty swatches are showing.

3 Hold down the Option key and click the fourth swatch in the last row to load PANTONE 5753 (the highlighted color in the list) into the empty swatch.

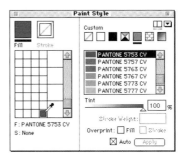

4 In the color list, scroll down further this time to find PANTONE Wm Gy 2 CV (gray color), and select it.

Note: *The abbreviation CV after the color name indicates that the color is a computer video simulation and may not match PANTONE identified solid color standards. It is strongly recommended that you use the current PANTONE® Color Reference Manuals for accurate color.*

5 Hold down the Option key and click the empty paint swatch to the left of the PANTONE 5753 (green color) swatch that you just filled.

CUSTOM CMYK EQUIVALENTS

The paint style palette can assist you in checking CMYK values for custom colors. This tip can be handy if you have a particular custom color in mind, but you want to print using the CMYK color process. By selecting the custom color, and then clicking the Process box, the values of the custom color will be converted to CMYK equivalents.

1 Click the Fill box and click the PANTONE Wm Gy 2 CV swatch you just created.

2 Click the Process box. Notice the CMYK percentages of the custom color appear in CMYK values.

Filling the shapes to apply overprint

1 Click the selection tool in the toolbox.

2 Select the circle to the left of the plane in the upper left corner.

3 Select the Fill box at the top of the Paint Style palette, and click the Pantone gray swatch.

4 Click the Stroke box and the None swatch. Then press Return.

5 Select the plane.

6 Click Fill, select the PANTONE green color, and then set the Stroke to None. Then press Return.

After you select the PANTONE colors, Adobe Illustrator prepares an assigned version for each PANTONE color you've chosen.

7 Choose Save As from the File menu, locate the Project folder, name the file *10Work*, and click Save.

Time-out for an Adobe Teach movie

If your system is capable of running Adobe Teach movies, you can see a preview of the techniques taught in this section. *Knockout, overprinting, choke trap,* and *spread trap* will be covered. Play the movie named *Adobe Teach 5.* For information on how to play Adobe Teach movies, see the "Getting Started" chapter at the beginning of this book.

UNDERSTANDING KNOCKOUT AND OVERPRINTING

In Adobe Illustrator, when an object such as your plane is placed on top of another object such as your circle and is separated in Adobe Separator, the area that falls beneath the top object is *knocked out.*

Viewing an electronic representation of a knockout

Note: This example is only a representation of what you would see if you printed film on two plates. In this case, the green plane knocks out of the gray circle.

1 Choose Knockout view from the View menu.

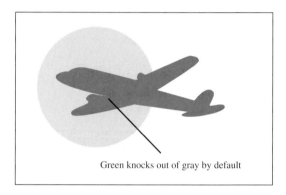

Green knocks out of gray by default

2 With the selection tool, click the plane select it.

3 Drag the plane (by the nose), about an inch to the right. Notice how the plane knocks out the object underneath it.

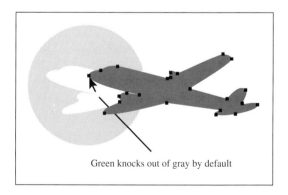

Green knocks out of gray by default

In this case, however, you want to create printed artwork where the color in the plane mixes with the color in the circle. You'll do this by *overprinting*, which causes a color to print transparently so that another color falls on top of it and mixes with it. Using overprinting prevents the automatic knockout and lets you create transparent effects in your separated artwork.

You'll try out the overprint technique now.

To overprint your artwork:

1 Choose Fit in Window from the View menu (Command-M).

2 Click the selection tool in the toolbox.

3 Select the plane in the upper left part of your Artboard.

4 In the Paint Style palette, click the Overprint Fill box in the lower-right panel.

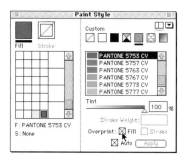

You'll probably notice that your artwork did not change after overprinting. The reason is that Adobe Illustrator does not show a representation of overprinting on-screen.

However, you can compare your plane with the one we have saved in a custom view.

5 Choose Overprint view from the View menu.

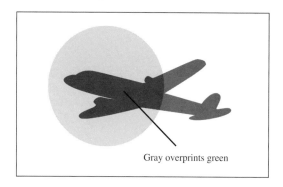

Gray overprints green

This plane has been simulated to show how the gray color overprints the green color.

6 Choose Fit in Window from the View menu (Command-M).

7 Choose Save from the File menu (Command-S) to save your work.

USING LAYERS

In the next few sections, you'll learn what misregistration is and how to correct it with trapping. You'll first display the Layers palette to turn on the Trapping layer to see the artwork you'll use in the trapping exercise.

To display the Layers palette:

1 Choose Show Layers from the Window menu (Command-Control-L). The Layers palette appears.

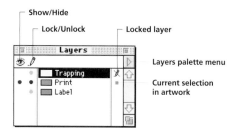

The Layers palette lists the layers in a document, starting with the frontmost layer. If any object on a layer is selected in the artwork, a colored dot appears to the right of the layer name in the palette.

Hiding and locking layers

You can hide and lock layers using the Layers palette.

To hide and lock layers:

1 Click the two dots to the left of Print to turn off its preview and lock it. The Artboard should be blank.

2 Click the Trapping layer to select it. Click below the eye and pencil icons and to the left of the Trapping layer to turn on the Preview and Write To options of the Trapping layer.

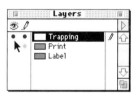

UNDERSTANDING TRAPPING

Often when there is press misalignment in an image, there is a gap where two inks should meet. This unintentional gap is called *misregistration*.

Examining a misregistration

1 Choose Gap zoom view from the View menu. Notice the white gap between the two ink colors.

To compensate for potential gaps, print shops traditionally have used a technique called *trapping*. Trapping creates a small area of overlap, called *trap*, between two adjoining colors.

In the following artwork of the Navigations logo with the plane and circle, you see an example of misregistration. In the next section you'll learn about various types of traps you can use to correct the problem.

Artwork with misregistration   *Trapping corrects misregistration*

Creating a spread trap

There are two basic types of trap: spread and choke. With *spread* trap, a lighter object overlaps a darker area and seems to extend into the area. The following illustrations show examples of spread trap.

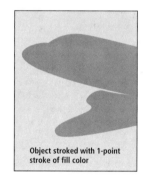
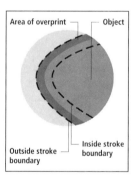

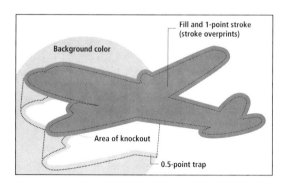

Creating a choke trap

With *choke* trap, a lighter area overlaps a darker object that falls within the area and seems to squeeze or reduce the object. The following illustrations show examples of choke trap.

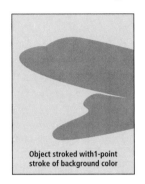

Object stroked with1-point stroke of background color

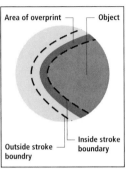

Area of overprint — Object
Outside stroke boundry — Inside stroke boundary

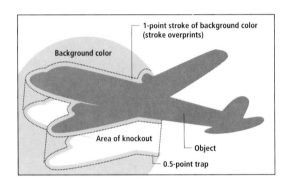

1-point stroke of background color (stroke overprints)
Background color
Area of knockout
Object
0.5-point trap

For more information on trapping, see the *Adobe Illustrator User Guide*.

Experimenting with trapping

You can create both spread trap and choke trap using Adobe Illustrator. To do so, you select the artwork that will overlap, or trap, into the object or background.

You set the artwork to overprint by selecting the Overprint option in the Paint Style palette. Typically, the lighter artwork overprints (traps into) the darker artwork.

You'll now experiment with trapping using some examples of the plane and circle.

Before creating trap, you'll need to decide whether you want to spread or choke the image. For best results, you should trap the lighter area into the darker area. In the plane artwork that you'll create, the gray circle (light object) will overprint the green plane (dark object) in the foreground. In this case, a choke trap is appropriate.

To create artwork with a trap:

1 Make sure the Gap zoom view is activated by choosing it from the View menu.

2 Click the selection tool in the toolbox.

3 Click the lighter color (the circle), and click Stroke in the Paint Style palette.

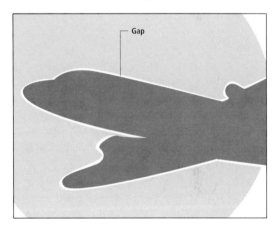

Gap

4 Click the light gray custom color and set the Stroke Weight to .5 and then press Return.

5 Choose Select None from the Edit menu (Command-Shift-A). Notice that the gap is smaller but it is still present.

6 With the selection tool, click the circle again, set the Stroke Weight to 2, and press Return. Notice that the gap between the plane and circle is now gone.

7 Press Command-Z to Undo the Paint Style, then press Command-Shift-Z to Redo the Paint Style. Notice the differences as you switch back and forth.

To create a spread trap:

In this exercise you'll create a sample spread trap using the circle and plane on the right side of the file. An example of a spread trap would be when a lighter object (plane) overlaps a darker background (circle) and visually seems to expand into the background.

1 Choose Spread trap view from the View menu.

2 With the selection tool, click the plane to select it.

3 Click the Stroke box and click the gray custom swatch.

4 Click the Overprint Stroke box in the Paint Style palette.

5 Set the Stroke Weight to 2 and then press Return. You've adjusted the gap so that misregistration will not occur.

You'll now use the other plane and circle in the reference file to create a choke trap.

To create a choke trap:

In this exercise you'll create a choke trap using the circle and plane on the left side of the file. An example of a choke trap would be when a lighter background object (circle) overlaps a darker object (plane) that falls within the background and visually seems to squeeze or reduce the object.

1 Choose Choke trap view from the View menu.

2 With the selection tool, click the plane to select it.

3 Click the Stroke box and click the custom gray swatch.

4 Set the Stroke Weight to 2 and press Return.

5 Make sure the Overprint Stroke box in the Paint Style palette is checked.

6 Choose Fit in Window from the View menu (Command-M).

7 Choose Save from the File menu (Command-S) to save your work.

You've just finished an extremely complicated technique to give you experience with trapping. If you still want more information, don't hesitate to experiment more on your own or read the chapter on trapping in the *Adobe Illustrator User Guide* to help clarify the technique.

PREPARING YOUR ARTWORK FOR SEPARATION

Every ink color, whether process or custom, is printed as an individual separation. In this part of the lesson, you'll prepare the Navigations luggage label for separation. Before separation, you need to do certain things to your artwork to prepare it. These steps include

- placing crop marks around the artwork

- saving the file for separation

- setting separation options for the print shop

You've already designed your luggage label, but you need to separate it and add crop marks to it.

To view another layer of the file:

1 In the Layers palette, click below the eye icon and the pencil icon to the left of the Trapping layer so you can not see or edit that layer. The Artboard should be blank.

2 Click below the eye icon to view the Label layer. The luggage label appears. Make sure you can see and write to the Label layer.

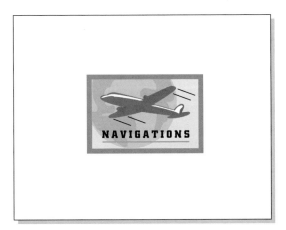

Placing crop marks

In your label artwork, you'll now place *crop marks* that indicate where the print shop should trim the image.

To place crop marks:

1 Click the selection tool in the toolbox.

2 Select the outer border box of the label.

3 Choose Copy from the Edit menu (Command-C).

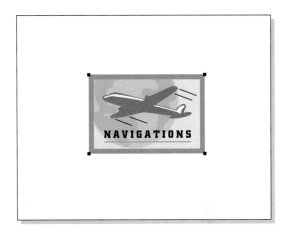

4 Choose Paste in Back from the Edit menu (Command-B). You do this so that you don't delete the original rectangle when adding the crop marks.

5 Choose Cropmarks from the Object menu and Make from the submenu.

Your artwork now has crop marks.

Adding bleed

You'll also add a *bleed* around the bounding box of your artwork. A bleed is ink that goes outside the crop marks. You include bleed in your artwork as a margin of error so that the ink will still be printed to the edge of the page after the page is trimmed.

If you don't do a bleed and the print shop crops the image based on the crop marks, you'll get the white paper edge if there is any misregistration in the cropped area.

To add a bleed:

1 With the selection tool, select the outer border box again. This time you'll add a *bleed* around the crop marks.

2 Double click the scale tool in the toolbox. The Scale dialog box opens.

3 Click Uniform, type 110 and make sure the Scale Line Weight option is checked.

4 Click OK. Notice that the color is outside the crop marks.

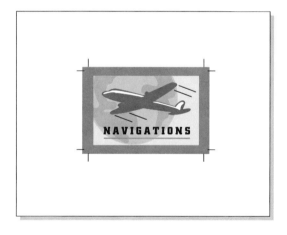

Saving your file for separation

Your file is just about ready to go to Adobe Separator for separation. However, before you take that step, you must save the file in the Preview mode of one of these file formats: None (Omit EPSF Header), None (Include EPSF Header), (Black & White Macintosh) and (Color Macintosh).

None (Omit EPSF Header) format can not be opened in Adobe Separator.

Note: *Do not save your file in the None (Omit EPSF Header) format if you plan to export the file to, or place the file in, another application. This format saves the document as an Adobe Illustrator file, but does not include an EPSF header and does not include a preview image of the artwork. The file can only be opened or printed using Adobe Illustrator, or an Adobe Illustrator compatible application.*

• *None (Include EPSF Header)* format saves the document as an Adobe Illustrator file and includes an EPSF header, but it does not provide a preview image of the artwork. The EPSF header allows the file to be recognized and printed by any software application that supports the EPS format.

• *Black & White Macintosh* format saves the file with an EPSF header and also saves a preview image in a black-and-white Macintosh Quick-Draw Pict format.

• *Color Macintosh format* saves the file with an EPSF header, and also saves a preview image in a color Macintosh QuickDraw PICT format. The preview image is limited to a maximum of 256 colors and 72 pixels per inch. (The color limit does not affect the number of colors in the saved document.)

To save your file as an EPS file:

1 Choose Save As from the File menu. The Save As dialog box appears.

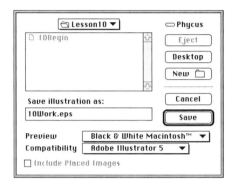

2 Change the file name to *10Work.eps.*

If you want to preview your file in Adobe Separator, you should select either the Color Macintosh option or the Black & White Macintosh Preview option, when saving your file.

3 Under Preview, choose Color Macintosh from the pop-up menu.

Note: When you save your file, the color information from your Adobe Illustrator file is retained with the file.

You can save your file in a version of Adobe Illustrator other than version 5. However, if you do, custom colors may be converted to process colors and any attributes specific to later versions of the program will be lost.

4 Under Compatibility, choose Adobe Illustrator 5 from the pop-up menu, if it is not already selected.

5 Make sure the Project folder is open and click Save.

6 Close your *10Work.eps* file.

You have now saved your artwork containing custom colors as an EPS file in Adobe Illustrator. But your job is not quite finished. Before you send the file to your print shop, you'll produce color separations. You'll use the Adobe Separator program to set the separation options.

SETTING THE SEPARATION OPTIONS

To set the separation options, you need to follow these steps:

• Open a color file to separate in the Adobe Separator program.

• Choose the separation options.

• Print or save the file.

You first must locate the folder where the Adobe Separator program is stored and then run Separator.

Running the Adobe Separator program

The Adobe Separator program is installed in the Separator & Utilities folder located in the Adobe Illustrator Application folder. If the Separator program is not installed on your computer, see the *Adobe Illustrator Getting Started Guide* for installation instructions.

To run the Adobe Separator program:

1 From the Adobe Illustrator icon in the title bar, hold the mouse and drag to choose the Finder.

2 From the Finder icon, choose Hide Others.

3 Locate the Adobe Illustrator Application folder on your computer, and double-click to open it.

4 Double-click to open the Separator & Utilities folder.

5 Locate the Adobe Separator 5 icon and double click to open it.

The Open dialog box appears and prompts you to open the file.

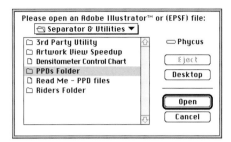

6 Locate the *10Work.eps* file in the Project folder, and double click to open it.

Note: *Although you may be able to select and open an incompatible (non-Encapsulated PostScript file) in the Open dialog box, the Adobe Separator program may not print separations of the file unless it has been saved in the proper format.*

After opening the *10Work.eps* file, one of two dialog boxes appears depending on whether you have previously run the Adobe Separator program.

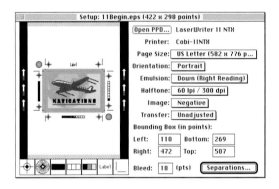

• If you are starting Adobe Separator for the first time, a dialog box appears and prompts you to open a *PostScript Printer Description (PPD) file.*

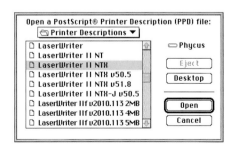

A PPD file contains information about your output device, including its resolution, available page sizes, line screen rulings, and screen angles.

For best results, use the PPD file that corresponds to your printer or imagesetter. To obtain PPD files not included with Adobe Illustrator, see the *Read Me–PPD Files* in the Separator & Utilities folder.

Note: *The printer or imagesetter you plan to use to print separations must match the PPD file you specified when setting up the separations. If the output device and the PPD file do not match, you may receive an error message, and the separations will not print.*

To open or change PPD files:

1 In the Separator window, click Open PPD. The Open dialog box appears.

2 Locate the Printer Descriptions (PPDs) folder that was placed in the Separator & Utilities folder when you installed the Adobe Illustrator program.

3 If you did not install the PPD folder when you installed Adobe Illustrator, install the folder now. See the *Adobe Illustrator Getting Started Guide* for instructions. If you installed the PostScript Printer driver, the program automatically finds the PPD files in the Printer Descriptions folder, located in the Extensions folder in the System folder.

4 Select a PPD file that corresponds to the output device you will use to print your separations, using the scroll bar as needed. The file names correspond to the printer or imagesetter name and model.

5 Click Open. The PPD file you select appears as its printer's name in the PPD text box in the Separator window.

To restore the default settings for the PPD file, choose Use Default Settings from the Settings menu (Command-T).

Using the Separator window

If you have previously run the Adobe Separator program, the Separator window appears with its default settings.

Your *10Work.eps* file appears in the preview window on the left side, and the Adobe Separator default settings appear on the right side.

Printer marks

When you modify the settings for your file, those settings are saved in the preferences (Prefs) file. If you open a file that has not been separated in Adobe Separator before (such as your *10Work.eps* file), the program will use the settings that were used on the last file you opened.

Understanding printer marks

When you prepare your artwork for printing, you need a number of *printer marks* on the artwork so that the print shop can precisely register the artwork elements and verify the correct color. Printer marks include registration marks, crop marks, color bars, and gradient tint bars.

You can create and move the printer marks in Adobe Separator, although in this lesson, you will not. However, you can later experiment on your own with printer marks.

Preparing your file for separation

You need to prepare your *10Work.eps* file for the print shop by specifying separation settings using the Separator window. These settings include

- printer you will use
- page size of printer
- image orientation
- emulsion side
- halftone screen ruling
- any tint adjustments for your separation

Note: *It is strongly recommended that you work closely with your local print shop before beginning your print job and during the time that your job is being processed.*

In this exercise, most of the separation settings will already be set correctly once you open your file. But you'll go through the steps so that you'll know how to set or change the options for future jobs.

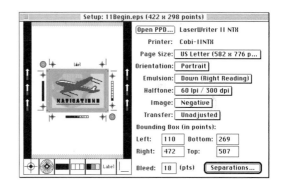

To specify the separation settings:

1 Select Chooser from the Apple menu.

2 Select the printer you will print to.

3 Close the Chooser.

The default is the currently selected printer, and its name is displayed in the Separator window.

4 Under Page Size, choose Letter from the pop-up menu, if not already selected. (The dimensions in point size are listed in parentheses next to the page size.)

The dimensions are the limits of the *imageable area*, which is the total page size less a border used by the printer or imagesetter to feed the media through the printer. No printer can print to the exact edge of a page.

The default is the page size in the PPD file for the selected printer. You can change the page size to any listed in the PPD file. Page sizes are listed by a familiar name, such as Letter.

You can specify a custom page size by choosing Other from the Page Size pop-up menu. The Page Size dialog box appears.

Note: The Other option appears on the pop-up menu only if you are using a printer that accommodates various page sizes, such as a high-resolution imagesetter. For example, the PPD file for a laser printer does not contain this option.

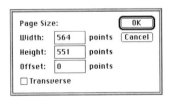

If you want to rotate your page 90 degrees, click the Transverse check box in the Page Size dialog box, and then click OK.

If you had the opportunity to click Transverse, the arrows in the margins of the preview window would be displayed horizontally, indicating that the imageable area has been rotated.

Transverse option off   *Transverse option on*

The offset option is also a choice you can adjust in the Page Size pop-up menu of some Imagesetters. This option allows you to change the placement of the page by entering a value in points in the offset field. The Offset value specifies the amount of space along the right side of the imageable area.

In some cases, you can significantly reduce the amount of film or paper needed for a print job by using the Transverse option in conjunction with the Offset option. Compare the following examples of an image printed by the Adobe Separator program with the Offset option on and off.

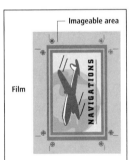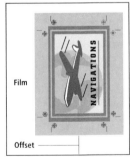

Offset option off   *Page moves up with Offset option on*

When both the Offset and Transverse options are selected, the Offset option controls the amount of space between the separations.

5 Under Orientation, choose Landscape from the pop-up menu if not already selected.

You can change the orientation of the image within the imageable area to either Portrait or Landscape.

• In *Portrait* mode, the top of the image is printed parallel to the short edge of the page; the arrow direction is vertical. In *Landscape* mode, the top of the image is printed parallel to the long edge of the page; the arrow direction is horizontal.

6 Under Emulsion, choose Down (Right Reading) from the pop-up menu if not already selected.

• *Emulsion* refers to the photosensitive layer on a piece of film or paper. Emulsion Down means that type is readable when the photosensitive layer is facing away from you.

Emulsion Up means that type in the image is readable (*right reading*) when the photosensitive layer is facing you. Check with your print shop to find out which emulsion direction it prefers.

Note: If you are printing a composite print (that is, CMYK, and any custom colors as one print versus several), and if Emulsion reads Up (Right Reading), the image will appear readable and not reversed.

7 Under Halftone, choose 60 lpi/300 dpi from the pop-up menu, if not already selected.

• *Halftone* refers to the line screen, or the lines per inch *(lpi)*, and the resolution, or dots per inch *(dpi),* of the printer or imagesetter that you'll use to print the color separations.

A high line screen ruling *(150 lpi)* spaces the dots used to create an image closely together to create a finely rendered image on the press. A low line screen ruling *(60 lpi to 85 lpi)* spaces the dots farther apart to create a coarser image. Some examples of lpi include

65 lpi–85 lpi: newspaper

85 lpi–133 lpi: magazine (low quality)

133 lpi and up: high quality

Consult with your print shop to find out how fine a line screen its press can hold, and then plan accordingly.

8 Under Image, choose Negative from the pop-up menu, if not already selected.

• The *Image* option determines the image exposure: negative or positive. Typically, print shops require negative film in the United States and positive film in Europe and Japan. Check with your print shop to find out which image type you should use.

Note: If you are printing a composite print sample, click positive instead of negative.

9 Under Transfer, choose Unadjusted from the pop-up menu.

• The *Transfer* option lets you compensate for discrepancies between the tint values specified in your artwork and the tint values actually printed by your printer or imagesetter. The condition of the chemicals used to process the film can also cause these variances.

By default, the setting is Unadjusted. Use this setting if you'll be sending your file to a service bureau. Most service bureaus calibrate their imagesetters daily, so you would not have to make additional transfer adjustments.

10 Under Bounding Box (in points), use the default values already entered.

Since you set crop marks in the label artwork earlier in this lesson you do not have to adjust them or the bounding box now.

However, if you'd like, you can experiment with changing the size of the bounding box by entering different values. Go ahead and type in some new numbers, and see how the bounding box changes.

11 Under Bleed, enter 18 next to (pts), if not already entered. The default value is 18. The maximum bleed you can set is 72; the minimum is 0.

Note: If you entered a bleed in Adobe Illustrator before opening the file in Adobe Separator you may not have to change the bleed.

Check with your print shop to find out the amount of bleed to use for your particular job.

12 Choose Print Composite from the File menu.

The output should be a one page sample of a reverse, negative composite image of the label art.

PRINTING THE SEPARATIONS

Now that you've set the options for the separations, you'll examine printing options. You can print

• a composite image

• all color separations

• selected separations

If you print (or save) selected separations, you can also overprint black. You can also convert custom colors to process colors and print them.

Printing a positive composite image

You may want to print a composite print of your image in the Adobe Separator program. The composite print can be positive or negative.

To print a composite image:

1 Make sure your printer and its PPD file are selected.

2 Under Emulsion, click Up (Right Reading).

3 Under Image, click Positive.

4 Choose Print Composite from the File menu.

The file will print on one piece of paper either in grayscale, if you are printing to a non-color printer, or color, if you are printing to a color printer.

Printing all separations

In this exercise you'll print all the color separations for your *10Work.eps* file. If you want to print all the process colors and custom colors in your file, you don't have to select all the colors first. The Adobe Separator program prints all the colors by default.

You'll also take a look at the other separation choices so that you'll know how to set or change the options for future jobs that you'll send to your print shop.

To print all separations:

1 Click the Separations button in the lower right corner of the window. The Separations dialog box appears.

2 Click in the Convert To Process column and click No next to the two PANTONE colors.

3 Click in both the PANTONE rows under Print and make sure the Print Column reads Yes next to each PANTONE color.

4 Choose Print All Separations from the File menu (Command-P). A progress bar appears as the separations print.

The program labels each printed separation with the color name assigned it in Adobe Illustrator. You will get six pages from your printer. One page for each process color CMYK (4), and one page for each custom color (2). In this case the custom colors are PANTONE WM GY 2CV and PANTONE 5753 CV.

In this example, if you were printing the luggage label at a print shop, six pieces of film would be generated, six printing plates would be created, and the print shop would run the press with six different inks. This example of a print run would be more costly than if you converted the two PANTONE colors to CMYK equivalents. If you converted the PANTONE colors to CMYK, you would have four pieces of film instead of six. You would also have four plates instead of six, and four inks instead of six.

Printing selected separations

If you want to print selected separations, you first select the process or custom color separations you want to print. You will specify to print only one separation below.

To print selected separations:

1 If the Separations dialog box is not already open, choose Separations from the File menu or click Separations in the Separator window to open it.

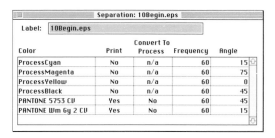

2 In the Print column next to PANTONE 5753 CV, click to change No to Yes. (Clicking *No* changes it to *Yes*, and vice versa.)

3 Make sure the Print column next to PANTONE Wm Gy 2 CV reads *Yes*. Make sure the print column for the other colors reads *No*.

4 Choose Print Selected Separations from the File menu.

5 The program labels each printed separation with the color name assigned it in Adobe Illustrator. The separation files for the custom colors is the output in this example.

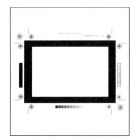 

Converting custom colors to process colors when printing

Imagine that you are working on a tight budget for printing the Navigations luggage label. One option is to convert the two custom colors in the artwork of the label to CMYK. The printer will then create four plates instead of six, and four inks will be used instead of six. Navigations is sure to be pleased with your smart management of the printing process.

You can also convert custom colors to process colors in your artwork for printing only, without affecting the original artwork. The conversion occurs only when you print selected separations, and the colors in your original artwork are not changed. However, if you save your separations using Adobe Separator, any color conversion will be saved in the separation files.

To convert custom colors to process colors when printing:

1 Make sure that the Separations dialog box is open.

2 In the Convert to Process column, click to select Yes next to both PANTONE 5753 CV and PANTONE Wm Gy 2 CV.

3 Choose Print All Separations from the File menu.

When you print your artwork, the Adobe Separator program converts the custom colors to CMYK equivalents and produce four pieces of film or paper.

Note: Your results from converting the custom colors to CMYK equivalents usually will not match the original custom color values exactly.

VIEWING AND PRINTING FILE INFORMATION

You can print a list of specific information about your file with the Get Info option. This is a useful feature if a service bureau will print your files, or if you have to troubleshoot color separation files.

To view and print information about artwork files:

1 Choose Get Info from the File menu. The Get Info dialog box appears.

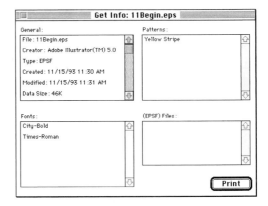

The General, Patterns, Fonts, and (EPSF) Files areas each list information about the file.

2 Scroll through the General area to see the kinds of information it contains.

Information in the Get Info dialog box may be useful to a service bureau when they are printing your separations. You can print the information.

3 Click Print. The Page Setup dialog box appears.

4 Click OK. The Print dialog box appears.

5 Click Print. A progress bar appears as the document information sheet prints.

6 Close the Get Info dialog box.

SAVING YOUR COLOR SEPARATIONS

You've completed all the prep work for saving your color separations. You have printed some sample separations and you may want to save them to disk. Saving the Setup will save PPD information, and any color conversions you may specify in the Separations dialog box. To save selected separations, select the process color and the custom color separations you want to save.

To save separations:

1 Make sure the Separations dialog box is open.

2 Choose Save All Separations from the File menu.

3 Make sure the Project folder is open.

4 Click Save to save each separator file to the Project folder. A dialog box appears and prompts you to save or cancel each separation.

If you choose Save Selected Separations, you will only save those separations that are clicked Yes in the Print column of the Setup dialog box.

After saving, you will have the original Adobe Illustrator file and the four individual PostScript files; in this case, a total of five files. The four Post-Script files can not be opened, but they can be downloaded to a PostScript printer. Be sure to keep the Adobe Separator files together and include all the separation files (in this case four), on the disk you send to the person generating the film on your project.

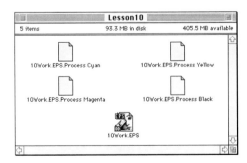

Note: If you use the default file name, the Adobe Separator program will append the file name with its color.

If you'll use a service bureau, consult them to find out if they want you to save the separations. For more detailed information on saving separations, see the *Adobe Illustrator User Guide.*

Right about now, your head is probably swirling from color separation overload as you finish up this lesson. It was a tough road but well worth the travel. Not only can you create fabulous artwork, you can use custom colors and then confidently make color separations for your print shop.

Cleaning up

1 Make sure you are in the Adobe Separator application.

2 Choose Close from the File menu to close all the files. Do not save changes.

3 Choose Quit from the File menu to close the Adobe Separator application.

4 Make sure the Adobe Illustrator application is open.

5 Close any Adobe Illustrator files that may have been open in Lesson 10.

Learning about overprinting, trapping and color separations may seem like a far cry from creating artwork. You're probably ready to get back to designing. In Lesson 11 you can work on the latest edition of the Navigations newsletter, a tabloid with an international flair.

LESSON 11: DESIGNING A NEWSLETTER

Navigations is getting nervous about a decline in their international business due to the increase of discount and cut-rate travel agencies. They have decided to create a unique travel newsletter. Budget restrictions require that they use the same newsletter for many different languages.

They want a high quality graphics presentation with universal themes that can be used as the backdrop of a multilingual newsletter. If you can provide a universal look, they'll provide the text in several languages.

While designing the newsletter, you'll

- work with custom colors

- use color tints

- convert process colors to custom colors

- fit copy into the newsletter

- import and specify type

- learn how to kern type

- use the paint bucket tool and eyedropper tools

- create patterns

It should take you two and a half to three hours to complete this lesson.

PLANNING THE PROJECT

The newsletter contains several pieces of placed art, including the Navigations logo and a vacation photo taken at the beach. Additional artwork includes a cruise ship and a famous Paris landmark, the Arc de Triomphe.

To open the reference file:

1 Open the Lesson 11 folder and the file named *11Final*. The document opens in Preview view.

Take a look at the newsletter to see what its components are. The newsletter consists of three vertical columns for the text, the sidebar containing the contents, and one horizontal row for the logo and title. The dimensions are 11 inches by 17 inches.

Here are a couple of keyboard shortcuts you can try while you look at the document.

2 Double-click the zoom tool in the toolbox. The view is changed to 100%, which is the document's actual size.

3 Use the scroll bars to look at different parts of the newsletter.

4 Double-click the hand tool in the toolbox. The view is changed to Fit In Window.

TIP: DOUBLE-CLICK THE HAND TOOL IN THE TOOLBOX TO FIT THE ARTWORK IN THE WINDOW. DOUBLE-CLICK THE ZOOM TOOL IN THE TOOLBOX TO CHANGE THE VIEW TO ACTUAL SIZE.

5 Resize your window, and drag the final file to a convenient location so you can access it when you need to.

SETTING UP THE DOCUMENT

To set up the document, you choose a page size and orientation, set the ruler origin, and create some guides.

1 Choose New from the File menu (Command-N).

2 Choose Document Setup from the File menu (Command-Shift-D). The Document Setup dialog box appears.

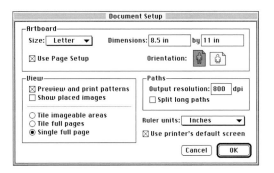

3 Change the page size by choosing Tabloid from the Size pop-up menu.

The page dimensions should be shown in inches (11 by 17). If they are not, change the Ruler Units to Inches and click OK.

4 Choose Fit in Window from the View menu (or double-click the hand tool in the toolbox).

5 Choose Page Setup from the File menu.

6 Enter 58 next to Reduce or Enlarge and click OK.

7 Click the page tool in the toolbox, and center the Artboard inside the page rectangles.

8 Choose Save As from the File menu and save your file as *11Work* in the Project folder.

Defining text and art areas

1 Choose Show Rulers from the View menu (Command-R).

2 Position the pointer in the box where the rulers intersect (in the lower right corner). Hold down the mouse button, and then drag the ruler origin to the lower left corner of the page.

3 Drag a guide from the right ruler to the 2½ inch mark on the bottom ruler.

4 Drag a guide up from the bottom ruler to the 14½ inch mark on the right ruler.

5 Click the rectangle tool in the toolbox.

6 Drag down from the upper left corner of the page along the 2½ inch guide to the bottom of the page to create a narrow column.

7 Position the pointer at the upper right corner of the page. Drag left and down along the 14½ inch right ruler guide to the left edge of the page.

You should have a column on the left edge of the page and a rectangle across the top.

8 Choose Select All from the Edit menu (Command-A).

9 Choose Pathfinder from the Filter menu and Divide Fill from the submenu. This filter divides the two rectangles into three separate objects. Notice the top left corner of the page.

10 Choose Ungroup from the Arrange menu (Command-U).

Drawing a circle

1 Click the oval tool in the toolbox.

2 Hold down the Option key and click the center of the upper left rectangle. The Oval dialog box appears.

3 Enter 1.85 inches for both the Width and Height, and click OK.

4 Click the selection tool in the tool box, and center the circle inside the rectangle.

5 Click away from the artwork to deselect everything.

6 Choose Save from the File menu (Command-S) to save your work.

USING CUSTOM COLORS

Next you'll use custom colors from the PANTONE MATCHING SYSTEM to fill various objects and columns in your newsletter. But first take a look at the Paint Style palette to see what colors are listed on the palette.

To check the color list in the Paint Style palette:

1 Choose Paint Style from the Object menu (Command-I) to open the Paint Style palette.

2 Click the Custom color box (fifth box on the top right side of the palette).

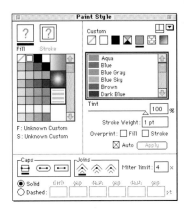

Notice the short list of custom colors on the right side of the palette.

Note: If you have not closed the Adobe Illustrator program since the previous lesson, the PANTONE colors will still all be listed, and you will not have to import them as described in the next section.

3 Double-click the name of any custom color.

The Custom Color dialog box appears. You can use this dialog box to create, name, and edit your own custom colors. For more information about creating custom colors, see the *Adobe Illustrator User Guide.*

4 Click Cancel to close the dialog box.

Next you'll use the Import Styles command to load the PANTONE custom colors.

To import the PANTONE Colors*(coated paper)* into the file:

1 Choose Import Styles from the File menu.

2 Open the Adobe Illustrator 5 folder.

3 Open the Color Systems folder located in the Adobe Illustrator 5 folder.

4 Double-click the file named PANTONE *Colors (coated paper).* The PANTONE Colors (coated paper) information appears in the Paint Style palette. Scroll the list to see them.

To make swatches for the PANTONE colors:

1 Scroll down and click to highlight PANTONE 5757 (green color) in the color list on the right side of the Paint Style palette. The PANTONE colors are listed numerically so you may have to scroll to the bottom of the list to find it.

2 On the left panel of the Paint Style palette, scroll down to the bottom of the paint swatches so that the empty swatches are showing.

3 Hold down the Option key and click the fourth swatch in the last row of empty swatches to load the PANTONE 5757 (green color).

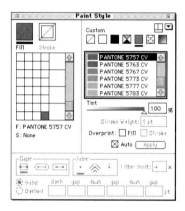

4 In the color list, scroll up this time to find PANTONE 3005 (blue color) and select it.

5 Hold down the Option key and click the empty paint swatch to the left of the PANTONE 5757 (green color) swatch that you just filled.

USING COLOR TINTS

You'll now fill a column and a row in your newsletter with a color tint.

To fill objects with a color tint:

1 Choose Artwork from the View menu (Command-E).

2 Click the selection tool in the toolbox.

3 Select the left edge of the page (the lefthand column).

4 Select the Fill box, and click the PANTONE 5757 green swatch you just created.

5 In the right panel of the Paint Style palette, enter 30 in the Tint box next to the Tint slider, and press Return. This creates a 30 percent screen of your PANTONE 5757 green color.

Although you don't see it in Artwork view, the left column is filled with a tinted custom green color.

6 Click the right edge of the small square in the upper left corner where you'll eventually place your Navigations logo.

7 In the Paint Style palette, click the Fill box and click the Black swatch.

8 Click the top right corner of the page on your Artboard to select the top rectangle (next to the small black rectangle).

9 In the Paint Style palette, click the Fill box, click Custom, and click the PANTONE 3005 blue swatch.

10 Click None for Stroke.

11 Drag the Tint slider to 30%, and press Return. This creates a 30 percent screen of your PANTONE 3005 blue color.

12 With the selection tool, click to select the oval.

13 Click the Fill box and click the White swatch.

14 Click the Stroke box and the None swatch.

15 Choose Preview from the View menu (Command-Y).

16 Choose Save from the File menu (Command-S) to save your work.

COPYING AND PASTING THE LOGO

Next you'll paste the Navigations logo into the upper left corner of the newsletter.

1 Choose Open from the File menu (Command-O).

2 Locate the Lesson 11 folder and the file named *11Logo*.

3 Use the selection tool in the toolbox to select the Navigations logo in the upper right corner of the file.

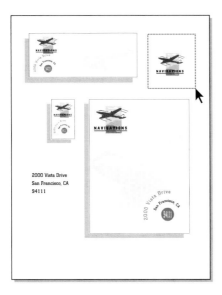

4 Choose Copy from the Edit menu (Command-C) to copy the logo.

5 Close the *11Logo* file.

6 Choose Paste from the File menu (Command-V).

7 With the selection tool, drag the logo to center it in the white oval.

8 Double-click the scale tool in the toolbox, and scale the logo to a Uniform scale of 120%.

9 Marquee zoom in on the white oval.

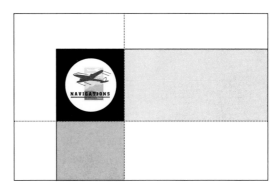

10 Choose Ungroup from the Arrange menu (Command-U).

11 Deselect all the objects (Command-Shift-A).

12 Choose Save from the File menu (Command-S) to save your work.

CONVERTING PROCESS COLORS TO CUSTOM COLORS

In this part of the lesson, you'll paint the different components of your logo with custom colors.

1 Use the selection tool to select the plane in the logo.

2 In the Paint Style palette, click the PANTONE 5757 green swatch to fill the plane. The green tint will stay at 100 percent.

3 Use the selection tool to select the line beneath the word *Navigations* in the logo.

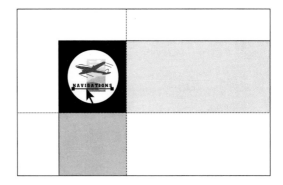

4 In the Paint Style palette, click the Stroke box and then click the PANTONE 5757 green swatch again. The underline becomes green.

5 Use the selection tool to select the mountain in the logo.

6 Click the Fill box and click the PANTONE 5757 green swatch. Enter 30 percent for the tint value. Click None for Stroke, and press Return.

7 Use the selection tool to select the background sky in the logo.

8 Click the Fill box and click the PANTONE 3005 blue swatch. Enter 25 percent for the tint value, and then click None for Stroke. Press Return.

9 Use the selection tool to select the water in the logo.

10 Click the Fill box, click the PANTONE 3005 blue swatch, and then enter 50 percent for the tint value; then press Return.

11 Choose Save from the File menu (Command-S) to save your work.

You have just converted all the components in the logo to PANTONE MATCHING SYSTEM colors from process colors.

COPYING AND SCALING OBJECTS

Next you'll copy and scale the airplane.

1 Click the selection tool in the toolbox.

2 Click the plane to select it.

3 Hold down the Shift key, and click to add the the two white highlights on the plane to the selection. Zoom in if you need a better view.

4 Choose Copy from the Edit menu (Command-C) to copy the plane and its highlights.

5 Double-click the hand tool in the toolbox (or choose Fit In Window from the View menu) to see the entire document.

6 Choose Paste from the Edit menu (Command-V) to paste the plane and its highlights.

7 Choose Group from the Arrange menu (Command-G) to group the selected objects.

8 Double-click the scale tool in the toolbox. The Scale dialog box opens.

9 Enter 600 for Uniform, and click OK.

10 With the selection tool, position the plane in the center of the blue rectangle. Be sure that the bottom of the tail is above the bottom line of the blue box and the upper wing overlaps the top of the page.

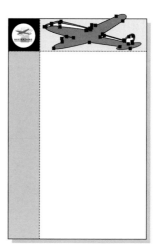

11 Choose Save from the File menu (Command-S) to save your work.

USING THE DIVIDE FILL FILTER

Next, you'll delete part of the plane's wing using the Divide Fill filter.

To use the Divide Fill filter:

1 Use the selection tool and the Shift key to add the blue box to the selection of the plane.

2 Choose Pathfinder from the Filter menu and Divide Fill. This filter creates independent areas, undivided by line segments that you can manipulate independently. The divided objects are grouped.

3 Choose Ungroup from the Arrange menu (Command-U).

4 Deselect all the objects (Command-Shift-A).

5 Use the selection tool to select the upper wing tip of the plane.

6 Press the Delete key to delete the upper wing tip.

7 Use the direct selection tool to select the plane. You need the direct selection tool because the plane is still grouped with the highlights.

8 In the Paint Style palette, click the Fill box, click the PANTONE 5757 green swatch, and then enter 30 percent for the tint value. Press Return.

9 Choose Select None from the Edit menu (Command-Shift-A) to deselect everything.

10 Use the direct selection tool and the Shift key to select the two white highlights of the plane.

11 In the Paint Style palette, click the Black swatch, and then enter 5 percent for the tint value. Press Return.

12 Choose Save from the File menu (Command-S) to save your work.

CREATING THE TRAVEL NEWS TITLE

Next you'll specify the type for the name, place the name, and then *kern*, or adjust the spacing, between two letters in the name.

1 Marquee zoom in on the rectangle containing the plane at the top of the page.

2 Click the type tool in the toolbox.

3 Click above the page and type **TRAVEL** (all uppercase letters), and press the Return key.

4 Type **News.**

5 Choose Select All from the Edit menu (Command-A).

6 Choose Character from the Type menu (Command-T). The Character palette appears.

7 Set the font to Madrone Regular and set the size to 57 points.

8 Make sure that Auto leading is checked, and press Return.

9 Choose Alignment from the Type menu and Center from the submenu (Command-Shift-C).

10 Drag to select the word News.

11 Set the font to Bellevue Regular.

TIP: COMMAND SHORT-
CUTS CAN BE USED TO
ADJUST KERNING. TO
KERN IN 100/1000 OF
AN EM SPACE, PRESS
THE OPTION AND
COMMAND KEYS AND
USE THE ARROW KEYS.
TO KERN IN 20/1000 OF
AN EM SPACE, PRESS
THE OPTION KEY AND
USE ARROW KEYS.

Kerning type

Take a closer look at the letters in the word *Travel*. There is too much space between the *A* and *V*. You'll *kern* the type, or adjust the space between two characters. See the *Adobe Illustrator User Guide* for more information on kerning.

To kern type:

1 Click to set an insertion point between the letters *A* and *V*.

2 In the Character palette, click the lever on the lower right corner of the palette to expand the palette.

3 Enter -400 (minus 400) in the Kerning text box and Press Return. The letters are moved closer together.

You can also use keyboard commands to kern.

4 Click between the letters *R* and *A*.

5 Hold down the Option key and press the left arrow key four times. Notice the value in the Kerning text box changes (in -20 increments) to -80 /1000 em.

6 Click the type tool in the toolbox to select the entire text object.

7 Use the selection tool to position the words *Travel News* in the center of the blue rectangle at the top of the page.

8 Choose Save from the File menu (Command-S) to save your work.

CREATING GUIDES FOR THE TEXT GRID

Next you'll set some guides in the columns of your newsletter before placing text in it.

1 Double-click the hand tool or choose Fit In Window from the View menu.

2 Drag a right ruler guide left to the 3 inch mark on the bottom ruler.

3 Drag a second right ruler guide left to the 6½ inch mark on the bottom ruler.

4 Drag a third right ruler guide left to the 7 inch mark on the bottom ruler.

5 Drag a fourth right ruler guide left to the 10½ inch mark on the bottom ruler.

6 Drag a ruler guide up from the bottom ruler to the ½ inch mark on the right ruler.

7 Drag a second ruler guide up from the bottom ruler to the 10 inch mark on the right ruler.

8 Drag a guide up from the bottom ruler to the 13½ inch right ruler mark.

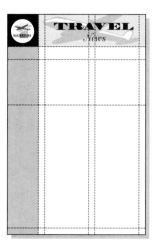

9 Choose Save from the File menu (Command-S) to save your work.

MAKING THE TEXT COLUMNS

You'll now make the columns in your newsletter where you'll place text.

1 Click the rectangle tool in the toolbox.

2 Click anywhere on the left side of the page.

3 Enter 3.5 for the Width and 9 for the Height, and click OK.

4 Use the selection tool to position the rectangle so that it sits on the ½ inch bottom ruler guide between the 3 inch and the 6½ inch vertical guides.

5 In the Paint style palette, click None for Fill and Black for Stroke.

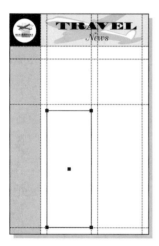

6 Use the rectangle tool, and click anywhere on the right side of the page.

7 Enter 3.5 for the Width and 13 for Height, and click OK.

8 Use the selection tool to position the rectangle so that the bottom corner aligns at the ½ inch bottom ruler guide and the 10½ inch vertical guide.

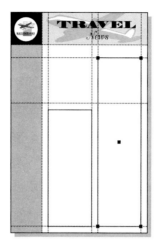

9 Use the rectangle took, and click near the left side of the page.

10 Enter 5.5 for the Width and 3.5 for the Height, and click OK.

11 Use the selection tool to position the rectangle so that it sits on the 10 inch horizontal guide and the right edge aligns with the 6½ inch vertical guide.

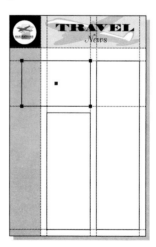

12 Choose Save from the File menu (Command-S) to save your work.

IMPORTING AND SPECIFYING TYPE

With the layout of your newsletter complete, you'll import some text files and specify the type for the text.

To import type:

1 Click the type tool in the toolbox.

2 Position the pointer just inside the edge of the upper left corner of the lower left column, and click when the round dotted line appears around the I-beam cursor. (Make sure that you don't click in the rectangle above the text column.)

The outline of the rectangular box disappears.

3 Choose Import Text from the File menu and open the file named *11Text1*. Some Italian copy appears in the text rectangle.

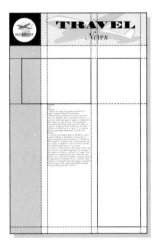

To specify type:

1 Marquee zoom in on the text.

2 Choose Select All from the Edit menu (Command-A) to select all the text.

3 Press Command-T to open the Character palette.

4 Set the font to AGaramond Regular, set the size to 16 points, set the leading to 20 points, set the tracking to -30, and press Return.

5 Choose Paragraph from the Type menu (Command-Shift-T). The Paragraph palette appears.

6 Under Alignment, click justified type (second box from the right).

When you *justify* type, you space lines of text so that the lines come out even at both margins.

7 Under Indentation, set the following values then press Return:

Left: 0
Right: 0
First line: 18

These values *indent,* or set in from the margin, only the first line of the text by 18 points. The remaining text is not be indented.

8 Click the Auto hyphenate check box.

The text is automatically hyphenated so that it fits in the text column.

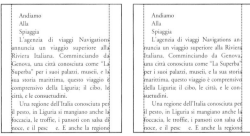

Before   *After*

Adjusting the title and the first line of text

You'll now adjust the title and the first line of the text in the column.

1 Click the type tool in the toolbox.

2 Hold down the mouse button and drag to select the first four lines of type.

3 In the Paragraph palette under Indentation, set the First line to 0.

4 With the type tool, drag to select the first three lines of text (the title).

5 With the top three lines selected, set the font to Madrone, set the size to 16 points, set the leading to 20 points, set the tracking to -30.

6 Click before the word *Alla*, and press Delete. The word is moved up to the top line of the headline.

7 Press the Space bar one time. This action places a space between the words.

Notice that the line changes.

Before   *After*

8 Choose Save from the File menu (Command-S) to save your work.

To import type into the right column:

1 Choose Fit In Window from the View menu (Command-M).

2 Click the type tool in the toolbox.

3 Position the cursor in the upper left corner of the right column, and click when the round dotted line appears around the I-beam cursor. Make sure that you don't click in the rectangle above the text column.

4 Choose Import Text from the File menu and open the file named *11Text2*. Some French copy appears in the text rectangle.

To specify type:

1 Marquee zoom in on the top of the right text column.

2 Choose Select All from the Edit menu (Command-A) to select all the text.

3 Set the font to AGaramond Regular, set the size to 16 points, set the leading to 20 points, set the tracking to -30, and press Return.

4 Choose Paragraph from the Type menu (Command-Shift-T). The Paragraph palette appears.

5 Under Alignment, click justified type (second box from the right).

6 Under Indentation, set the following values and then press Return:

Left: 0
Right: 0
First line: 18

7 Make sure the Auto hyphenate box is checked.

The text is automatically hyphenated so that it fits in the text column.

Before   *After*

Adjusting the right column title and text

You'll now adjust the title of the text in the right column.

1 Click the type tool in the toolbox.

2 Hold down the mouse button and drag to select the first four lines of type.

3 In the Paragraph palette under Indentation, set the First line to 0.

4 Hold down the mouse button and drag to select the top three lines of type.

5 With the top three lines selected, set the font to Madrone, set the size to 16 points, set the leading to 20 points, set the tracking to -30, and press Return.

6 Click before the word La, and press Delete.

7 Press the Space bar one time.

Notice that the line breaks.

Before   *After*

8 Double-click the Hand tool (or Choose Fit in Window from the View menu.

9 Choose Save from the File menu (Command-S) to save your work.

IMPORTING GRAPHICS

With the text now placed in your newsletter, you'll import some graphics to stimulate the travel appetites of your prospective clients for some far-away adventures. Then you'll mask the photos. These photos were scanned and turned into duotones in Adobe Photoshop.

To import the beach photo:

1 Click the selection tool in the toolbox, and then choose Place Art from the File menu.

2 Select 11*Beach* and click Place.

3 Use the selection tool to drag the photo into the box above the left column of text.

4 Choose Send To Back from the Arrange menu (Command-hyphen) to send the photo to the background.

To mask the photo:

1 Hold down the Shift key and click the outer rectangle so that both objects are selected.

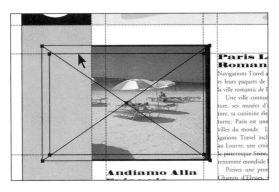

2 Choose Masks from the Object menu and Make from the submenu.

To import the Arc de Triomphe photo:

1 Choose Place Art from the File menu.

2 Select *11Arch* and click Place.

3 Use the selection tool to drag the photo left and off the page.

4 Click the oval tool in the tool box.

5 Hold down the Option key and click the center of the photo.

6 Set the Width and Height of the circle to 3.3, and then click OK.

7 Use the selection tool to make sure that the circle is centered on the photo.

8 Hold down the Shift key and click the photo so that both the circle and the photo are selected.

To mask the photo:

1 Choose Masks from the Object menu and Make from the submenu.

2 Deselect the selection.

You'll make a slightly larger circle and group it with the type. This circle will provide a nice border around the round photo when the type is wrapped around it.

3 Select the circle outline.

4 Choose Copy (Command-C) from the Edit menu.

5 Choose Paste In Front (Command-F) from the Edit menu. The new circle is pasted right on top of the other circle.

6 Double-click the scale tool in the toolbox.

7 Set Uniform to 120 and click OK.

8 Use the selection tool to select the photo mask, outer circle, and inner circle.

9 Choose Group from the Arrange menu (Command-G) to group the objects.

10 Drag the grouped circle to the center on top of the two text columns at the 1/2 inch guide line.

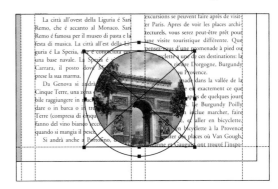

To wrap type:

1 Hold down the Shift key and select the left text column, then add the right text column. Make sure the grouped circles and the two columns are selected.

2 Choose Make Wrap from the Type menu. The type is wrapped around the outer circle around the photo.

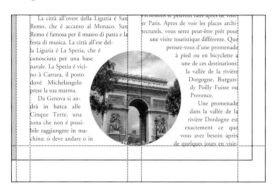

Note: When you wrap type, the object must be in front of the type in the stacking order.

3 Choose Select None from the Edit menu (Command-Shift-A).

4 Choose Save from the File menu (Command-S) to save your work.

Creating a dividing line between text columns

Between the two text columns, you'll now add a dividing line in the *gutter*, or white space adjoining two margins.

1 Click the pen tool in the toolbox.

2 Click the top center of the gutter at the 13½ inch vertical guide.

3 Hold down the Shift key, and then click at the 4¼ inch horizontal guide (top of the arc) in the center of the gutter.

4 In the Paint Style palette, click the Stroke box, click the Black swatch, and set the Stroke Weight to 1 point.

5 Use the selection tool and center the line in the gutter if needed.

6 Choose Save from the File menu (Command-S) to save your work.

CREATING AND PLACING TYPE

You'll now place some type above the beach photo.

1 Scroll up a little so that the area above the beach photo is visible.

2 Click the type tool in the toolbox.

3 Click the area above the beach photo.

4 Type **Volume 1**, space, press Option-8 (to make a bullet), space, and type **Spring 1994** (no period).

5 Choose Select All from the Edit menu (Command-A).

6 In the Character palette, set the font to Madrone, set the size to 18 points, and then set the tracking to 180.

7 Click the Fill box, click the PANTONE 5757 green swatch, and then set the tint to 60 percent.

8 Make sure that the Stroke box is set to None.

9 Use the selection tool and drag to center the type above the beach photo and below the blue plane rectangle.

10 Choose Save from the File menu (Command-S) to save your work.

Placing and filling the sidebar rectangles

Notice the sidebar in the lower left corner of the final file. You'll create the sidebar now.

To fill the sidebar with a custom color:

1 Double-click the hand tool (or choose Command-M) so you can see the entire file.

2 Click the rectangle tool in the toolbox.

3 Click to the left of the page, enter 2 for the Width and 4.5 for the Height, and click OK.

4 In the Paint Style palette, click Fill, click the PANTONE 5757 green swatch, and then set the tint to 10 percent. Press Return.

The sidebar rectangle is filled with light green.

5 Marquee zoom in on the sidebar rectangle you just made.

6 Click the rectangle tool in the toolbox.

7 Click the top left corner of the new rectangle, enter 2 for the Width and .5 for the Height, and click OK.

8 In the Paint Style palette, click Fill, click the Black swatch, and then set the tint to 75 percent. Press Return.

The smaller rectangle on top of the side bar rectangle is filled with black.

9 If needed, use the selection tool to center the smaller rectangle so that it sits directly on top of the large rectangle.

10 Choose Save from the File menu (Command-S) to save your work.

Importing, filling, and placing text

You'll now import some text into your sidebar and fill the text with a custom color.

To import, fill, and place text:

1 Click the rectangle tool in the toolbox.

2 Click to the left of the sidebar rectangle. The rectangle dialog box appears.

3 Enter 2.3 for the Width and 4.5 for the Height, and click OK.

4 Click the type tool in the toolbox.

5 Position the pointer on the left edge of the rectangle, and click the mouse button.

6 Choose Import Text from the File menu and open the file named *11Text3*.

7 Choose Select All from the Edit menu (Command-A) to select all the text.

8 In the Character palette, set the font to Madrone Regular, set the size to 9, set the leading to 13, set the tracking to 0. Press Return.

9 Choose Alignment from the Type menu and Center from the submenu.

10 Click the type tool in the toolbox.

11 Hold down the mouse button and drag to select the word "Contents."

If the word *contents* does not fit on one line, you can switch to Artwork view, and use the direct selection tool to drag the right edge of the rectangle to the right to increase the width. Then return to Preview.

12 In the Character palette, set the size to 10 points and press Return.

13 In the Paint Style palette, click the Fill box, and then click the White swatch to fill the word *Contents* with white.

14 With the selection tool, click the Contents text box, drag the text to the sidebar rectangle and center the word *Contents* on the black rectangle.

15 With the selection tool, drag a narrow rectangle over the left edge of the new text shape and two rectangles.

16 Choose Group from the Arrange menu (Command-G).

17 Double-click the hand tool or choose Fit In Window from the View menu.

18 Use the selection tool to drag the sidebar with the text you just created so that the right edge of the green rectangle aligns with the 2½ inch right ruler guide, and the lower edge of the sidebar sits on the ½ inch bottom ruler guide.

19 Choose Save from the File menu (Command-S) to save your work.

Time out for a hot tip

As you work in the Adobe Illustrator program, you'll open and close many of the palettes during a work session. If you have a small screen, you need to close some palettes before you open others. You can use keyboard commands to close the palettes. The same keyboard command that opens a palette will close it. You can open the Paint Style palette by pressing Command-I. If the palette is already open, you can close it by pressing Command-I. This is also true for other palettes. Give it a try.

PLACING, SIZING, AND ROTATING A GRAPHIC

You'll add the final artistic flair to your newsletter by placing, sizing, and then rotating the cruise ship in the center of the newsletter.

1 Choose Place Art from the File menu, select *11Boat*, and then click Place.

2 Use the selection tool and drag to center the cruise ship on the two columns of text.

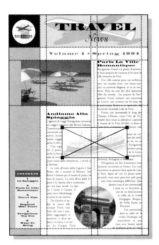

The Info palette shows the horizontal and vertical distance traveled from the *x* and *y* axes, the absolute horizontal and vertical distance measured, and the angle measured. In addition to simple measuring, the Info palette is useful for checking a scale factor. One way to access the Info palette is to choose Show Info from the Window.

Another way to see the Info palette is to click the measure tool in the toolbox and click or drag in the drawing area. Although you won't measure anything right now, you'll use the shortcut to open the Info palette to help you scale the cruise ship.

3 Click the measure tool in the toolbox.

4 Click anywhere on the page. The Info palette appears.

5 Click the scale tool in the toolbox.

6 Click the upper left corner of the cruise ship box, hold down the Shift key, drag diagonally up and left, and watch until the percent value (in the third column in the Info palette) gets close to 130 percent.

| X: 4.253 in | W: 6.668 in | W: 130.11% |
| Y: 8.431 in | H: 3.036 in | H: 130.11% |

To rotate the graphic:

1 Click the rotate tool in the toolbox.

2 Click the lower left corner of the cruise ship box, hold down the mouse button and drag diagonally up. Watch the third column in the Info palette, and drag until the percent value gets close to 17 degrees. (It's a little difficult to get the exact angle, so close to 17 degrees will be okay.) The cruise ship is now rotated.

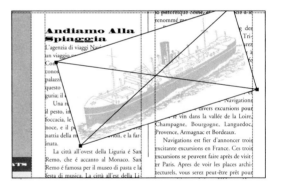

3 Use the selection tool and drag the cruise ship so that it is centered on the two columns of text.

4 Choose Send to Back from the Arrange menu (Command-hyphen).

5 Zoom in to see your cruise ship floating in a sea of text.

6 Choose Save from the File menu (Command-S) to save your work.

Note: If you click the Type tool in the toolbox while the Info palette is open, you'll see type characteristics of the last type you created. If you use the Type tool to select some type, you'll see some of the attributes of the selected type.

CREATING PATTERNS

The Adobe Illustrator program builds a pattern from a pattern tile, which consists of a pattern object (or artwork) surrounded by a rectangle, called a bounding rectangle. The bounding rectangle becomes the pattern's background. The rectangle must have square corners to tile properly and must be the backmost object in the stacking order.

You can create patterns from scratch with any of the tools in the Adobe Illustrator program. Once you create a pattern, you can customize it by resizing the pattern, moving or transforming it, or coloring its objects.

While creating the pattern, you'll get some practice using the eyedropper and paint bucket tools.

Creating a rectangle for a pattern

1 Choose Fit in Window from the View menu.

2 Scroll to the right side of the newsletter and make sure you have some empty space to work in.

3 Choose Select None from the Edit menu.

4 Make sure the Paint Style palette is open, the Fill box is selected with a fill color of white.

You will create a few patterns and then apply those patterns to the leftmost vertical column of the newsletter.

5 Select the rectangle tool in the toolbox.

6 Click in the white area to the right of the newsletter. The Rectangle dialog box appears.

7 Type 1 for Width, click on the word Height and click OK.

Using the eyedropper and paint bucket tools

You can use the eyedropper tool to copy attributes from an object to the Paint Style palette, and the paint bucket tool to apply the current paint attributes to an object.

Together, these tools let you copy the paint attributes from one object in your artwork to other objects in the same or in different documents. You can use these tools with the Paint Style palette open or closed.

1 Click the eyedropper tool in the toolbox.

2 Click the large light green plane in the headline to select the color.

Next you'll use the paint bucket tool to copy the paint attributes from one object in your artwork to another.

3 In the Paint Style palette make sure Fill is selected and Stroke is None.

Note: The fill color should be the green color you just selected with the eyedropper tool.

4 Click the paint bucket tool in the toolbox.

5 Position the paint bucket tool over the rectangle you just created and click. The rectangle is now filled with green.

Creating an airplane pattern

1 Click the selection tool in the toolbox.

2 Click to select the plane in the logo located in the top left corner of the newsletter. Zoom in if you need to.

3 Begin to drag down and right to the location of the rectangle you just created, then hold down the Option key to make a copy.

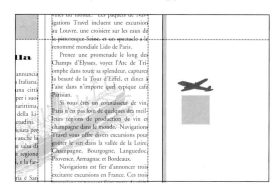

4 With the plane selected, click the scale tool in the toolbox.

5 Hold down the Option key and click on the copy of the plane. The Scale dialog box appears.

6 Type 75 for Uniform and click OK.

7 Marquee zoom in on the area of the plane and the rectangle.

8 With the selection tool, drag the plane over the rectangle.

Keep in mind that you are creating a pattern tile with the rectangle and the airplane.

Because the logo was created before the rectangle, you must change the stacking order by bringing the plane in front of the rectangle.

9 Choose Bring to Front from the Arrange menu.

10 With the selection tool, drag a marquee around the rectangle with the plane to select both the objects.

11 Choose Pattern from the Object menu. The Pattern dialog box appears.

12 Click New. Notice the preview of the pattern.

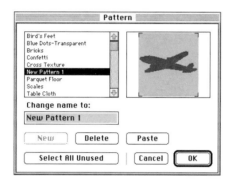

13 Type **My Plane Pattern** for the pattern name and click OK.

14 Choose Fit In Window from the View menu.

Applying the pattern to the newsletter

1 With the selection tool, click the left green column of the newsletter.

2 In the Paint Style palette make sure that the Fill box is selected and Stroke is None.

3 In the right side of the Paint Style palette, click the Pattern box.

4 Scroll and select *My Plane Pattern*. Notice the plane pattern fills the area of the column.

Transforming the plane pattern

1 With the pattern fill column selected, double-click the scale tool in the toolbox. The Scale dialog box appears.

2 Type 50 for Uniform. Click to deselect Objects, and make sure Pattern Tiles is checked. Click OK. Notice the plane pattern has been scaled down 50%.

3 With the pattern column selected double-click the rotate tool in the toolbox. The Rotate dialog box appears.

4 Type -45 (minus 45) and click to deselect Objects. Make sure Pattern Tiles is checked, and click OK. Notice the plane pattern has been rotated.

Now that you've had some practice with patterns, you'll repaint the rectangle.

5 In the Paint Style palette, click the Custom box and click the PANTONE 5757 CV green swatch.

6 Set the tint to 30 and press Return.

7 Choose Save from the File menu (Command-S).

Cleaning up

1 Choose Fit in Window from the View menu (Command-M).

2 With the selection tool, drag a selection marquee around the pattern tile (plane in rectangle) in the Artboard area to select it.

3 Press the Delete key. Although you have deleted the pattern artwork, the pattern is still retained with the file in the pattern list.

4 Choose Select None from the Edit menu.

5 Close all the files except the *11Work* file.

Printing the newsletter

You'll now print your newsletter. If you have a printer that can handle tabloid-sized paper, you can print the document at 100%.

If your printer handles letter-sized paper, you can print the document at the 58% reduction.

To print the document:

1 Choose Page Setup from the File menu.

2 Check the Reduce or Enlarge percentage. To print on letter-sized paper make sure that 58 is the percent next to Reduce or Enlarge and click OK.

3 Select the page tool in the toolbox.

4 Position the pointer on the page and surround the newsletter.

5 Choose Print from the File menu (Command-P). The Print dialog box appears.

6 Click Print.

7 Close the file.

CREATING A CUSTOMIZED WORK FILE

Patterns, graph designs, gradients, and custom colors are always saved with a document when you save a file.

In this part of the lesson you'll make a customized file that contains some of the special elements you've created just for Navigations. This file will be useful if you want to begin another project and use any of these elements.

Note: Although you won't change them here, the Document Setup, Page Setup, zoom level, window size, and viewing options are also saved with the file.

First you'll quit the Adobe Illustrator program and then re-open it, so you'll be starting with a file that has no extra added ingredients.

You'll begin by opening a new file. Then you'll import the other elements into it.

To create a clean file:

1 Choose Quit from the File menu.

2 Restart the Adobe Illustrator program.

3 Choose Save from the File menu.

4 Name the file *Navigate* and save it in the Project folder.

5 Click the graph tool in the toolbox.

6 Drag to draw a graph of any size.

7 Click OK in the Graph Data dialog box.

8 Choose Graphs from the Object menu and Design from the submenu.

Notice that no graph designs are listed.

9 Click OK to close the dialog box.

To import styles:

1 Choose Import Styles from the File menu.

2 In the dialog box, locate the file named 08Work and click Import.

Note: If you didn't complete Lesson 8, you can use the file named 08Final.

The styles from that file are imported into the current file.

3 Choose Graphs from the Object menu and Design from the submenu. The graph designs from the Lesson 8 file are now available and are a part of the current file. You can click the design name to see a preview. Click Cancel.

4 Choose Import Styles from the File menu.

5 Locate the file named 11Final and click Import.

6 Click the Custom box in the Paint Style palette.

7 Scroll through the list and notice that the PANTONE colors are now listed.

Note: If you import the PANTONE or other color files into any file you can easily delete the unused colors. Choose Custom Color from the Object menu, and click Select All Unused. Click delete and click OK.

8 Choose Save from the File menu and click OK.

9 Close the file.

As you can see, making your own files with specific designs, colors, and patterns is a snap.

You're almost to the end of your Navigations journey. In the next lesson you'll review a lot of the techniques you've learned while creating a background for a multimedia presentation. You'll see how you can use other Adobe applications to create even more exciting visual effects.

LESSON 12: DESIGNING WITH OTHER ADOBE APPLICATIONS

A combination of Adobe Systems products is perfect for multimedia presentations. You'll see a preview of the possibilities of combining Adobe Systems applications such as Adobe Illustrator, Adobe Premiere™, Adobe Photoshop™, Adobe Streamline™, Adobe Dimensions, and Adobe Acrobat™ to design a presentation. While designing with other Adobe Systems applications, you'll

- review the pen tool techniques

- import files from Adobe Streamline and Adobe Dimensions

- use new filters and build on filters you've already used in previous lessons

- learn more advanced gradient techniques

It should take you about 2½ to 3 hours to complete this lesson.

BEGINNING THIS LESSON

First you'll run a demo containing a multimedia presentation created for Navigations. The demo shows the front lobby of Navigations with two video screens. One screen is displaying a spinning globe while the other shows a deliriously happy client who has just returned from a vacation arranged by Navigations.

The drawing components in this demo were created with products from Adobe Systems. The globe was created in Adobe Dimensions and exported into Adobe Illustrator. The globe's ribbon and type were added in Adobe Illustrator, and then the entire globe file was saved as an EPS file in Illustrator. The videos displaying on the pillars were created in Adobe Premiere. The photo of the palm tree in the background was screened back using Adobe Photoshop, opened in Adobe Streamline for automatic tracing, and then brought into Adobe Illustrator. The Adobe Illustrator file and the Adobe Premiere files were then assembled using MacroMind Director™ (which is not an Adobe Systems product).

This lesson provides step-by-step instructions for creating some of the elements that were used in the multimedia presentation.

Note: *You will* not *design an actual multimedia presentation, but you will create some of the elements used in the demo.*

RUNNING THE DEMO

If you are running System 7 or higher, you can run the demo.

1 From the Adobe Illustrator icon in the title bar, hold down the mouse button, and drag to choose Finder.

2 Locate the Adobe Illustrator CIB folder, and double-click to open it.

3 Double-click to open the Lesson 12 folder.

4 Double-click to open the Lesson 12 Demo folder.

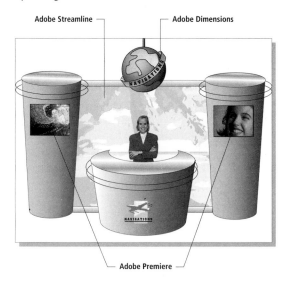

5 Double-click the file named *12Demo*. This file was assembled in MacroMind Director.

The multimedia QuickTime movie now plays in the file that was created in Adobe Illustrator.

6 After you are done watching the demo, press Command-period to quit.

7 To return to the Adobe Illustrator program, position the pointer on the Finder icon in the title bar, hold down the mouse button and drag to select Adobe Illustrator.

PLANNING THE PROJECT

Now that you've run the demo and have seen just a glimpse of what multimedia is all about, you'll have the opportunity to create in Adobe Illustrator the background artwork for a multimedia presentation.

1 Open the Lesson 12 folder and the file named *12Final*.

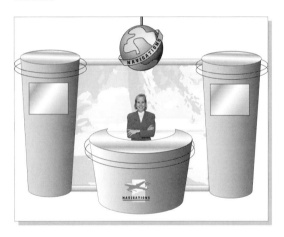

Take a look at the file to see what the drawing components are.

You created some of the components and effects in previous lessons. The beach photo creates a backdrop with a travel flair for the lobby. The Navigations logo creates an accent on the front of the counter. The counter, video screens, and pillar top all have highlights. Any highlights will be drawn after the underlying object has been created. In addition, the Navigations globe has a 3D effect.

2 Choose Artwork from the View menu (Command-E), and take a look at the paths in the drawing.

3 Choose Preview from the View menu (Command-Y).

4 Resize the window to make it smaller.

5 Choose Fit in Window from the View menu (Command-M).

6 Drag the image to a convenient location on your screen.

SETTING UP THE DRAWING AREA

Before you can lay out your presentation, you'll set up your page size, image orientation, and ruler guides.

To open the working file:

1 Choose New from the File menu Command-N).

2 Choose Fit in Window from the View menu (Command-M).

3 Choose Page Setup from the File menu.

4 Click the landscape orientation icon (the second icon), and click OK.

To create ruler guides:

1 Choose Show Rulers from the View menu (Command-R).

2 Hold down the mouse button and drag the ruler origin from the ruler to the lower right corner of the page.

3 Position the pointer inside the bottom ruler, and drag one guide up to 6¾ inches.

4 From the bottom ruler, drag a second guide up to 1¼ inches.

5 Position the pointer in the right ruler and drag one guide left to 8½ inches

6 From the right ruler drag a second guide left to 2½ inches.

This lays out the placement of the photo backdrop.

7 Choose Save As from the File menu, locate the Project folder, and name the file *12Work*.

PLACING A BACK WALL INTO THE LOBBY

The wall in the background of the lobby is actually one of the photos you worked with in an earlier lesson. The photo is an Adobe Photoshop scan that was brought into Adobe Streamline and then saved as an Adobe Illustrator file.

Adobe Streamline is a software application that will quickly convert any black-and-white bitmapped image or color-pixel image into flexible PostScript language line art. Once the images are converted, you can edit them any way you want or scale them to size while their lines stay sharp and clear.

In this part of the lesson, you'll place the photo into your working file. But before you do that, you'll watch an Adobe Teach movie that shows you how the photo was converted in Adobe Streamline.

 If you are able to run Adobe Teach movies on your system, play the movie named *Adobe Teach 6*. For information on how to play Adobe Teach movies, see the "Getting Started" chapter at the beginning of this book.

To place a streamlined image:

1 Make sure the *12Work* file is selected.

2 Choose Open from the File menu.

3 Locate the Lesson 12 folder and select the file name *12Palm* and click Open.

This file was converted from a pixel based scanned photograph to line art in Adobe Streamline.

4 Choose Select All from the Edit menu (Command-A).

5 Choose Group from the Arrange menu (Command-G).

6 Copy the palm art image.

7 Close the *12palm.art* file.

8 Paste the palm art image into the *12Work* file.

9 With the selection tool, center the illustration between the left and right bottom guides.

10 Move the illustration so that the bottom edge of the artwork is flush with the 1¼ inch right ruler guide.

Note: The Auto Color swatches in the Paint Style palette are saved with the Adobe Streamline image so that you have those color values at your finger tips to use in Adobe Illustrator.

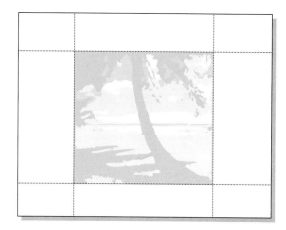

11 Choose Save from the File menu (Command-S) to save your work.

12 Click the rectangle tool in the toolbox, and click on the top left corner of the palm illustration.

13 Enter 6 inches for Width. Enter .25 for Height, and click OK.

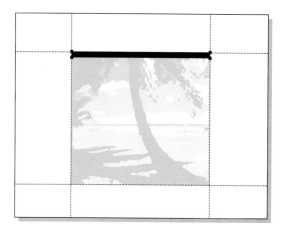

The bar should be aligned with the top edge of the photo.

To color with a gradient fill:

1 Press Command-I, click Fill in the Paint Style palette, and click the Gradient box.

2 Click Black & White in the gradient list.

3 Click the Stroke box and click Black.

4 Enter .5 for the Stroke Weight and press Return.

5 Zoom in to 100 percent.

6 Click the gradient vector tool in the toolbox.

7 Position the pointer at the top center of the bar, hold down the Shift key, and drag straight down to approximately ⅛ of an inch below the bar.

8 Click the selection tool in the toolbox.

9 Click to select the bar; hold down the Option key, start to drag, then hold down the Shift key, and drag a copy of the bar to the bottom of the Artboard so that the bottom edge of the bar aligns with the bottom edge of the illustration. As you drag down, the window will scroll.

10 Choose Zoom Out from the View menu.

11 Choose Save from the File menu (Command-S) to save your work.

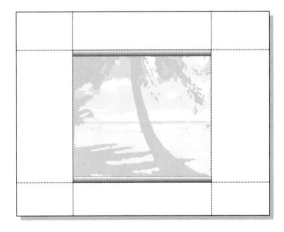

MAKING THE VIDEO PILLARS

With the background wall now in place, you'll begin creating the video pillars for the lobby.

1 Click the rectangle tool in the toolbox.

2 Move the pointer to the left of the palm art in the drawing area, and click the mouse button.

3 Enter 2.6 for the Width.

4 Enter 5.5 for the Height and click OK.

5 In the Paint Style palette, click the Fill box, then click the None swatch.

6 Click the Stroke box in the Paint Style palette. Make sure that Black is selected.

7 Set the Stroke Weight is .5 and press Return.

8 Click the oval tool in the toolbox.

9 Position the pointer in a white area above the rectangle, click and then release the mouse button.

10 Enter 2.6 for the Width. Enter .6 for the Height, and click OK.

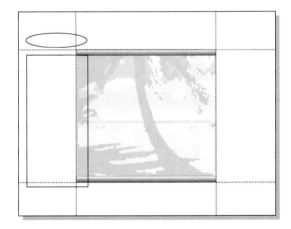

Moving the oval

1 Click the selection tool in the toolbox.

2 Position the pointer on the center point of the oval.

3 Hold down the mouse button and drag until the oval centers on the bottom line of the pillar.

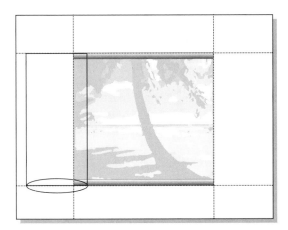

4 Position the pointer on the center point of the oval.

5 Hold down the Option key, start to drag, then press the Shift key. Drag up until the second oval centers on the top line of the rectangle.

6 Position the pointer on the center point of the oval.

7 Hold down the Option key; start to drag, then press the Shift key, drag upwards and position the third oval above the pillar in a white area.

8 Deselect everything.

Uniting the pillar parts

You'll now put together the pieces you've created to form the video pillar by using one of the Pathfinder filters with the Unite filter.

Note: *The Pathfinder filters (including the Unite filter) require a math coprocessor and cannot be installed nor run without one.*

To unite the pillar parts using the Pathfinder filter:

1 Select the lower two ovals and the rectangle.

Note: *Do not select the top oval above the pillar.*

2 With the pillar parts selected, choose Pathfinder from the Filter menu and Unite from the submenu.

3 Choose Select None from the Edit menu (Command-Shift-A).

4 Choose Save from the File menu (Command-S) to save your work.

CHANGING THE PILLAR SHAPE

You're now going to use the Free Distort filter to *pinch* the bottom of the pillar inward. This filter lets you change the size and shape of an object by dragging the corner points in a Distort box. As you drag the corner points of the box, the object's shape is distorted accordingly.

To distort the pillar:

1 Select the pillar.

2 Choose Distort from the Filter menu and Free Distort from the submenu.

3 Click the bottom left anchor point.

4 Move the anchor point in about $\frac{1}{8}$ to $\frac{1}{16}$ of an inch.

5 Repeat steps 3 and 4 for the bottom right anchor point.

6 Click OK.

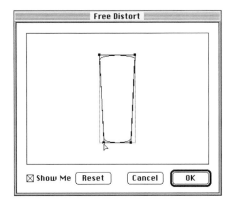

PAINTING THE PILLAR

You'll paint the pillar with a gradient fill.

To create a gradient:

1 Choose Select None from the Edit menu (Command-Shift-A) to deselect everything.

2 Choose Gradient from the Object menu. The Gradient palette appears.

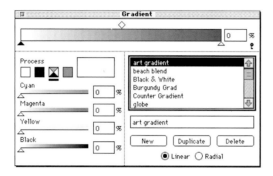

3 Click New and type **MyPillar** for the gradient name.

4 Click the Process box.

5 Make sure the triangle at the left end of the gradient bar is selected, define the starting color as follows;

 Cyan.......... 29 %
 Magenta...... 0 %
 Yellow.......... 8 %
 Black .... 12 %

6 Press Return when you have finished.

7 Click the triangle at the right end of the gradient bar to select it for defining the ending color of the gradient.

8 Click the Process box in the Gradient palette and set the ending color as follows:

 Cyan.......... 89 %
 Magenta.... 56 %
 Yellow.......... 0 %
 Black .... 66 %

9 Press Return when you have finished.

10 Move the center diamond above the gradient bar to the right to 70% .

11 Close the Gradient palette.

12 Choose Save from the File menu (Command-S) to save your work.

To apply the gradient fill:

1 Use the selection tool to select the pillar you just created.

2 Make sure the Paint Style palette is open.

3 Click the Fill box and click to select the Gradient box.

4 Click *MyPillar* in the list, and press Return.

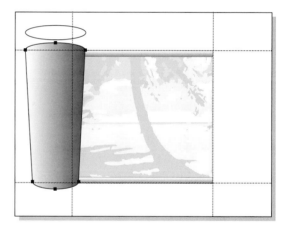

The selected pillar is filled with the gradient.

MAKING A METALLIC TOP FOR THE PILLAR

You'll now make a second gradient fill to paint the top of the pillar with a metallic color.

To create a gradient fill:

1 Choose Select None from the Edit menu (Command-Shift-A) to deselect everything.

2 Choose Gradient from the Object menu. The Gradient palette appears.

3 Click New and type **MyMetallic** for the gradient name.

Creating new gradient fill points

To make the second gradient fill, you are first going to create some gradient points. You'll click three equal points under the gradient bar to create new gradient points for the gradient fill. These points are represented by the three new triangles inserted between the left (starting color) triangle and the right (ending color) triangle. The diamond above the bar represents the midpoint of the blend—the point at which each color is 50 percent, or halfway, between the two colors. For more detailed information on the gradient bar in the Gradient palette, see the *Adobe Illustrator User Guide.*

Note: *Each click under the gradient bar is similar to making a tab in a word processing program.*

The gradient bar should look like this when you finish adding and moving the points.

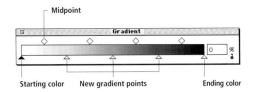

Midpoint
Starting color   New gradient points   Ending color

To add gradient points to the gradient bar:

1 Position the pointer about an inch to the right of the left triangle under the gradient bar, and then click the mouse button.

2 Repeat step 1 two more times to add two additional triangle markers to the three triangle markers that are now there.

3 Move the three new triangles to the following locations on the gradient bar:

Second Δ... 25 %
Third Δ ..... 50 %
Fourth Δ ... 75 %

To apply color values to the triangles:

1 Click the first triangle, and then click the Process Box. The values should be

Cyan ....0 %
Magenta ......0 %
Yellow ....0 %
Black............0 %

2 Press Return.

3 Click the second triangle, and then click the Process box. The values should be

Cyan 21%
Magenta ......0 %
Yellow ....0 %
Black..........40 %

4 Press Return.

5 Click the third triangle, and then click the Process Box. The values should be

Cyan ....0 %
Magenta ......0 %
Yellow ....0 %
Black..........15 %

6 Press Return.

7 Click the fourth triangle, and then click the Process box. The values should be

Cyan ....25 %
Magenta ......0 %
Yellow ....0 %
Black..........32 %

8 Press Return.

9 Click the fifth triangle, and then click the Process box. The values should be

Cyan ....19 %
Magenta ......0 %
Yellow ....0 %
Black..........38 %

10 Press Return.

11 Close the Gradient palette.

To apply the gradient fill:

You'll apply the metallic gradient to the top of the pillar.

1 Use the selection tool to select the oval above the pillar shape.

2 Click the Fill box in the Paint Style palette.

3 Click to select the Gradient box in the Paint Style palette.

4 Click *MyMetallic* in the list, and press Return.

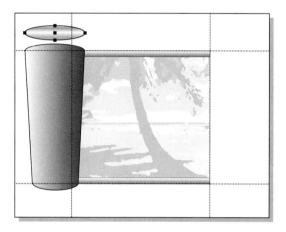

5 Click the gradient vector tool in the toolbox.

6 Hold down the mouse button and drag down from the top of the oval to the bottom of the oval.

To move the oval:

1 Click the selection tool in the toolbox.

2 Drag the oval to the top of the pillar, aligning it with the top of the pillar.

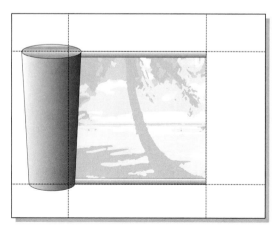

3 Hold down the Shift key, and click the pillar to add it to the selection.

4 Drag the pillar and its top to the left of the palm artwork. Use the final file as a reference for the position.

5 Choose Save from the File menu (Command-S) to save your work.

MAKING THE VIDEO SCREEN

In this part of the lesson, you'll make the video screen that appears on each of the pillars.

To make the video screen:

1 Click the rectangle tool in the toolbox.

2 Click in the upper one-third of the pillar.

3 Enter 1.7 for Width.

4 Enter 1.3 for Height, and click OK.

The fill in the Paint Style palette is the same as that of the top of the pillar.

5 Click the gradient vector tool in the toolbox and drag from the upper left corner of the video screen to its lower right corner. (This changes the direction of the gradient fill to give it a 45-degree angle.)

6 With the selection tool, position the video screen so that it is centered on the upper one-third of the pillar.

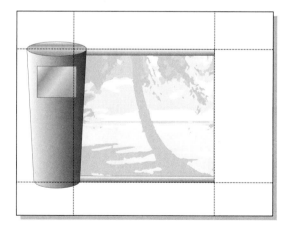

7 Choose Save from the File menu (Command-S) to save your work.

You now have the video screen on your pillar ready to view some exciting travel scenes.

ADDING ACCENT OVALS TO THE PILLAR

To enhance the pillar, you'll add two accent ovals.

To add the accent ovals:

1 Click the oval tool in the toolbox.

2 Click near the top of the pillar.

3 Enter 3.12 for the Width.

4 Enter .8 for the Height and click OK.

5 In the Paint Style palette, click the Fill box, and click None.

6 Click the Stroke box, and click the Black swatch. Set the Stroke Weight to .5 and press Return.

7 Marquee zoom in on the upper one-third of the pillar, to about 1 inch on either side of the pillar.

8 Click the selection tool in the toolbox.

9 Position the oval so that it is centered on the pillar with the top of the oval on the 6¾ inch right ruler guide.

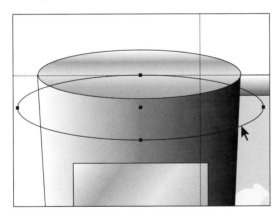

You'll now make a second accent for the pillar.

10 Position the pointer on the top center anchor point of the accent oval.

11 Hold down the Option key, and begin to drag; then hold down the Shift key, and drag the copy of the oval upward about an eighth of an inch above the original oval.

You'll cut away the part of the accent oval that shows on top of the pillar.

To cut away part of the accent oval:

1 Click the scissors tool in the toolbox.

2 Click the point where the top accent line intersects the pillar on the left and right sides.

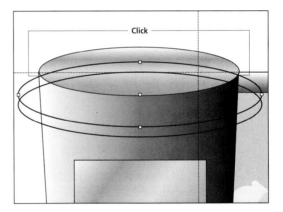

3 Click the selection tool in the toolbox.

4 Click the top center point of the accent oval, hold down the mouse button and drag up ½ inch. Notice that the oval has been cut.

5 Press the Delete key to delete the cut.

6 Repeat steps 2 through 5 for the bottom oval.

7 Choose Fit In Window from the View menu (Command-M).

8 Choose Save from the File menu (Command-S to save your work.

Copying the pillar

After creating the pillar, you'll group and copy it so that you'll have a duplicate pillar to place on the other side of the receptionist's counter in the lobby.

To group the pillar units:

1 Choose the selection tool in the toolbox.

2 Drag a marquee over the left side of the pillar, the ovals, the rectangle and the top.

3 Make sure the oval top, two circles, screen and pillar are selected.

Do *not* select the background shapes.

4 Choose Group from the Arrange menu (Command-G).

5 Press Option, start to drag, press the Shift key and then drag to the right until the left edge aligns with the right edge of the palm illustration (the left edge of the pillar aligns with the 2½ inch ruler guide).

6 Press Command-S to save your work.

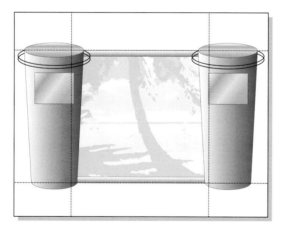

7 Choose Select All from the Edit menu (Command-A).

8 Choose Lock from the Arrange menu.

MAKING THE RECEPTIONIST'S COUNTER

With the pillars for the lobby copied, it's now time to create the receptionist's counter for the front lobby.

1 Click the rectangle tool, hold down the Option key, and then click between the two pillars.

2 Enter 4.6 for the Width.

3 Enter 2.5 for the Height, and click OK.

4 In the Paint Style palette, set the Fill to None, the Stroke to Black with a .5 Stroke Weight. Press Return.

5 Click the oval tool in the toolbox, hold down the Option key, and click between the two pillars.

6 Enter 4.6 for Width.

7 Enter 1.16 for Height and click OK.

8 Make sure the Stroke is Black, and the Stroke Weight reads .5 and press Return.

9 Click the selection tool in the toolbox.

10 Position the pointer at the bottom edge of the rectangle, and drag down so that the bottom edge of the rectangle is at the 3/4 inch mark in the right ruler.

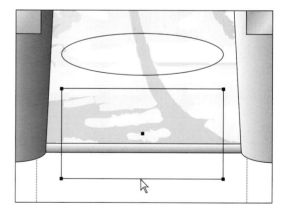

11 Center the rectangle between the two pillars.

To make additional oval copies:

1 Hold down the Option key, and drag the oval down so that the copy of the oval centers on the top line of the rectangle.

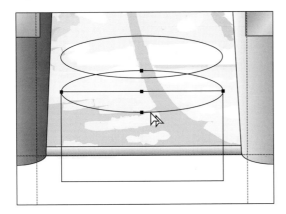

2 Hold down the Option key, start to drag, hold down the Shift key, and then drag down again so that the third oval centers on the bottom line of the rectangle.

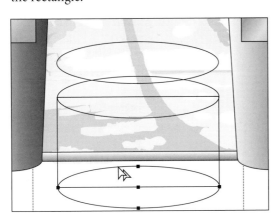

To unite the counter objects:

1 With the oval selected, hold down the Shift key and click the middle oval and the rectangle to select all the counter parts. Make sure that the top oval is *not* selected.

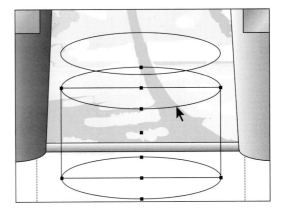

2 With all the counter parts selected, choose Pathfinder from the Filter menu and Unite from the submenu.

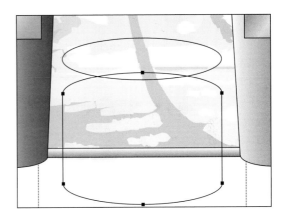

3 Hold down the mouse button and drag the remaining oval over the top of the counter shape.

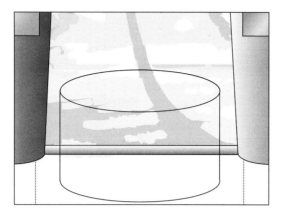

Making the cutout shape of the counter

Next you'll remove part of the counter top, the cutout where the receptionist stands.

To make the cutout:

1 Click the scale tool in the toolbox.

2 Hold down the Option key and click the center point of the large oval. The Scale dialog box appears

3 Click Uniform and enter 65.

4 Make sure that Scale line Weight Option is *not* checked, and click Copy.

5 Click the selection tool in the toolbox.

6 Position the pointer on the top anchor point of the small oval.

7 Hold down the mouse button, start to drag and press the Shift key. Drag the small oval down, as shown in the next figure.

8 If necessary, center the small oval between the left and right sides of the counter.

9 Hold down the Shift key and select the counter top (the two top ovals are selected).

10 Choose Pathfinder from the Filter menu and Back Minus Front from the submenu.

The Back Minus Front filter traces the backmost path in the stacking order, ignoring any areas overlapped by paths more forward in the stacking order.

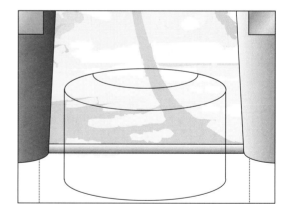

11 Choose Save from the File menu (Command-S) to save your work.

Changing the counter shape

1 With the counter top selected, hold down the Shift key and select the base of the counter.

2 Choose Distort from the Filter menu and Free Distort from the submenu.

3 Move out the left and the right corner anchor point of each side of the counter a little bit and click OK.

4 Position the pointer on the bottom center anchor point of the counter.

5 Drag up so that it is centered between the two pillars about ½ inch above the bottom edge of the page.

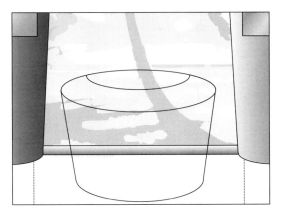

6 Click in a white area to deselect everything.

7 Select the top of the counter.

8 Choose Bring to Front from the Arrange menu (Command-equal).

To **apply the gradient**:

1 Use the selection tool to select the base of the counter.

2 Make sure the Paint Style palette is open.

3 Click the Fill box, and click the Gradient box.

4 Choose the Burgundy gradient.

5 With the selection tool, click the counter top.

6 Click the Fill box, and click the Gradient box.

7 Choose Metallic from the list, and press Return.

8 Click the gradient vector tool. Position the pointer on the bottom center edge of the counter and drag straight up about 1 inch. (This changes the direction of the gradient fill to be horizontal.)

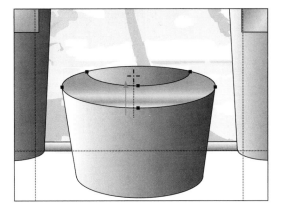

Deleting the back path of the counter

1 Click the direct selection tool in the toolbox.

2 Click the top back edge of the burgundy counter to select it. Do *not* select the metallic counter top.

3 Click the top center point.

4 Press the Delete key.

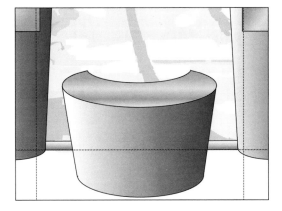

ADDING THE FRONT COUNTER ACCENT RINGS

1 Marquee zoom in on the front counter.

2 Select the oval tool and click once.

3 Enter 4.75 for the Width.

4 Enter 1.5 for the Height and click OK.

5 In the Paint Style palette, click the Fill box, and then click None.

6 Click the Stroke box, click Black, and make sure the Stroke Weight is set to .5 and press Return.

7 Click the selection tool in the toolbox.

8 Position the pointer on the bottom center anchor point of the oval.

9 Drag the oval so that the bottom edge of the oval is ½ inch below the edge of the counter top and centered on the counter.

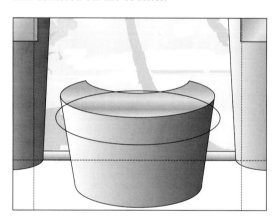

10 Position the pointer on the bottom center anchor point of the oval.

11 Hold down the Option key, and start to drag. Hold down the Shift key, and drag up ¼ inch.

To cut away part of the counter accent:

1 Click the scissors tool in the toolbox.

2 Zoom in to the left corner of the counter if needed.

3 Click the point where the top accent line intersects the counter on both sides.

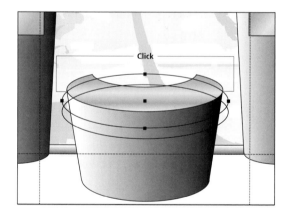

You may have to scroll to see the right side of the counter.

4 Click the selection tool in the toolbox, click the top center point of the oval, and press the Delete key.

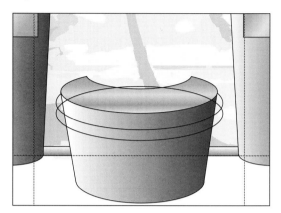

5 Repeat steps 1 through 4 for the bottom oval.

6 Click the selection tool in the toolbox.

7 Hold down the Shift key and click each counter part (top, front, and accent rings).

8 Choose Group from the Arrange menu (Command-G).

9 Choose Fit In Window from the View menu (Command-M).

10 Choose Save from the File menu (Command-S) to save your work.

IMPORTING THE RECEPTIONIST

You'll import a photo of the receptionist into the Adobe Illustrator program.

To place the receptionist behind the counter:

1 Choose Place Art from the File menu.

2 Locate the Lesson 12 folder, select the file named *12Art*, and then click Place.

To scale the receptionist:

1 With the photo selected, select the scale tool.

2 Hold down the Option key, and click the photo.

3 Click Uniform, type 45, click the Scale Line Weight box to select it, and click OK.

4 Click the selection tool in the toolbox.

5 Click the counter to select it.

6 Choose Bring To Front from the Arrange menu (Command-equal).

7 Zoom in on the photo to 200 percent.

8 With the selection tool, position the receptionist so that she is centered behind the counter. (The bottom edge of the receptionist is at the back edge of the counter top.)

9 Choose Save from the File menu (Command-S) to save your work.

Tracing the receptionist

You'll now trace the edge of the photo.

1 Click Fill in the Paint Style palette and click None.

2 Click Stroke in the Paint Style palette and click None and press Return.

3 Select the freehand tool from the toolbox and begin tracing the edge of the photo.

4 Loosely trace the edges of the photo, and click the origin point to end close the path).

5 Edit the path, if needed, using the direct selection tool.

To mask the receptionist:

1 Click the selection tool in the toolbox.

2 With the path selected, hold down the Shift key, and select the white rectangle behind the receptionist.

3 Choose Masks from the Object menu and Make from the submenu. You have masked the receptionist.

4 Choose Group from the Arrange menu (Command-G).

5 Choose Fit in Window from the View menu (Command-M).

6 Choose Save from the File menu (Command-S) to save your work.

IMPORTING THE GLOBE

You'll add a little travel flavor to the lobby atmosphere by placing a Navigations globe above the lobby counter. You'll do this by importing a file created in Adobe Dimensions. With Adobe Dimensions software, you can give objects a 3D appearance in a two-dimensional (2D) drawing program, such as Adobe Illustrator.

In this part of the lesson, you'll place the globe into your working file.

To place the globe:

1 Choose Place Art from the File menu.

2 Locate the Lesson 12 folder, select the file named *12Globe* and then click Place.

3 After importing the globe, position it above the receptionist and centered on the photo (between the pillars).

4 Click the scale tool.

5 Hold down the Option key, and click the selected globe. The Scale dialog box appears.

6 Enter 80 for the Uniform Scale, and click OK.

7 With the selection tool, reposition the scaled globe.

IMPORTING THE NAVIGATIONS LOGO

1 Open the Lesson 12 folder and the file named *12Logo*.

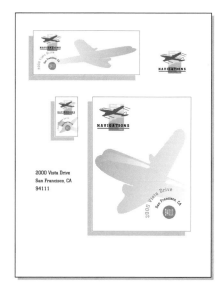

2 Select the Navigations logo in the upper right corner, and choose Copy from the Edit menu (Command-C).

3 Close the *12Logo* file.

4 Paste the copy of the logo (Command-V) and center it in the lower half of the front counter.

5 Choose Save from the File menu (Command-S) to save your work.

6 Choose Print from the File menu and click OK.

7 Close the Lesson 12 files.

UNDERSTANDING ADOBE ACROBAT

In this part of the lesson, you'll learn how you can use the Adobe Acrobat application to have other Navigations branch offices review your artwork. But before you do that, you'll watch an Adobe Teach movie that shows you how to create a PostScript file from Adobe Illustrator, distill the file, and then open it in Adobe Acrobat Exchange.

 If you are able to run Adobe Teach movies on your system, play the movie named *Adobe Teach 7*. For information on how to play Adobe Teach movies, see the "Getting Started' chapter at the beginning of this book.

Adobe Acrobat is a family of software programs from Adobe Systems that allows you to easily exchange documents, regardless of the platform, typefaces, operating system, or application software used to create the document. Once you install Adobe Acrobat software, the documents produced on your computer with your favorite applications can be converted into a Portable Document Format (PDF) file. Any computer with Acrobat Reader or Acrobat Exchange software can read the PDF description even if the computer lacks the originating software or fonts.

Let's say you need to send out the artwork you just finished creating for review immediately to the marketing manager of Navigations European and Canadian branch offices. There's no time for express mail or interoffice mail. You need to send it instantaneously.

The solution is electronic mail to ensure that the contacts at the two offices can review this document.

The marketing managers have different computer platforms—one has a Macintosh, the other a PC, but they both have Adobe Acrobat Reader installed on their computers. Adobe Acrobat files can be viewed on either platform, regardless of the typefaces and original application the artwork.

Documents lengthy in text are easy to convert to the Portable Document Format (PDF). You simply use the PDF Writer, and then print to a file instead of a printed page. Then you can enclose the file in your electronic mail application and send your message. For complex, graphically rich documents the Adobe Acrobat Distiller™ program will produce the highest quality output.

In this lesson, you saw how Adobe Systems products can be used to create an exciting multimedia presentation. Then you used many of the features of Adobe Illustrator to design some of the same elements that were used in the presentation.

Taking off on your own

You've finally traveled all the way from Explorations to Multimedia, with stops along the way for the beach, the wine country, and the Pacific Rim. You've created a tremendous amount of artwork for Navigations.

We hope you had a good time on the way to learning Adobe Illustrator. Most of all, we hope the techniques you've learned on this journey will help you the next time you want to create your very own designs and artwork.

Au revoir.

Index

Colophon

Project and Illustration Designs: Andrew Faulkner, *Andrew Faulkner Design and Illustration*

Written by: Sue Crissman

Illustrations: Jeffrey Schaaf, John Woodell

Art Direction: Sharon Anderson

Cover Design: Sharon Anderson

Book Production: Jeffrey Schaaf, John Woodell

Writing Assistance: Pat Cook, Kisa Harris

Book Production Management: Kisa Harris

Publication Management: Kisa Harris

Technical Support Advisors: Lynn Dalton, Jim Ryan

Adobe Teach Movies: Jonathan Caponi, Joan Mackrell

CD Cover Design: Dean Dapkus

Film Production: Cheryl Elder, Karen Winguth

Translators: Serge Paxton, J. T. Wheeler

Legal Advisor: Paul Klein

Special thanks to: Patrick Ames, Frank Gomez, Tom Harmon, Carita Klevickis, Glen Pierre, Sarah Rosenbaum, Nora Sandoval, Sean McKenna

Alpha Test-Teach Class Participants:

Sharon Anderson, Art Director
Kelly Lang, Adobe Inside Sales
Joan Mackrell, Mackrell and Associates
Kate Oliver, Adobe International Administrator
Sylvia Wanderaas, Adobe Dealer Sales

Beta Test-Teach Class Participants:

Tim Dirks, The Tech Museum
Patrice Anderson, Computer Attic
Terrie Kerth, Director, Adobe Customer Services
Wendy Nugent, Nurse and designer
Lynn Dalton, Adobe Technical Support Specialist
Roma Swenson, Adobe Librarian.

Self-paced Testing Participants:

Jim Meehan, Engineer
Joan Mackrell, Mackrell and Associates

PRODUCTION NOTES

This book was created electronically using Frame-Maker on the Macintosh Quadra 800. Art was produced using Adobe Illustrator, Adobe Photoshop, and SnapJot on the Quadra 800. Working film was produced with the PostScript language on an Agfa 5000 Imagesetter. The Minion and Frutiger families of typefaces are used throughout this book.